Louis Kahn and staff at work on a site model of the capitol building of Bangladesh, the Sher-e-Bangla Nagar of 1962–1983 in Dhaka, in his Philadelphia office, May 10, 1964. The most revered architectural educator of his time, he often used students to help develop his designs.

Makers of
Modern Architecture
Volume III

Governor Nelson Rockefeller looking at a model of the
World Trade Center with its architect, Minoru Yamasaki,
at the New York Hilton Hotel, Manhattan, January 19, 1964;
photograph by John Campbell (New York Daily News/Getty Images)

Makers of
Modern Architecture
Volume III

Martin Filler

NEW YORK REVIEW BOOKS

New York

*Publication of this book was made possible in part by
a generous grant from Elise Jaffe + Jeffrey Brown.*

THIS IS A NEW YORK REVIEW BOOK
PUBLISHED BY THE NEW YORK REVIEW OF BOOKS
435 Hudson Street, New York NY 10014
www.nyrb.com

MAKERS OF MODERN ARCHITECTURE VOLUME III
Copyright © 2018 by Martin Filler
Copyright © 2018 by NYREV, Inc.

Library of Congress Cataloging-in-Publication Data

Filler, Martin, 1948–
    Makers of modern architecture / By Martin Filler.
    p. cm.
    ISBN-13: 978-1-59017-227-8 (alk. paper)
    ISBN-10: 1-59017-227-2 (alk. paper)
    1. Architecture, Modern — 20th century. I. Title.
NA680.F46 2007
724'.6—dc22

                                                        2007004176

ISBN 978-1-68137-302-7
Also available as an electronic book; ISBN 978-1-68137-303-4

Printed in the United States of America on acid-free paper
1 3 5 7 9 10 8 6 4 2

For
Barbara Novak and Brian O'Doherty
and for
John Richardson
Scholars, exemplars, and friends

Contents

Acknowledgments

THE DEATH OF Robert Silvers on March 20, 2017, at the age
of eighty-seven, brought to an end the career of the greatest
literary editor of modern times, and deprived me of the most
important figure in my development as a writer. This third
collection of my pieces for Bob—fourteen of its nineteen
chapters began as articles he commissioned and edited—
continues an idea he had in the 1980s when he suggested that
I embark on a series of reassessments of major modern architects, both historical masters and contemporary practitioners, which could eventually be assembled into a book.
Thus my *Makers of Modern Architecture* (2007) and *Makers
of Modern Architecture, Volume II* (2013) came into being,
and our thirty-two-year collaboration culminates with this
collection.

Bob's work ethic was the stuff of literary legend. As many
of my fellow *New York Review* contributors attested in the
outpouring of tributes prompted by his death, Bob's fear-
some mental acuity stayed astonishingly intact until the very

end. Well into old age he could exhaust successive teams of young assistants during his prodigious weekend marathons, edit copy with flabbergasting speed and laser-like incisiveness, and come back to the office after a dinner party or a night at the opera and resume his labors until the small hours of the morning. But it was in the concluding weeks of his life that Bob's superhuman dedication to one all-consuming task—putting out the next issue (a total of 1,127 in his fifty-four years as editor)—assumed heroic proportions. Early in 2017 he edited my last two pieces for him, on the redevelopment of New York's World Trade Center site (chapter 17) and, finally, Louis Kahn (chapter 10), even though he was emotionally shattered and very ill following his return to New York after the death in Switzerland of his beloved companion of four decades, Grace Dudley. This devoted couple now lie in Lausanne's verdant Cimetière du Bois-de-Vaux.

A large part of Bob's genius stemmed from his ability to personalize the editorial process to a degree I have never experienced with anyone else. Employing a technique that I and others have likened to the patient/therapist transference in psychoanalysis—an odd analogy, perhaps, given the amount of editorial space he gave over the years to one famously outspoken critic of Freud—Bob would patiently, expansively, and insightfully talk his contributors through the topic at hand (he knew a very great deal about everything) and draw from us thoughts we were not yet fully conscious that we held.

Those exhilarating consultations on a Sunday afternoon—when I usually would hear from him—rank among the peak experiences of my life. (My wife has said that she always knew when I was talking to Bob on the telephone because my voice went up one octave and I spoke very loudly.) But far from trying to impose his own point of view, Bob was intent on motivating us to think at our sharpest, write at our clearest, and produce what he knew could be our best, even if we were not so sure.

In time Bob became so synonymous with the *Review* that it was increasingly difficult to imagine its existence without him. The extent to which my colleagues shared this apprehension became clear to me at a gathering after his memorial at the New York Public Library, when a fellow contributor forlornly said to me, "I don't know who to write for now." To my surprise I found myself instantly replying, "Well, I do, because even though he's not going to be reading it, I will always write for Bob." This was the first realization I'd had that what I call my Inner Bob did not depend on his being alive, and that I would be able to go on without him, wrenching though his death has been.

Rather than encouraging a personality cult—despite the intense devotion of his writers—what now seems evident to me is that Bob methodically built an institution that would not only survive him but could thrive after he was gone if the high standards he set were maintained. Here principal credit must go to the *Review*'s publisher since 1984, Rea Hederman, whom Bob designated the executor of his estate, which added further to his burden as he steered the paper through an unprecedentedly difficult period, to say nothing of an even darker phase in our nation's history.

However, the steadfastness Rea demonstrated throughout this dreaded transition came as no surprise to me, given the calm resolve he manifested in the five months following August 2014, when the *Review* and I were sued for libel by Zaha Hadid over an article in which I mistakenly claimed, because of a fact-checking lapse, that a large number of workers had died on the construction site of a project of hers that had not yet begun to be built, for which we quickly issued a retraction and an apology.

Throughout this difficult episode and the tsunami of unwelcome publicity it unleashed, Rea extended to me without hesitation the full legal representation of the *Review*'s law firm, Satterlee Stephens Burke & Burke. The partner in charge of our case, Mark A. Fowler, Esq., was a wise and judicious presence throughout, and a source of sound advice on matters large and small. (My friend and fellow writer Michael Z. Wise had gallantly offered to organize a legal defense fund on my behalf, but under the circumstances it was not needed.)

To Rea's wife, Angela Hederman, I owe a debt of gratitude for her having suggested, in 2006, that a compendium of my essays from the preceding two decades would make a worthwhile addition to the New York Review Collections, published by New York Review Books. That imprint's editor and the *Review*'s deputy editor, Michael Shae, has once again been an ideal partner in reshaping these essays, most of which he helped edit in their original format. Michael's importance to the *Review* since he arrived there in 1994 cannot be overstated. Apart from his highly developed editorial skills, superb taste, and tact comparable to Bob's in dealing with authors, his temperamental equanimity is exceptional, as is his characteristic self-effacement. Not long ago he excised, without comment, a phrase in one of the pieces included here that would have been an enormous gaffe had it gone into print. But when I thanked him profusely for saving me, he replied, "This is what we do."

Also repeating her much-valued contributions to the earlier volumes is Louise Fili, whose original dust jacket design has proven remarkably adaptable to later installments in this series, just as Borden Elniff's classic typographic design pleases me whenever I open one of these books. I have again been lucky to have Alaina Taylor conduct the photographic research. Working with a relatively small budget, she has wrought small miracles of resourcefulness in finding the perfect image for each building I wanted to illustrate. And I am honored to have had my author's photo taken by Brigitte Lacombe, one of today's foremost portrait artists, whose work I have greatly admired.

Parts of four chapters (on Jan Duiker, Frei Otto, Renzo Piano, and Alexander Gorlin) were originally written for the *NYR Daily* and edited by Hugh Eakin, who began overseeing that online feature of the *Review* in 2009. His colleague and fellow senior editor, Gabriel Winslow-Yost, was a frequent participant in bringing those pieces to publication. To them and to the *Review*'s digital editorial director, Matthew Howard, I am immensely grateful for helping to present my writing to the larger readership afforded by electronic and social media.

A source of understandable anxiety among the *Review*'s contributors was how their offerings would be received by its new editor, Ian Buruma, who, with commendable bravery, in 2017 accepted Rea Hederman's offer to succeed such a formidable predecessor. I was therefore pleased and relieved by Ian's positive response to the first of my pieces to be edited under his tenure (chapter 12, on the Japanese-American architect Minoru Yamasaki), especially because of his expertise in East Asian culture. I am not alone among the *Review*'s contributors in feeling that the paper again resides in eminently qualified hands.

Two chapters of this book—on Frank Gehry and Renzo Piano—resulted from an unforgettable trip that my wife and I made to Paris in the fall of 2014 as the guests of our close friends Robert and Meryl Meltzer. Bob's sudden death in April 2017 was a huge loss to all who knew him as well as to the world of art and architecture. A distinguished connoisseur and generous donor, he had served as president and board chairman of the American Federation of Art and was an early supporter of the Institute for Architecture and Urban Studies, the New York think tank that defined an international avant-garde from 1967 to 1984. Above all, Bob was a dear, lovable, endlessly thoughtful friend—a true life-enhancer—and we will miss him deeply.

ACKNOWLEDGMENTS

For a wide range of assistance—from providing access to buildings not open to the public or viewing exhibitions privately, and most importantly for sharing their ideas—I thank, among others, George Baird, Barry Bergdoll, Francesca Bianchi, Giorgio Bianchi, Cynthia S. Brenwall, Mark Carroll, Christiane Crasemann Collins, Anne Edgar, Marian Wright Edelman, Alexander Gorlin, Pedro E. Guerrero, Robert A. Heintges, Rebecca Lewis, Mary McLeod, Guy Nordenson, Renzo Piano, Bernard Plattner, Renée Price, Thorsten Sahlmann, Suzanne Stephens, Jewel Stern, Wallace Turbeville, Gijs van Hinsbergen, and Christian Witt-Dörring.

Aware that there is sometimes no better way to present an idea than to quote the unimprovable words of others, for my excerpts from their printed works I am indebted to, *inter alia*, Jay D. Aronson, Reyner Banham, Stephen Bayley, Julian Brash, George Collins, James Glanz, Dale Allen Gyure, Ada Louise Huxtable, James A. Jacobs, Juliet Kinchin, Martin Kitchen, Barbara Miller Lane, Wendy Lesser, Zeuler R. M. de A. Lima, Eric Lipton, Jan Molema, Guy Nordenson, John Ochsendorf, Nikolaus Pevsner, Peter Rice, Timothy M. Rohan, Judith Rohrer, Lynn Sagalyn, Stephanie Saul, Vincent Scully, Eduard Sekler, Kathryn Smith, Gavin Stamp, Louise Story, Despina Stratigakos, James F. Williamson, Carol Willis, Mabel O. Wilson, and Olgivanna Lloyd Wright.

The fact that I have survived to complete this book—especially since my work on its two precursors was interrupted by life-threatening illnesses—is owed in no small part to the vigilance and skill of Dr. Timothy C. Dutta, MD, my primary care provider and cardiologist. Several years ago Bob Silvers asked me, after his longtime physician died, if I could ask Dr. Dutta to take him on as a patient as well, which he agreed to do at once. He doubtless extended Bob's life, and attended him during his final illness with extraordinary personal concern and sensitivity.

This book is dedicated to three giants of modern culture who have been paragons to me throughout my adult life. When I arrived at Columbia College as a freshman in 1966, Barbara Novak was a rising star of the university's art history faculty, which then included such titans as Julius Held, Meyer Shapiro, and Rudolf Wittkower. Her teaching explored what was still the terra incognita of nineteenth-century American art, and she was spoken of by the brightest students with awe for her penetrating intellect, vibrant personality, and arresting appearance. Yet to come was her magisterial trilogy: *American Art of the Nineteenth Century: Realism, Idealism, and the American Experience* (1969); *Nature and Culture: American Landscape Painting, 1825–1875* (1980); and *Voyages of the Self: Pairs, Parallels, and Patterns in American Art and Literature* (2006)—altogether a towering accomplishment in the historiography of art. As if that were not enough, she is also a novelist, watercolorist, and playwright who has achieved distinction in each of those mediums as well.

By the time I heard of Professor Novak, my future wife, Rosemarie Haag Bletter, had already taken her Barnard courses and found in her a role model at a time when women rarely attained top academic positions, and often seemed not to be having much fun, which she clearly was. Novak's husband since 1960, the physician/artist/critic/novelist Brian O'Doherty, was already familiar to me as an art critic for *The New York Times* and later through his pioneering televised art commentaries on *The Today Show*. In addition to his renown as a conceptual and installation artist under his anonym Patrick Ireland, O'Doherty's fame skyrocketed with his 1976 *Artforum* series that comprised "Notes on the Gallery Space," "The Eye and the Spectator," and "Context as Content." Reissued in book form as *Inside the White Cube: The Ideology of Gallery Space* (1999), by then they had long been regarded as classic texts. (I have jokingly referred to the *White Cube* as Brian's Golden Albatross because it has so overshadowed all other aspects of this polymath's multifaceted career.) In the 1980s Rosemarie and I came to know Barbara and Brian better through our many mutual art world connections, and they've since become two of our most treasured friends, as well as our ideal of the proverbial but all-too-rare "marriage of true minds."

It was also during the 1980s that I got to know this book's third dedicatee, John Richardson, when he began writing for *House & Garden* at Condé Nast, where I then worked as an editor. I was immediately dazzled by John's charismatic manner, encyclopedic knowledge of cultural and social history past and very recent, wicked wit, and unselfishness in sharing his deep stores of expert opinion and arcane information with fellow writers. My reliance on him increased later in that decade when we both were contributing editors to *Vanity Fair* and he began the great undertaking of his career, the multivolume *A Life of Picasso* (1991, 1996, 2007 et seq.), universally praised as the definitive study of the artist and a landmark in the history of biography.

In a bravura display of late-life intellectual vigor akin to that of his great friend Bob Silvers—who asked John to become a contributor to the *Review* in 1964, a year after it began publication—he found time to spin out two scintillating memoirs, *The Sorcerer's Apprentice: Picasso, Provence, and Douglas Cooper* (1999) and *Sacred Monsters, Sacred Masters* (2001). I was never more flattered than when Bob asked me to write about the stupendous exhibition John curated at New York's Gagosian Gallery in 2009, "Picasso: Mosqueteros," which completely reversed my estimation of the artist's late works.

Although Barbara, Brian, and John are all quite different as scholars, what links them in my mind is the breathtaking quality of their writing. I often turn to their books when I need verbal inspiration, yet even when I consult those volumes for specific information, what invariably holds me, page after page, is the sheer beauty of their prose. I present this book to these masters of art history and the English language with the Flemish words Jan Van Eyck inscribed on his paintings: *Als Ik Kan* (As best I can).

Distraught on the day of Bob Silvers's death, I blurted out to my wife that there were only two people whose opinion of my work I really cared about, and now one of them was gone. Although that cri de coeur contradicted my quite genuine desire to reach a large audience through my writing, the outburst did reflect the truth that for me, she and Bob have been in a class all their own, and made me even more aware of how central Rosemarie has been to my life and work. After four decades together, she remains my first, best, and most valued reader. As a peerless scholar of the Modern Movement in architecture, she has guided me through the subject matter of this trilogy so thoroughly, and with such particular attention to important nuances that most other architectural historians generally overlook, that this must be seen as her work as much as mine. For that, and for every day of these many years enlivened by the love we have shared, I will always be thankful.

—MARTIN FILLER
New York City
March 20, 2018

Introduction

SINCE THE 1980s, when I began writing the essays that comprise my *Makers of Modern Architecture*, of which this is the third volume, the building art has undergone such a thoroughgoing transformation that it would be largely unrecognizable to most of the figures included in this open-ended series of career assessments. This should not be surprising, given that the oldest of my subjects, Frederick Law Olmsted, was born nearly two centuries ago (one indication that the Modern Movement in architecture, of which he was an important precursor, has long become a historical development). However, the most extreme changes have occurred during the three decades when these texts were originally published in *The New York Review of Books*. Technological advances that emerged during that period in architecture are no less remarkable than those from horse-drawn vehicles to space travel, handwritten communications to electronic media, or phrenology to gene therapy.

For example, although there are striking formal similarities between the work of two major figures discussed in this volume, Antoni Gaudí and Frank Gehry—both of whom designed idiosyncratic, biomorphic structures wholly at odds with the predominantly rectilinear rule of Western architecture since Classical antiquity—the means by which they realized their heterodox visions could not have been more different. Gaudí drew on millennia of ingenious fabrication techniques indigenous to his native Catalan region, a tradition that began with Roman colonists but remained localized until the nineteenth century and the international dissemination of those techniques by an older compatriot of his, Rafael Guastavino. The execution of Gaudí's marvelously bizarre designs also depended on the availability of cheap artisanal labor, for although the architect plotted his innovative structures with an exceptional but largely intuitive knowledge of engineering, he still needed the help of skilled craftsmen, who were often required to improvise onsite adjustments that no amount of forethought, in those low-tech times, could have anticipated.

Gehry, in contrast, ingeniously co-opted computer software devised for the aviation industry to plot the increasingly irregular forms of his buildings, a conceptual masterstroke that opened a new universe of architectural design for him and an emergent generation of coprofessionals. But the technical innovations of the past three decades have not been limited to the digital realm and include a host of new building materials once undreamed of, such as translucent concrete that transmits light through load-bearing walls, powerful adhesives that enable the installation of huge windows without intrusive mullions, and biodegradable plastics as strong as aluminum but half its weight. And although natural methods of passive climate control have been part of vernacular building traditions since time immemorial, the LEED (Leadership in Energy and Environmental Design) rating system of the United States Green Building Council—a private, nonprofit architectural sustainability group founded in 1993—has promoted a wide array of energy-conservation strategies that have profoundly changed business-as-usual attitudes toward the issue of climate change.

As with the two preceding installments of this series, the chapters in this volume are arranged more or less chronologically, by the subject's date of birth or the approximate order in which she or he rose to prominence. And although none of these books purports to be a full-fledged narrative of modern architecture, taken as a whole they offer a veritable mosaic of the profession's major protagonists from the mid-nineteenth century to the present day. There are several notable reappearances here. Frank Lloyd Wright, a figure of fathomless depth to scholars and perennial interest to the general public, appears in all three volumes, a sign of his unparalleled place in the American architectural pantheon. Renzo Piano likewise is included in each book, although that has had more to do with his having commanded so many of the most coveted cultural commissions of the past thirty years, when he has reigned as the world's most prominent designer of performing- and visual-arts buildings. (Le Corbusier—more important in the global picture than either Wright or Piano—was in Volumes I and II.)

Two chapters, in Volume I and the present collection, are devoted to Louis Kahn, who, along with Robert Venturi and Denise Scott Brown (discussed in Volume I) and Gehry (Volumes I and III), can be safely cited as the most significant American architects in the six decades since Wright's demise. Also in both the first and third volumes are estimations of the work of David Childs and Santiago Calatrava, whose headline-making schemes at New York's Ground Zero gave them extraordinary visibility during the decade and a half that it took them to execute those projects. As with its two predecessors, the components of this book were prompted by a variety of topical occurrences, including the completion of culturally significant public buildings (such as Piano's addition to Kahn's Kimbell Art Museum in Fort Worth and Gehry's Fondation Louis Vuitton in Paris); the emergence of new structural forms (the super-tall, super-thin condominium towers that began to appear in Midtown Manhattan during the second decade of the new millennium); major museum exhibitions (including retrospectives on Wright, the Wiener Werkstätte, and Gehry); and, as always at a paper devoted to reviewing books, new architectural publications.

In recent years many of those have been monographs that focus on architects of a half-century earlier whose heyday was followed by a period of posthumous obscurity. This often happens when tastes and fashions change, and it falls to a younger generation of scholars to look with fresh eyes at buildings that can seem embarrassingly dated. In Volume II, I discussed the revival of interest in Eero Saarinen and Edward Durell Stone, and the renewed enthusiasm for what is now known as Midcentury Modern continues in this collection with similar reevaluations of Paul Rudolph, Minoru Yamasaki, and their many contemporaries whose tough-looking concrete structures earned them the label of New Brutalists. Even the developer-built suburban housing tracts that so altered the postwar character of middle-class American habitation have lately been the beneficiary of scholarly analyses referred to in these pages.

Such studies are often undertaken by graduate students in search of unclaimed dissertation topics, but apart from that impetus there is always good reason to reexamine the merits of discredited or neglected architecture after contemporary prejudices subside. However, in reconsidering the fifty-five chapters of this series, it now seems to me that the most fascinating rediscoveries are not of postwar male architects but rather of women architects who managed not only to prevail but to excel in a profession that remained so adamantly male-dominated and openly misogynistic for most of the twentieth century. The most notable example of such myopia—to give this habitual omission its most charitable definition—was the absence of Lina Bo Bardi from the canon of indispensable twentieth-century architects, and even the most cursory overview of her accomplishment indicates that she would have long enjoyed her current high critical status were she a man.

In general, the prospects of women entering architectural practice today are much improved in comparison with those thirty years ago, to say nothing of sixty, when even the leading female figures in the profession were routinely subjected to discrimination and harassment. Natalie de Blois, for example, who died in 2013 at the age of ninety-two, was among the few women of her generation to reach the highest echelons of architectural practice in this country. Blois, who as a senior partner at Skidmore, Owings & Merrill helped design several of the firm's most noteworthy buildings of the 1950s and 1960s, was fired from an earlier job because she rejected a male superior's sexual overtures. But even at SOM, the period's paradigm of corporate architectural culture, she had to endure repeated humiliations, such as being excluded from meetings with prospective clients and from group photographs with her male colleagues. When Blois was pregnant with one of her three children, Gordon Bunshaft, the firm's cantankerous design principal ("He took all the credit and she did all the work," as one feminist advocate has explained their collaborative dynamic), told her that she should not attend the opening of a corporate headquarters they'd worked on together if she had not given birth by then.

Although social mores may change in the short term, human nature rarely does in any significant manner. Thus I believe that the specifically personal approach I have taken in these essays, far from reinforcing a discredited Great Man approach to history, helps to explain the inner workings of an art that has become increasingly mysterious to the general public since the professionalization of building design began during the second half of the nineteenth century. To be sure, for millennia the construction industry remained very much a closed shop, with knowledge of the building art jealously guarded as a trade secret transmitted by familial dynasties or trade guilds intent on monopolizing lucrative sources of income. Yet to a far greater extent than was possible in the Industrial Age, the lay public in premodern times could closely observe the building process and gain some understanding of its nature, or even, as with the scores of cathedrals erected throughout Christendom during the Middle Ages, directly participate in the creation of a monument used by the entire community.

No wonder that this lost ideal of social integration was invoked by Modernist architects in the immediate aftermath of World War I, most movingly by the founders of the Bauhaus, the cover of whose founding manifesto of 1919 was decorated with Lyonel Feininger's Expressionist woodcut *Kathedrale*. (Indeed, the very name of this multidisciplinary design school has echoes in the word *Bauhütte*—a builder's lodge adjacent to those great medieval churches, the equivalent of the far less prepossessing job-manager's trailers we now see on modern construction sites.) Overall, though, the social aspects of architecture today are quite different from those of earlier epochs, and have depended much more on the interpersonal relations between architect and client than, say, those between master mason and clerical hierarchy.

At the heart of this customary imbalance of architectural

power—the perpetual tug-of-war between economic necessity and artistic desire—lies the basic fact that nothing can get built unless someone agrees to pay for it. Although distinguished architects of the modern period, from the Adam brothers in the eighteenth century onward, have been able (given the financial backing of others) to create structures that can be sold on speculation—most often residences but also office buildings—the profession for the most part remains in the thrall of patronage. Except for a recent increase in design/build architects, who act as their own contractors and developers, there has been no widespread change equivalent to the one that began with the rise of a middle-class market for paintings in seventeenth-century Holland, which removed the creation of art from complete dependency on princely patronage.

The ability, indeed the necessity of architects to convince others to employ them—whether on the basis of their social insight (Olmsted, Bo Bardi), otherworldly spirituality (Gaudí, Kahn), extraordinary charm (Calatrava, Rafael Viñoly), political ideology (Albert Speer, Gerdy Troost), or technological expertise (Frei Otto, Piano), to name just several of the practitioners I discuss in this book—cannot be discounted as an integral component of their exceptional success. Highly developed social skills can propel architects of mediocre artistic ability to great heights, as was demonstrated by the stellar careers of Philip Johnson and I. M. Pei, neither of whom was a very talented designer.

Conversely, a lack of what's known colloquially as "people skills" can doom even the most gifted professional. When I served as an adviser on an architectural search committee in the early 2000s, I watched in dismay as the perfect person for the job lost the commission by never once establishing eye contact with his potential clients as he gave his presentation. Instead he talked right over their heads, which one member of that committee cited as the determining reason not to hire him. In one-on-one situations this architect can be delightfully engaging, but his tendency to seem remote and aloof in more formal settings is at painful odds with such virtuosos of the client pitch as Piano, whose lyrical evocations of architecture as the noblest of human endeavors have likely won him as many projects as his lengthy roster of superbly executed buildings.

Yet no matter how high-minded they may be, all architects know that if they do not have a client, they do not have a building. (Gaudí coped with the countless human vicissitudes that hampered the progress of his masterwork, the church of the Sagrada Família, by insisting that "God is my client," while the Lord's representatives on earth made this saintly master builder miserable.) But even when it comes to architects whose work I do not much admire (Rudolph and Calatrava, to name but two included here), one cannot question the seriousness with which they addressed their tasks or the strong confidence their patrons had in them.

As with every other human undertaking there is a dark side to architecture, which was exposed most sinisterly during the modern period in the Third Reich, whose leader was a frustrated architect and urban planner manqué. For decades after World War II, any serious discussion of Nazi construction was strictly *verboten* in academic circles, as if acknowledging the central part that architecture played in the Führer's comprehensive takeover of the arts in German culture implied approval of his malign program for political subjugation through every possible medium. Once it became permissible to talk about this long-suppressed subject, a parallel increase of interest in traditional styles during the 1970s and 1980s emboldened some contrarians, most notably the neoconservative Postmodernist Léon Krier, to openly admire Nazi architecture. Thus encouraged, Hitler's chief architect, Albert Speer—who survived a postwar prison term and made a second fortune from best-selling memoirs unparalleled in their mendacity—expected the critical rehabilitation of his architectural corpus despite the atrocities he perpetrated as a high-ranking member of the Nazi regime.

Apart from the centrality of technological matters, the most salient aspect of the building art since the millennium has been the exponential growth (though "metastasis" might be the better term) of the cult of celebrity, which has taken the long-standing emphasis on individual inspiration in this necessarily collaborative medium to grotesque new extremes. Today's relentless commercial emphasis on "branding" has been a setback for those who want to acknowledge that the creation of architecture would be impossible without the participation of numerous specialists on each project. However much a principal architect might drive the process, in the same way that a movie director is the auteur of a production, it is hugely misleading to perpetuate persistent stereotypes of the individual genius.

To their credit, two of today's most important architects have insisted that their firms' corporate identities stress the collaborative nature of their work: the Office for Metropolitan Architecture, of which Rem Koolhaas is the most widely recognized principal, and the Renzo Piano Building Workshop, which even though it highlights the name of its founder implies a more generous sharing of credit than the customary "and Partners" or "and Associates." It might be said that both Koolhaas and Piano are both secure enough about their own celebrity not to worry about what their offices are called, and concerned that the future livelihoods of their coworkers not be dependent on their firms' sole identification with one all-too-mortal individual.

But such nomenclature straddles an earlier tendency to name architectural practices after their principals—McKim, Mead & White; Skidmore, Owings & Merrill—and the recent preference for cryptic titles believed to efface such personal associations and epitomized by Ennead Architects (formerly Polshek Partnership, a change made upon the founder's retirement, and based on a Greek-derived term for a group of nine, the number of remaining partners in that practice). But the allure of a widely recognized name dies hard, and even though James Polshek's office was renowned for its dependably fine if rarely spectacular work, his successors preferred a concocted moniker more reminiscent of a sport-utility vehicle than an architectural atelier.

Today's mania for constant extrapersonal validation—especially through our all-pervasive electronic media—threatens the most likely means we have, and have always had, for gauging the successful outcome of a building commission: through some direct understanding by architects of what their clients want and, reciprocally, clients who trust that an architect understands and is willing to act upon their requirements. In rare circumstances such transactions rise above the level of mere expediency and enter the realm of art. That condition is never dependent on high expenditure, as evidenced in the last chapter of this book by Maya Lin's Riggio-Lynch Chapel, a church humble enough for Saint Francis of Assisi but grand enough for Dr. Martin Luther King. In some essential way this small but powerful sanctuary expresses the "quiet inner voice" I wrote about in my initial 1999 essay on Piano. That expression of architecture's ability to elevate life in countless ways can still be heard from time to time in the profession, drowned out though it often is by the distracting modern clamor of money, fame, and self-interest. To the heroines and heroes who appear in this book and its two forerunners, I give thanks for my fruitful career in helping to document their struggles and triumphs in this most daunting of all art forms, a task I have attempted to fulfill as sympathetically as possible.

I

FREDERICK LAW OLMSTED

THE NEARLY UNIVERSAL acclaim that greeted New York City's High Line—the linear greenway built between 2006 and 2014 atop an abandoned elevated railway spur that opened in 1934 on Manhattan's Lower West Side—reconfirmed the transformative effect parks can have on the quality of urban life. Well before the project's completion, real estate prices began to soar in the vicinity of this one-and-a-half-mile-long wonder of adaptive reuse. The surrounding neighborhood subsequently became among the trendiest and costliest in town, and thousands visit it daily, many from abroad. Yet however much the High Line has enriched the megalopolis (economically not least of all), its social effects pale in comparison to the revolutionary vision of the public park as promulgated by its greatest American exponent, the nineteenth-century polymath Frederick Law Olmsted.

Besides being an experimental farmer, prolific journalist, crusading publisher, military health-care reformer, and insightful social critic, Olmsted was also the greatest advocate and impresario of the public realm this country has ever produced. Now best remembered as the codesigner, with the British-born architect Calvert Vaux, of New York's Central Park of 1857–1873, he was even more important as the veritable inventor of landscape architecture as a modern profession (see Illustration 1a). For apart from Olmsted's exceptional and apparently innate abilities as a horticulturist—he had little formal training—he systematically conceived the large-scale reshaping of the natural terrain to an extent unimaginable to such illustrious and influential antecedents as Capability Brown in Georgian England and Andrew Jackson Downing (Olmsted's beloved mentor) in pre–Civil War America.

Olmsted can also be said to have Americanized high-style landscape design, despite all he learned from British sources about felicitous composition. He created vistas like a series of Constable paintings with an almost cinematic revelation of one breathtakingly arranged Arcadian tableau after another, but whenever possible he used native species to make his schemes seem like spontaneous emanations of the ecology rather than artificial impositions. Though he was hardly averse to transporting the best available plant material over long distances, and had mature trees and shrubs for Central Park shipped in quantity from England, Olmsted always closely studied local settings for indigenous characteristics that he reproduced with astounding fidelity. Likewise he shunned the strenuous exoticism of Victorian gardening, with its cedars of Lebanon, Argentinian pampas grasses,

Mexican agaves, Chilean monkey puzzle trees, and Norfolk Island pines that flaunted horticulture's new imperial scope. Olmsted and his collaborators created scores of parks large and small—in Boston and Fall River, Massachusetts; Baltimore; Bridgeport, Hartford, New Britain, and New London, Connecticut; Chicago; Detroit; Louisville, Kentucky; Milwaukee; Montreal; Buffalo, Newburgh, and Rochester, New York; Newport, Rhode Island; Philadelphia; and San Francisco. He also laid out campuses for the University of California at Berkeley, Stanford University in Palo Alto, and the University of Chicago; Mountain View Cemetery in Oakland, California; as well as one of America's earliest planned suburbs, Riverside, Illinois. He was responsible for the nation's first state park—the Niagara Reservation, which got rid of the commercial mess that disgraced the famous waterfalls. At his urging the Yosemite Valley was put under federal jurisdiction, the first public land to be thus protected, and his 1896 report to Congress about the valley is now seen as a mission statement for the then-nascent National Park movement.

Central Park, which launched Olmsted's landscaping career and inspired communities across the country to commission similar projects from him, emerged at a pivotal moment in the recognition of our environmental treasures and their increasing endangerment. A distinctively American form of nature worship—exalted through the writings of the Transcendentalists Ralph Waldo Emerson and Henry David Thoreau, the poetry of William Cullen Bryant, and the art of

Hudson River School painters, including Thomas Cole and Frederic Edwin Church—grew into a widely accepted non-sectarian sort of spirituality. This resulted in a significant change in public attitudes toward the environment, which for the first two centuries of European settlement in the Western Hemisphere were more about despoilment than preservation. Lewis Mumford later called this shift "an effort to make reparations to nature."

The saga of Central Park began in 1844, when Bryant wrote a *New York Post* editorial that urged the country's burgeoning metropolis to establish an appropriately grand public pleasure ground. The idea languished in the politically corrupt city, where no official activity was free from favoritism and graft. Under the so-called spoils system, the elected party had absolute control over public funds and distribution of municipal jobs, with abrupt shifts in allocations and appointments when power changed hands, which it did with surprising frequency in mid-nineteenth-century New York City. High among Olmsted's many accomplishments was his ability to buck this entrenched self-interest and bring his dream to fruition.

The seed of that vision was planted in 1850 during his trip to Europe to study new farming methods, though as always Olmsted's restless eye absorbed everything of interest. Soon after debarking in Liverpool he visited Birkenhead Park of 1841–1847 in the eponymous town across the River Mersey from the great seaport. Laid out by Joseph Paxton—the landscape gardener who with the engineer Charles Fox designed the Crystal Palace of 1850–1851 in London—the 125-acre Birkenhead tract was the earliest urban park in Britain developed with public funds and open to all classes. This represented an enormous advance in the gradual democratization of civic culture that began during the Enlightenment. Just as the establishment of the first public museums in the late eighteenth and early nineteenth centuries extended the audience for art beyond the aristocracy, so Paxton improved upon forerunners such as Green Park and Hyde Park in London, which were created from former royal hunting preserves but open only to gentlefolk.

Olmsted's perceptive 1851 report on this innovation, "The People's Park at Birkenhead, near Liverpool," is among the forty-seven essays, memoranda, and excerpts from his travel dispatches, along with sixty letters, collected in the Library of America's thoroughly inspiring *Frederick Law Olmsted: Writings on Landscape, Culture, and Society* (2015), authoritatively edited by the preeminent expert on the master, Charles Beveridge. Also in 2015, publication of the ninth volume of Olmsted's correspondence culminated the heroic project initiated by Johns Hopkins University Press in 1972. If this collection does not numerically surpass the forty-six volumes of Adams family papers issued by Harvard University Press since 1954, it nonetheless represents the most ambitious initiative of its kind on behalf of an American artist or designer in any medium, and deservedly so.

Olmsted's seminal essay on the People's Park epitomizes not only his breezy, conversational, inimitably American voice, but also predicts, in startlingly prescient detail, what by the end of the decade would become Central Park. His text reveals that it was not stylistic considerations that took precedence for him, but rather a design's social implications. As he wrote of that momentous field trip:

> In studying the manner in which art had been employed to obtain from nature so much beauty,...I was ready to admit that in democratic America, there was nothing to be thought of as comparable with this People's Garden. Indeed, I was satisfied that gardening had here reached a perfection that I had never before dreamed of....We passed through winding paths, over acres and acres, with a constant varying surface, where on all sides were growing every variety of shrubs and flowers, with more than natural grace, all set in borders of greenest, closest turf, and all kept with most consummate neatness. At a distance of a quarter of a mile from the gate, we came to an open field of clean, bright, green-sward, closely mown, on which...a party of boys...were playing cricket.
>
> Beyond this was a large meadow with rich groups of trees, under which a flock of sheep were reposing, and girls and women with children, were playing. While watching the cricketers, we were threatened with a shower, and hastened back to look for shelter, which we found in a pagoda.... It was soon filled... and I was glad to observe that the privileges of the garden were

enjoyed about equally by all classes. There were some who even were attended by servants, and sent at once for their carriages, but a large proportion were of the common ranks, and a few women with children, or suffering from ill health, were evidently the wives of very humble laborers....

All this magnificent pleasure-ground is entirely, unreservedly, and forever the People's own. The poorest British peasant is as free to enjoy it in all its parts, as the British Queen.

During the 1840s, New York City was flooded by somewhere between a million and a million and a half immigrants, mainly Irish and German, who were largely unaccustomed to living in a dense, heterogeneous urban setting. Olmsted grasped how a park like Birkenhead could serve New York as a vast outdoor classroom for mass acculturation, where uneducated newcomers would be on an equal footing with the established citizenry and observe modes of improving behavior—in dress, deportment, and leisure pursuits—that they otherwise might not encounter. Also in Olmsted's article we find a veritable checklist of features later realized in the 843-acre Central Park: the serpentine pathways, the Mall shaded by American elms, the grassy Sheep Meadow, the glades and underbrush of the Rambles, and the spacious ball fields of the Great Lawn. Even the Greensward Plan, the name that Olmsted and Vaux gave their competition-winning New York design, is prefigured here.

Central Park was laid out four decades before Manhattan's first automobile fatality in 1899, but urban equine traffic was also often deadly; in 1900 there were some two hundred horse-related deaths in New York City. Thus Olmsted and Vaux's strict division of circulation in the park acknowledged the ever-present danger of such accidents by consigning heavy east–west vehicular traffic to crosstown transverses sunk well below surface level, while above-grade pedestrian footpaths dipped beneath north–south roadways through small bridges and short tunnels. (The partners, who until they ended their partnership refused individual credit for any specific design solution, seem to have gotten this idea from a pedestrian underpass in John Nash's Regent's Park of 1812–1835 in London.)

Their concept of dual circulation soon became an article of faith among progressive planners in the United States and Europe. Clarence Stein and Henry Wright's much-praised 1929 design for Radburn, New Jersey—touted as the "New Town for the Motor Age"—so effectively segregates cars and people that children can walk to local schools and playgrounds without crossing a street. Stein, whose Central Park West apartment overlooked the 65th Street Transverse, said that he discovered what became known as "the Radburn idea" simply by peering out his front window.

Yet for all the priority Olmsted and Vaux gave to traffic patterns, it remains hard to believe that almost everything one now sees in Central Park is man-made (see Illustration 1b). This impression depends entirely on their adherence to the naturalistic ethos of the eighteenth-century British Romantic landscape movement, which supplanted the strictly formal, symmetrical, geometric approach typified by the seventeenth-century French master André Le Nôtre, who in turn drew on earlier Italian Renaissance models. In contrast, the softly undulating outlines and gentle contours of a new British landscape style that came into vogue around 1750 evoked the so-called line of beauty expounded by William Hogarth and other aesthetic theorists, who believed that the graceful Rococo S-curve was the basis for all visual harmony.

Capability Brown and his principal follower, Humphry Repton, sought to make their landscapes seem as though they had evolved naturally over time rather than being newly formed by the hand of man, exactly what Olmsted achieved time and again in his work. Renderings and photographs of Central Park in its early years remind us that it took four decades for it to grow into the mature form we recognize today. Olmsted's ability to imagine how a barren stretch of urban wasteland could be turned into an idyllic glade that looks as if it had been there forever is further demonstrated in several of his before-and-after sketches of Central Park. These and other visual documents make it clear how complicated that task was, with a host of now invisible infrastructural underpinnings that needed to be put into place—foundations for roads and paths, soil emendation and storm drainage, rerouting existing streams and ponds, dynamiting rock outcroppings—before any planting could begin.

Frederick Law Olmsted was born in 1822 to a successful

Hartford merchant who long remained his son's financial mainstay, much as that other towering nineteenth-century design and social reformer William Morris was supported by a rich parent until he finally found his professional footing. Olmsted received an excellent secondary education at the Phillips Academy in Andover, Massachusetts, but poor health kept him from matriculating at Yale as planned. He then began a fitful decade of assorted occupations—from dry goods clerk to apprentice seaman on a China trade ship that sailed to Canton and back in 1843–1844—before his father staked him to a 125-acre farm on Staten Island. (Miraculously, the old Olmsted homestead still stands, though in decrepit condition, near that outer borough's busy Hylan Boulevard. It was bought by the city of New York in 2006 to prevent its destruction, and ought to be restored as befits an important cultural landmark.)

Throughout his life, Olmsted displayed an extraordinary ability to immerse himself in a new subject and fully master it. To better cultivate his Staten Island property he studied the emergent applied science of progressive farming and land management enabled by recent discoveries in plant biology, industrial chemistry, and agricultural machinery. Yet the young would-be agronomist had many competing interests, and found that the relentless dawn-to-dark drudgery of farm work kept him from other pursuits. His watchful father saw the problem and admonished, "Your farm will require your *close & undivided personal* attention at all times & I hope no extraneous or unimportant matters...will take up your mind & time."

However, important matters continued to distract the endlessly curious Fred, mainly journalism, a direct outgrowth of the acute powers of observation and thoughtful analysis so evident in his personal correspondence. Setting aside full-time farming, he served a two-year stint as an editor of *Putnam's Magazine*, founded in New York in 1853 as an American-minded alternative to the Anglocentric literary journal *Harper's New Monthly Magazine*. This job ended when *Putnam's* foundered after the Panic of 1857, not the last time a nationwide financial crisis affected his career.

Olmsted's extensive travels throughout the southern and southwestern United States during the 1850s to report on social and economic conditions for *The New-York Daily Times* produced sharply perceptive columns that were subsequently collected in three volumes, the first and best of which—*A Journey in the Seaboard Slave States* (1856)—remains a classic on a par with Alexis de Tocqueville's endlessly cited American critique of a generation earlier. Although Olmsted was not an abolitionist, he supported the proposal that slave owners should be compensated for the value of their freed human chattel as the most equitable and practicable means of avoiding the looming conflict between North and South. That solution—which likely would have been far less costly than the Civil War in money, let alone blood—was of course never implemented.

The Cotton Kingdom, a compendium of his travel writings published in 1862 during the Civil War, gave a harsh view of the region's inhabitants, and debunked even their much-vaunted southern hospitality:

> The citizens of the cotton States...work little, and that little, badly; they earn little, they sell little; they buy little, and they have little—very little—of the common comforts and consolations of civilized life. Their destitution is not material only; it is intellectual and it is moral....They were neither generous nor hospitable....

When hostilities broke out Olmsted had already completed his principal work on Central Park, and was thus able to transfer to the war effort the formidable executive skills he'd developed in marshaling the huge platoons of contractors and workmen for a logistically complex job. He became head of the US Sanitary Commission, an agency created after the incompetence of the US Army's Medical Department became a national scandal. Long before the founding of the American Red Cross (1881) and the Department of Veterans Affairs (1930), the Sanitary Commission tried to ameliorate the appalling conditions inflicted on wounded and diseased soldiers. Of the 620,000 men who lost their lives in the Civil War, two thirds succumbed to illness, and Olmsted struggled to stem that toll in a period when the very basics of hygiene and sanitation were doubtful.

After the war he returned to finish his work on Central

Park, and with Vaux began planning the sequel that some consider an even more exquisite composition: their 585-acre Prospect Park of 1865–1873 in nearby Brooklyn. But Olmsted still kept a hand in the literary world as a financial backer of *The Nation*, the liberal political journal founded in 1865, to which he was an occasional contributor. Olmsted and Vaux dissolved their firm in 1872 after increasing disagreements, but the Panic of 1873 deterred Olmsted's rapid rebound. When economic conditions improved he quickly reestablished himself with the help of two new partners—his nephew and adopted son John Charles Olmsted and his younger biological son, Frederick Law Olmsted Jr., who headed the firm until he retired in 1949. Olmsted Brothers finally went out of business in 1980.

By the first half of the 1890s—the period covered by the ninth volume of the Olmsted correspondence—the grand old man had become not merely a national but a continental eminence, as demand for his services impelled him to shuttle continually among far-flung projects from Maine to California and Michigan to Kentucky. Most experimental among them was his comprehensive planning of the Biltmore Estate in the North Carolina Blue Ridge Mountains for George Washington Vanderbilt II. The centerpiece of this 125,000-acre property is Richard Morris Hunt's Biltmore House of 1889–1895, still the largest private residence in America, a French Renaissance Revival château like those favored by Vanderbilt's plutocratic kin and kind on New York's Fifth Avenue. Olmsted urged his client, who had run the Vanderbilt family farm on Staten Island, not far from Olmsted's old property, to rise above the empty ostentation of Gilded Age display and instead turn the surrounding land into a model of modern sustainable forestry, an idea the multimillionaire admirably endorsed. The Biltmore Estate, now owned by a family trust, has become a hugely popular tourist destination and attracts more than a million visitors each year.

Not all of Olmsted's late projects were so happy. His work at the World's Columbian Exposition of 1893 in Chicago fell victim to the rigid formality of the fair's Beaux Arts–inspired layout, in which monumental Classicizing buildings were surrounded by enormous lagoons that impeded easy circulation. One critic wrote that although Olmsted's contribution was "unquestionably very fine to look at," it was "totally unsuited for practical purposes." The designer conceded as much, and wrote that the fair would have been much better without "perhaps a third of all that was exhibited and ... an innumerable lot of trifling concession coops and shantees with slight regard to the landscape design."

But this was a rare flub in an otherwise unbroken sequence of successes that gave many American cities their finest civic features, especially Boston's dazzling "Emerald Necklace" park system (which comprises the Back Bay Fens, the Arnold Arboretum, and Wood Island Park, among other things) and the refashioning of Buffalo's topography through parkways, squares, and lakefront improvements. In 1895, the seventy-three-year-old Olmsted began to notice short-term memory lapses, and though his letters from that year show no sign of cognitive impairment, his sons also recognized his increasing decline and eased him out of the family business. Before long he had full-blown dementia, and he lived out the last five years of his life in a cottage at the McLean Hospital near Boston, where he died in 1903 amid grounds he had laid out long before.

Olmsted's status as a national figure was confirmed by the invitation in 1874 to landscape the grounds of the United States Capitol in Washington, D.C., a tricky assignment that gave this sprawling and oddly proportioned structure—erected in fits and starts to the designs of several different architects throughout the first half of the nineteenth century—a softening frame of majestic trees and a virtual pedestal of shrubberies worthy of the project's grandeur. This deeply symbolic scheme also paid indirect homage to a national heritage of unparalleled natural splendor, which Olmsted, more than anyone save the pioneering conservationists George Perkins Marsh and John Muir, identified, celebrated, enhanced, extended, and preserved. Yet even Olmsted, for all his uncanny foresight about how his parks would function in a future beyond his possible imagination, could never have predicted how instructive they would be in our polarized postmillennial America, so different from the egalitarian society his unifying designs vigorously promoted.

2

ANTONI GAUDÍ

ALTHOUGH SACRED STRUCTURES of all sorts have been central to every culture throughout history, religious architecture has attained even greater importance in times of social upheaval. This was certainly true in mid-nineteenth-century Barcelona, the ancient Mediterranean seaport that had lately become an economic powerhouse with the advent of industrialized textile manufacturing. As the strains caused by this rapid shift from small workshop to large factory production worsened, many felt that the Roman Catholic Church was unresponsive to the travails of increasingly downtrodden urban laborers. Thus during the 1870s pious (and wealthy) *barcelonés* conceived a monumental building project for a working-class neighborhood that they hoped would stem religious disaffection by harking back to the devotional fervor, communal brotherhood, and civic pride fostered by the construction of grand cathedrals during the Middle Ages.

The result is one of the most celebrated shrines in Christendom, known in Catalan as the Temple Expiatori de la

Sagrada Família (Expiatory Temple of the Holy Family). It was begun in 1882 using the conventional neo-Gothic designs of Francisco de Paula del Villar, who after two years of persistent quarrels with diocesan supervisors quit and handed the job over to his largely untested assistant Antoni Gaudí. Over the next four decades Gaudí worked toward a church that would be both intensely personal yet embracingly universal, startlingly unprecedented though rooted in tradition, and altogether far more rich and strange than anything del Villar ever dreamed of (see Illustration 2a).

Although many cathedrals feature elaborate ensembles that depict scenes from the Gospel, the program of the Sagrada Família sculptures makes most others seem rather subdued. Gaudí's jam-packed Nativity Façade, executed between 1894 and 1930, offers a paradisiacal vision of (holy) family life amid a panoply of grottoes dripping with stalactites, dense with leafy bocage, and alive with all sorts of fauna and flora. You have to look closely to find Jesus, Mary, and Joseph through all the busy detail, a bit like some divine "Where's Waldo?" game. One can scarcely imagine what this teeming jumble would have looked like had it been painted in polychrome, as Gaudí wanted to do in the manner of ancient Greek sculpture and architecture.

Above the sanctuary rise eight elongated sugarloaf spires (four were completed before the Spanish civil war, and another quartet has been added since, with another ten yet to come). Their surfaces are multicolored mosaic and they are surmounted by torqued and faceted pinnacles topped with marvelous finials like radiant monstrances. Unfurled down the sides of the towers, where only angels can read them, are trompe l'oeil scrolls joyously inscribed "Excelsis," "Hosanna," and "Sanctus."

Contrary to the common misnomer, the Sagrada Família is not a cathedral—site of a bishop's throne, or cathedra—though it was elevated to the status of a "minor basilica" when Pope Benedict XVI consecrated the half-finished church in 2010. Still under construction after more than a century and a quarter of financially and politically related fits and starts, it is scheduled to conclude in 2026, the centennial of the architect's death. (Gaudí succumbed at seventy-three after he was hit by a tram on his way from the Sagrada Família to the parish church where he attended vespers every evening.)

The Sagrada Família, Barcelona's top tourist attraction, welcomes some three million visitors annually—nearly twice the city's population—and their admission fees have been the major source of revenue for completing the edifice. The architect is a cult figure not only in his native region, where he exemplifies the unruly Catalan spirit to political separatists, but as far away as Japan. There in 2011 the hugely popular manga artist Takehiko Inoue—whose usual subject is basketball—published a book that seeks to pinpoint the source of Gaudí's inspiration, an ultimately futile task when it comes to such a complex, and to some extent inexplicable, figure.

The architectural historian Judith Rohrer has written that the Sagrada Família (originally meant to house pharos-like searchlights in its pinnacles) was intended to "serve as a beacon of faith, proclaiming the revived piety of the Spanish people, while atoning for the sins, both public and private, of a modernist, materialist age." The strain of deep conservatism implicit in that formulation—which brings to mind the militant antimodernism of Pope Pius IX, who died shortly before the Sagrada Família's inception—makes one understand why proletarian radicals did not necessarily view this costly exercise in spiritual advertisement as a social improvement program.

The new church was dedicated to the Holy Family because Saint Joseph was a carpenter with whom the city's laborers might personally identify. But empathetic feelings among that target audience were perhaps undermined when the architect's iconography for the Temptation portal (one of several thematic groupings that in addition to the Nativity include the Rosary, the Way of the Cross, and the Crucifixion) revealed a figure of a demon proffering a workman a spherical Orsini bomb—the handheld weapon favored by fin-de-siècle anarchists.

Thus despite the populist appeal of the Sagrada Família's exuberant forms and idiosyncratic decoration, a severely critical undertone lodged in some people's minds. Lingering resentment took a violent turn when in 1936, during the Spanish civil war, Republican rioters broke into Gaudí's old studio and destroyed his plaster models for the church. Indeed, as late as the 1960s, when my wife, Rosemarie Haag Bletter, did research as a graduate student in Barcelona on

Gaudí's lesser-known contemporary Josep Vilaseca, she was habitually quizzed by different factions about her attitude toward the completion of Gaudí's church, a political litmus test under the Franco regime, which looked upon *gaudísme* as a cover for seditious Catalan dissidents.

This was a tricky question to answer in any case, because Gaudí certainly realized that no one designer could live long enough to see such a grandiose endeavor through to completion. And although he left detailed instructions for parts of the structure still unbuilt during his lifetime, he expected (and accepted) that other designers would put their own, likely quite different, stamp on it, as happened with cathedrals such as Chartres, with its mismatching early Gothic and Flamboyant spires.

"Great temples were not the work of one architect," Gaudí observed, but those in charge at the Sagrada Família today have drawn on his work to the exclusion of all other possibilities. To be sure, a highly skilled, deeply dedicated group of architectural, engineering, and decorative arts professionals was directed from 2012 onward by the Barcelona architect Jordi Faulí (who spent the preceding two decades as an associate on the project). The team hewed as faithfully as possible to the letter of Gaudí's vision, but one wonders about the spirit. As a visit to the Sagrada Família today indicates, there is such a thing as being too conscientious. Employing the most advanced computer imaging technology, it has been possible to reconstitute elements once thought irretrievably lost after Gaudí's models were shattered. Yet the newest portions of the Barcelona landmark utterly lack the tactile quality of the parts of the Sagrada Família carried out while Gaudí was alive. The sense of an artist being physically involved is conspicuously missing from the most recent additions there.

Gaudí's conception evolved in three distinct phases—1890, 1913–1915, and 1921–1926—marked by models that varied significantly from one to the next. Rohrer suggests why the version being realized today, based on that final revision, seems somehow less Gaudíesque than might have been expected:

> There is a certain angularity to the forms that emerge in this model, less fluid in its continuity than Gaudí's earlier work. While not abandoning the ruled surfaces of double curvature that were so much a part of his structural thinking, he nevertheless turned in the last phase of his work toward intersecting and interlocking polyhedral geometries that yield an angular, prismatic, crystalline, almost cubist effect.

Although translating Gaudí's reconstituted designs for the Sagrada Família into building components has been made infinitely easier by digital scanning programs, there is a world of difference between the sharply rendered parts that emerge from this process and the far more improvisational results Gaudí was able to coax from artisans on site, his habitual working method. Given the figurative arthritis that set into Gaudí's supple organic forms late in his career, strict fidelity to those last pieces of work might not have been the wisest course, either. The completed nave of the Sagrada Família looks disturbingly fake, and in many places jarringly slick, especially the grid-patterned, polished stone floor that brings to mind the lobby of a 1980s corporate headquarters by Philip Johnson. Perhaps in the fullness of time all this bright, precision-cut stonework will mellow into pleasing decrepitude, but that now seems unlikely. Few mainstream architects have dared emulate Gaudí directly. Today's most obvious claimant to his mantle as maverick master is Frank Gehry, whose Olympic Fish pavilion of 1989–1992 in Barcelona (part of the Olympic Village erected for the 1992 games) exudes the antic energy of his antecedent's biomorphic fantasias. However, the steel-mesh skin of Gehry's design is uniformly detailed and tastefully monochromatic in a High Modernist mode antithetical to Gaudí's colorful and irregular surface treatments. Much more Gaudíesque in its decorative flair is Gehry's *A Rose for Lilly*, a fountain dedicated to the memory of Lillian Disney, widow of the famed animator and film producer, in the garden adjacent to his Walt Disney Concert Hall of 1989–2003 in Los Angeles. The surfaces of this biomorphic sculpture, shaped like the honoree's favorite flower, are inlaid with shards of broken china similar to the Catalan architect's work in Barcelona's Park Güell. Tellingly, the alacrity with which the civic sponsors of Gehry's Guggenheim Museum Bilbao (1991–1997) accepted his wildly unorthodox scheme says much about the persistence of the adventurous cultural attitudes Gaudí fostered in Spain a century earlier. Artists in other mediums have responded to Gaudí's example with more abandon. Although it remains unclear how much the Italian-American outsider sculptor Simon Rodia knew about him, there is no question that Rodia's Los Angeles landmark, known as the Watts Towers (1921–1954), bears a striking resemblance to the Sagrada Família in the outlines of its spires and its hand-molded mortar surfaces studded with discarded china fragments. And from the 1950s onward, the eccentric Austrian artist Friedensreich Hundertwasser fabricated a series of oddly shaped, brightly colored, and whimsically patterned houses in several European locales that led to his being dubbed "the Austrian Gaudí."

Astonishingly, given his current réclame, Gaudí languished in critical limbo for three decades after his death, in part because of the Spanish civil war and the cultural pariahdom visited on the Franco regime long afterward. The architectural historian Nikolaus Pevsner, single-minded in his promotion of a Modernist machine aesthetic, focused on Gaudí's decorative impulse but largely ignored his considerable structural achievements. In his polemical *Pioneers of Modern Design* (1936), Pevsner finds Gaudí's fairy-tale-Gothic episcopal palace at Astorga (1887–1893) "nightmarish" and his mysteriously organic chapel at the Colònia Güell (1898 and 1909–1915) "horrible." He discerns in Gaudí's creations not a miraculous inventiveness but a "frantic desire for the unprecedented" and a "delight in the arbitrary curve."

However, there was nothing at all capricious about Gaudí's parabolas and catenaries, which he calibrated just as scientifically as his great engineering contemporaries did their innovations, and without any of the high-tech aids architects now routinely rely on. Although he scorned the use of buttresses as a lazy structural crutch and was determined to find other ways to support the Sagrada Família's high, thin walls, he also sought to avoid Gothic horrors like the collapse of the choir of Beauvais cathedral in 1284 or the tower of Ely cathedral in 1322.

Gaudí gauged the strength of his arches and vaults with mock-ups from which he suspended sandbags on ropes to simulate the gravitational forces that would bear on the executed masonry, rather than depending solely on the mathematical formulae through which he arrived at his structural configurations. "I am a geometrician," the architect insisted, a riposte to those who saw only willfulness in his deceptively arbitrary-looking forms. Nonetheless, neurotic menace lurks everywhere in Pevsner's fretful surveys. Gaudí's roofs are "like the backs of dinosaurs" and the ironwork of his balconies "might stab you at any moment." Although Pevsner remained obtusely immune to the sheer bravura that has made Gaudí arguably the world's most beloved architect, he later softened his tone somewhat and attributed that animus to an excess on his part of pro-Modernist zeal. Yet his earlier position helps explain why Gaudí's work was hardly appreciated at the mid-twentieth century.

Although the Expressionists and Surrealists esteemed

Gaudí as a fellow visionary, popular attitudes began to change dramatically in the 1960s, a decade of worldwide social and cultural ferment that made Gaudí's work speak to a young generation alert to imaginative and expressive qualities long dismissed as pathologically bizarre, especially in architecture. Indeed, there is something almost psychedelic in his freewheeling aesthetic, characterized by distorted forms, propulsive patterns, kaleidoscopic colors, and quirky materials. The rediscovery of Art Nouveau during the 1960s carried Gaudí along with other newfound fin-de-siècle heroes of the burgeoning counterculture, including Aubrey Beardsley, Alphonse Mucha, and Louis Comfort Tiffany. Growing public interest was reflected in shows of Gaudí's work held at Richmond's Virginia Museum of Fine Arts (1964) and New York's Museum of Modern Art (1966).

Ulrich Conrads and Hans G. Sperlich's illustrated history *Phantastische Architektur* (1960) contained several Gaudí designs and found an even wider audience in its English-language edition, *The Architecture of Fantasy: Utopian Building and Planning in Modern Times* (1962). Published that same year, *Antoni Gaudí*, by the Barcelona-born Modernist architect Josep Lluís Sert and James Johnson Sweeney (then director of the Guggenheim Museum), stressed not the architect's phantasmagoric bent but instead an unexpected pragmatism. As Sweeney and Sert write:

> It is curious to note that Gaudí always designed taking into consideration the practical methods by which his

plans could be carried out. He chose warped surfaces because model makers and masons can construct them easily, as both the hyperboloids and the hyperbolic paraboloids are ruled surfaces which can be easily reinforced by straight steel rods, thus providing a considerable economy.

Gaudí has never wanted for admirers among his countrymen, but it was the American architectural historian George R. Collins (1917–1993) of Columbia University who made a long-overdue reappraisal that became one of the most successful attempts to elevate an artist's critical standing in modern times. During a 1959 research trip to Spain, Collins came upon a large cache of unpublished Gaudí drawings, and the following year published *Antonio Gaudi*, the first English-language monograph on the architect (using the then-prevalent Castilian, not the now preferred Catalan, version of the subject's first name). Although only 136 pages long, this tour de force of concision and insight definitively verifies Gaudí's structural genius and remains an unsurpassed introduction. Collins followed his breakthrough with further publications (including a pioneering bibliography) and influential exhibitions.

Gaudí's emergence followed and paralleled that of Rafael Guastavino (1842–1908), a decade-older Catalan contractor-builder who studied at the same Barcelona technical college where Gaudí later went, and who worked for at least one major Gaudí client, the Batlló textile manufacturing clan.

Just as Gaudí drew on a host of age-old local construction traditions, including a method for spanning large overhead spaces, Guastavino regularized and industrialized the low-tech, cost-efficient Catalan method of tile vaulting. This technique can be traced back to fourteenth-century Spain but may have had its origins in similar methods devised by the ancient Romans who colonized Iberia.

In search of international markets for his tile-vaulting concept, Guastavino displayed a proposed scheme for "Improving the Healthfulness of Industrial Towns" at the 1876 Centennial International Exposition in Philadelphia, where it won an honorable mention. This encouraged him to immigrate to the United States five years later, when he arrived in New York with a $40,000 nest egg but soon lost it in a Manhattan tenement construction speculation. He recovered financially when in 1885 he filed the first three of his firm's two dozen patents (a third of which were for acoustical improvements to make tiled interiors less noisy) for the Arch System, in which thin, grooved, slightly curved terracotta tiles are layered to form a continuous curved surface with more tensile strength than a single thicker stratum, and set with fast-drying plaster. His favored mortar—which included Portland cement (an early-nineteenth-century invention, mixing limestone and clay)—added further strength to vaults that were sometimes a mere two inches thick.

This allowed a space to be spanned without the full scaffolding needed for conventional brick or stone vaulting, which supports itself only after the central keystone is inserted into the apex of an arch. Guastavino's system was quicker and cheaper than traditional masonry methods because it significantly reduced labor time and preparatory materials. Furthermore, the result was not only sanitary (impervious to damp and rot, plus easy to clean) but, most important, fireproof, a widespread public safety concern following several catastrophic nineteenth-century urban conflagrations. Guastavino's first big American success was his work on McKim, Mead & White's Boston Public Library of 1887–1895. In a tour de force of design variation, he came up with different ceiling patterns for each room in the large structure, a veritable three-dimensional catalog for his product's versatility. Significantly, he left the handsome structural tile work fully exposed rather than covering it with plaster, an attitude that anticipated the Modernist practice of celebrating functional elements by letting them show. Thereafter his thriving company supplied Catalan-style roofs and ceilings to hundreds of architectural firms over the next eight decades.

In 1961, a crucial connection occurred to Collins at a memorial service in I. N. Phelps Stokes's St. Paul's Chapel of 1904–1907 on the Columbia campus, when he had an epiphany about how closely the structure's exposed Guastavino vaulting resembled the work of Gaudí. This eureka moment changed how architecture scholars understand a crucial chapter in the history of modern design and suggested a missing link between Catalonia and the Americas. A year later, when the Guastavino family business folded and its records were about to be discarded, Collins secured them for his school's Avery Architectural and Fine Arts Library, an invaluable act of cultural salvage. The Guastavino office's meticulous working drawings allow a full understanding of a structural methodology that would otherwise be lost to us today. In fact, many large architectural firms for whom the family worked would confidently leave portions of their own blueprints blank but labeled "Guastavino here" to indicate that vaults would be skillfully filled in by their trusted collaborator. No wonder the city of Barcelona in 1999 renamed a street bordering Gaudí's Finca Güell of 1884–1887 the calle George Collins.

Antoni Plàcid Guillem Gaudí i Cornet was born in Catalonia in 1852, though it remains unclear whether that occurred in the town of Reus, where his father and grandfather worked as coppersmiths, or in the family's ancestral village of Riudoms. The architect attributed his innate sense of volumetric enclosure to his antecedents' skilled craftsmanship of boilers, kettles, and other heating devices. Whether or not Gaudí's virtuosic grasp of irregular forms was genetic or acquired through close observation, he certainly could visualize space in three dimensions, an attribute far from common among the general public and not to be taken for granted among design professionals, either.

As the art historian Gijs van Hensbergen relates in his absorbing *Gaudí: A Biography* (2001), the future architect from an early age displayed an exceptional aptitude for mathematics, and as a teenager he and two friends dreamed up an imaginative if overreaching scheme to turn a derelict local monastery into a full-service tourist destination. Gaudí's father, instead of encouraging his progeny to continue in the family trade as was usual at that time, sold inherited land to help finance the medical studies of Antoni's older brother and then his second son's architectural education at Barcelona's Escuela Superior de Arquitectura.

There have been numerous studies of Gaudí's many sources of influence, especially the authoritative French architect and theorist Eugène-Emmanuel Viollet-le-Duc, whose combination of eclectic historicizing motifs and modern industrial materials is everywhere evident in Gaudí's oeuvre. But there is also a psychological complexity to the Catalan master's work that sets him above and apart from not only other European practitioners of his time but also from the most talented of his contemporaries in Barcelona. For all his stunning ingenuity, Gaudí did not emerge from a cultural vacuum, and he was but one—albeit the most extravagantly gifted—among an extraordinary generation of local architects who espoused the new credo of Modernisme, the distinctive Catalan variant of Art Nouveau, which drew heavily on the Romantic revivalist Renaixença (renaissance) movement of mid-nineteenth-century Spain.

This brilliant cohort included Lluís Domènech i Montaner (creator of Barcelona's stupendous Palau de la Música Catalana), Josep Vilaseca i Casanovas (who designed the city's neo-Moorish Arc de Triomf), and Josep Puig i Cadafalch (whose step-gabled Casa Amatller stands next to Gaudí's saurian-roofed Casa Batlló of 1905–1907 on the Passeig de Gracia, Barcelona's street of Modernisme dreams). There was a strong measure of competitive display among Barcelona's new industrial elite, and they vied with one another in hiring these and other exponents of the new architecture to design domestic showplaces of unabashed grandeur.

If a tycoon's town palace could directly advertise the source of his wealth, so much the better, as Gaudí achieved with his first major residential commission, Casa Vicens (1878–1880), a multicultural extravaganza for a brick and tile manufacturer that has been restored and is now open to the public. This learned exercise in the Mudéjar style—the term refers to Muslims who remained in Spain after the expulsion of the Moors—juxtaposes panels of blue and white tiles in a bold checkerboard pattern against tawny brick worked into daring variations on traditional themes of the Mozarabic Arabs (Iberian Christian Arabs who lived under Moorish rule). But as accomplished as Casa Vicens is, it exhibits none of the curvaceous organic continuity that Gaudí attained in his later and most famous works, exemplified by Casa Milá (1905–1910), a six-level Barcelona apartment building with an undulating façade that turns a chamfered corner between two perpendicular streets. Clad in limestone, this landmark is popularly known as La Pedrera (the quarry) because of its craggy, cliff-like elevation and the flowing horizontal lines of the projecting cornices on each story, which evoke the layering of geological strata (see Illustration 2b).

Another hallmark of Gaudí's architecture is ceramic embellishment. Although mosaics had been incorporated into buildings since Classical antiquity, he eschewed purpose-made components and instead appropriated irregular shards of domestic pottery in a Catalan technique called *trencadís*.

Irregular pieces of broken dishes and teacups are readily identifiable on the crazy-quilt surfaces of several of the architect's constructions in the Park Güell (1900–1914), where a quite unmenacing *trencadís*-encrusted dragon welcomes visitors at the entrance stairway, and the undulating Sea Serpent Bench, similarly enriched with recycled crockery, offers a dazzling resting place and vantage point on the central terrace overlooking Barcelona and the sea beyond.

Gaudí's most important private patron was the textile magnate Eusebi Güell i Bacigalupi, for whom he executed five major commissions in and around the Catalan metropolis. The first of these was for Bodegas Güell (1882–1897), a winery in the seaside town of Sitges southwest of the city, which remained in operation until 1936. Next came Palau Güell (1885–1889), an imposing mansion erected not in a plutocratic enclave but in what was then the city's artists' quarter (during the early 1900s the young Picasso's studio was directly across the narrow street). The building's otherwise severe masonry façade is dominated by a powerful pair of parabolic entry and exit arches screened with intricate ironwork in the form of coiled snakes that surround the initials "E" in one portal and "G" in the other. The architect's expansion of the industrialist's country estate, Finca Güell

(1887), was followed by his primitive chapel at Colònia Güell (1898–1915), the enlightened industrialist's company town. With its cavernous interiors and mysterious lighting, this jewel-like sanctuary seems a direct precursor of Le Corbusier's Ronchamp chapel. Last in this remarkable series was the phantasmagoric Park Güell, a hillside residential development more practically based in planning terms on recent English Garden City prototypes. However, it failed as a real estate speculation and was turned into a municipal park. On this forty-two-acre site Gaudí designed a host of endearingly strange infrastructural features, including cascading stairways, snakelike pergolas, arcades composed of tilting columns, as well as habitable follies for caretakers of the lushly landscaped property.

The architect himself lived in one of those outbuildings for many years, but toward the end of his life moved into makeshift quarters at the Sagrada Família to save time on commuting. This increasingly solitary and fanatically devout monomaniac—a celibate vegetarian who never married and was often mistaken for a vagrant because of his disheveled appearance and distracted demeanor—was looked upon in his old age as a secular saint, especially after 1910, when he forswore new jobs and devoted himself solely to his all-consuming masterwork. And although intimations of mortality weighed heavily on this phenomenally ambitious artist, we can only hope that he believed the words long attributed to him when he was urged to speed up production: "My client is in no hurry."

3

FRANK LLOYD WRIGHT

FEW THINGS ARE more satisfying in the arts than unjustly forgotten figures at last accorded a rightful place in the canon, as has happened in recent decades with such neglected but worthy twentieth-century architects as the Slovenian Jože Plečnik, the Austrian Margarete Schütte-Lihotzky, the Austrian-Swedish Josef Frank, and the Italian-Brazilian Lina Bo Bardi, among others. Then there are the perennially celebrated artists who are so important that they must be presented anew to each successive generation, a daunting task for museums, especially encyclopedic ones that are expected to revisit the major masters over and over again while finding fresh reasons for their relevance.

Barry Bergdoll, the Columbia professor who served as the Museum of Modern Art's chief curator of architecture and design from 2007 to 2013, confronted that dilemma when he was asked to curate a show at MoMA in honor of Frank Lloyd Wright's sesquicentennial in 2017. The result was "Frank Lloyd Wright at 150: Unpacking the Archive" (which he organized with Jennifer Gray, a project research assistant at MoMA), and it turned out to be a more hazardous proposition than its universally beloved subject might have indicated. Despite the seeming effortlessness with which MoMA has spun out popular Picasso and Matisse shows decade after decade, Bergdoll wanted to avoid rehashing its 1994 Wright retrospective or repeating material covered in more specialized exhibitions on the architect held in New York at the Whitney in 1997 and the Guggenheim in 2009.

He decided instead to organize this anniversary tribute around a mere twelve projects, including rarely discussed unexecuted designs such as Wright's Depression-era plans for a self-sufficient agricultural community and his postwar scheme for the world's tallest skyscraper. These and others were illuminated by some 450 drawings, documents, photographs, models, and architectural fragments selected from the mountain of objects obtained by MoMA and Columbia's Avery Architectural and Fine Arts Library when they took possession of the architect's archives from the economically troubled Frank Lloyd Wright Foundation in 2012. Financial details of the arrangement were never been revealed, but it was rumored that a transfer of money was involved, on terms said to be very favorable for the acquiring institutions.

The sheer numbers involved in this transcontinental move were staggering: 55,000 drawings, 300,000 sheets of correspondence, 125,000 photographs, 2,700 manuscripts, and a panoply of miscellanea, including architectural details, working and presentation models, documentary films, and home movies, all of which had been kept at Taliesin in Spring Green, Wisconsin, and Taliesin West, the foundation's headquarters in Scottsdale, Arizona. (The archive is now on the Columbia campus, with conservation done at the museum.) There is a piquant irony to the final disposition of Wright's architectural estate, for this supreme egotist never forgave MoMA for what he deemed the slighting treatment he received from Philip Johnson and Henry-Russell Hitchcock in their epochal "Modern Architecture: International Exhibition" of 1932, which he felt should have revolved around him, his characteristic worldview. Tellingly enough, "Frank Lloyd Wright at 150" was the eleventh MoMA exhibition in which he has been included, and although some of those were relatively minor mountings devoted to single projects, Wright has tallied more cumulative gallery time there than any other architect (even though Ludwig Mies van der Rohe has been given three solo retrospectives, another MoMA architectural record).

To arrive at the dozen projects featured in the exhibition, Bergdoll asked each member of a team of scholars to select a single work from the archive—the less familiar the better—and discuss it in depth. Although MoMA officials proudly stressed that they engaged a younger generation of untapped talent instead of what Bergdoll called "the usual suspects," only two of the catalog's sixteen authors were in their thirties, with more than half older than fifty, and five in their sixties and seventies.

These demographics seem to confirm what academicians

warned of decades ago: that the restrictive control of the master's archives for a quarter-century after his death in 1959 by his widow, Olgivanna (who died in 1985), would set back Wright studies for a full generation, if not longer. Dissertation advisers prudently steered doctoral candidates away from Wright topics because of the extortionate research and reproduction fees charged at that time by his foundation, as well as the editorial approval it demanded for publications that used material from the Taliesin archive. The rise of poststructuralist criticism further eroded younger scholars' interest in an architect whose uniquely personal approach to architecture had little to do with the period's fascination with linguistic theory.

The detailed attention given in "Wright at 150" to discrete aspects of his output rather than its broad outlines risked a certain unevenness, and lesser-known work by great artists is often obscure for good reason. Happily, despite its many participants, the show cohered better than one had expected. It included renderings of many projects well known to the public, including Unity Temple of 1905–1908 in Oak Park, Illinois, an inward-turning concrete monolith that reopened in June 2017 after a two-year, $25 million restoration; Fallingwater of 1934–1938 in Bear Run, Pennsylvania, with its breathtakingly cantilevered balconies perched above a woodland cascade; the Johnson Wax Building of 1936–1939 in Racine, Wisconsin, a streamlined reconception of the corporate workplace as a light-filled forest grove; and Taliesin West of 1936–1959, the architect's miragelike desert home and studio.

A highlight of the exhibition was Bergdoll's investigation of Wright's hypothetical Mile-High Illinois skyscraper of 1956—a 528-story tower intended for an unspecified site in Chicago and nearly twice as high as the tallest building executed since then—which made one wonder why, given the postmillennial mania for super-tall, super-thin engineering, it has taken so long for this stupendous oddity, more publicity stunt than serious proposal, to be reexamined so thoughtfully. Bergdoll interprets the architect's eight-foot-tall, foot-and-a-half-wide presentation drawing, which resembles some ancient scroll when opened to its full height, as a revealing artistic last will and testament prepared for posterity three years before his death at ninety-one. On it the needlelike visionary structure extends from the bottom—where its "taproot" foundation burrows into the earth as deep as the Empire State Building is tall—to little over the halfway mark, with lengthy autobiographical inscriptions occupying the uppermost portions.

The two other most engrossing schemes selected for the show emphasized Wright's long engagement with several of the most advanced currents in American society. This began in infancy when his mother, Anna Lloyd Jones Wright, introduced him to the innovative pedagogical practices of the German education reformer Friedrich Fröbel; continued throughout his youth with exposure to the preaching of his renowned social activist and pacifist uncle, the Unitarian minister Jenkin Lloyd Jones; included immersion in the early twentieth century's most advanced feminist ideas, which were shared by his freethinking companion Mamah Borthwick; and extended to ecological preservation, as signified by his being made an honorary member of the Friends of Our Native Landscape, an early environmental advocacy group founded in 1913. (Wright's subsequent support for the isolationist America First Committee between the outbreak of World War II in Europe and Pearl Harbor is often seen as a conservative retreat from those formative progressive principles, but he always insisted that his opposition to US involvement in foreign conflicts was solely pacifist, not political.)

Although Wright's principal response to the Great Depression is commonly seen as his founding in 1932 of the Taliesin Fellowship—the idealistic work-study commune that served as both an architecture school and his architectural office—between the world wars he accepted two commissions that displayed his ability to imaginatively rethink social issues. The Little Farms Unit project of 1932–1933 was intended for a back-to-the-land initiative on Long Island that would have fostered small regional agriculture as a means of making people self-sufficient at a time of widespread economic collapse and catastrophic unemployment (see Illustration 3b). The low-rise, streamlined, multipurpose food-processing and marketing facility that Wright devised as a replicable prototype for this experiment in modern subsistence farming was underwritten by the businessman Walter V. Davidson.

A former advertising executive for the Larkin Soap Company, whose monumental Buffalo headquarters of 1903–1906 Wright designed, Davidson commissioned a Prairie

House from the architect in 1908 (as did Darwin D. Martin, another Larkin executive whose Buffalo residence of 1903–1905 is now open to the public). Decades later Davidson returned to Wright to help realize this utopian rural rescue mission, which never moved beyond the planning stage despite Davidson's obsessive projections. Wright's sleekly Modernist concept looks more like the contemporaneous work of the Dutch De Stijl architect J. J. P. Oud, and both the jaunty model unearthed for the show and the inspiring story behind it made this a major rediscovery.

Of equal significance as socially motivated design is Wright's unrealized Rosenwald School of 1928 for the Hampton Normal and Agricultural Institute in Virginia (see Illustration 3a). Sponsored by the Chicago philanthropist Julius Rosenwald—president and later chairman of Sears, Roebuck and Company, then the world's largest catalog retailer—the project was meant to give architectural distinction to a charitable vocational education program dedicated to freeing poor rural blacks from an intractable cycle of poverty. Wright's scheme departed from the neo-Colonial daintiness of previous designs that had been pursued under the widely admired "Hampton Ideal," and proposed a cloister-like unit dominated by a dramatic central structure, with twin-peaked roofs as if two A-frame houses had been laterally conjoined, quite unlike the earth-hugging structures generally associated with him. In her probing analysis of this long-lost scheme for the MoMA catalog, Mabel O. Wilson, a professor at the Columbia architecture school, does not rationalize the paternalistic undertone of racial condescension inescapable in Wright's hope that through his design "the Darkies would have something that belonged to them. Something exterior of their own lively interior color and charm."

Indeed, to say that Wright—born just two years after the death of Abraham Lincoln (and originally named Frank Lincoln Wright in memory of the martyred president)—was simply echoing the prevalent racial attitudes of his time might seem like special pleading. But others who knew him well, including his longtime official photographer, the Mexican-American Pedro E. Guerrero, who himself was subjected to bigotry in the pre-war Southwest, have averred that amid the racism of mid-twentieth-century America, Wright was at heart among the least prejudiced men they had ever known.

Although Wright was a born draftsman—as proven by his intricate yet ethereal early drawings, such as his 1892 depiction of a bronze gate for the Wainwright Tomb in St. Louis, designed by his boss Louis Sullivan—from the very start of his independent practice the following year he hired talented renderers to create presentation drawings of his projects. The 2017 exhibition went to great lengths to stress this fact by identifying specific hands at various points in his career, especially one of Wright's earliest collaborators, Marion Mahony.

Like Wright, Mahony was entranced by the woodblock prints of Japanese masters that had become all the rage among Western artists during the second half of the nineteenth century. Her delicately toned rendering of one lesser-known Prairie House—his DeRhodes residence of 1906 in South

Bend, Indiana—mimics the flattened planes, strong outlines, and suggestive voids typical of the ukiyo-e style. Lest this point be lost on us, beneath her signature she added, "After FLLW and Hiroshige." Wright, who had a deeply acquisitive streak that impelled him to buy beautiful things even when he could not pay his grocer's bills, amassed such a large hoard of Japanese graphics that like many other compulsive but impecunious collectors he perforce became a dealer, both to balance his books and to further feed his habit.

In 1913, when Wright's architectural practice had come to a veritable halt because of the public outrage he caused by leaving the mother of his six children and setting up housekeeping with Mamah Borthwick, a client's wife, he traveled to Japan with the express purpose of raising cash by buying and selling prints. Bankrolled by two rich Boston aesthetes, the Spaulding brothers, the out-of-work architect, as he later wrote,

> established a considerable buying power and anything available in the ordinary channels came first to me... until I had spent about one hundred and twenty-five thousand Spaulding dollars for about a million dollars' worth of prints.

Proof of Wright's discriminating eye was evident in another sesquicentennial exhibition, small but exquisite, "The Formation of the Japanese Print Collection at the Art Institute of Chicago: Frank Lloyd Wright and the Prairie School," at the museum where the architect arranged a show with some of the same pieces in 1908, not least to create a local market for his lucrative sideline.

Because of further personal scandals (the murder of Borthwick and her children at Taliesin in 1914; a sordid divorce from his second wife; and the birth of a final child, out of wedlock), as well as changing architectural tastes—which encompassed the demise of the Arts and Crafts Movement, a resurgent Classical revival in the US, and the emergence of more radical forms of Modernism in Europe—Wright saw his job prospects go dormant for a crucial midlife decade when architects customarily receive their most important commissions. It was only the sheer force of his titanic will and capacity to constantly readapt his protean talents to new conditions—for example by taking up the new technique of concrete-block construction in Southern California during the 1920s and devising affordable "Usonian" houses for middle-class Americans in the 1930s—that gave him a triumphant second career during his final quarter-century, wholly different from but comparable in inventiveness to his Prairie School period of 1900–1914.

Once he at long last shifted into that unbroken two-decade professional upswing after the late 1930s, he spent even more time exploiting his public persona. The degree to which he became America's most recognizable architect between Stanford White and Philip Johnson through his skillful manipulation of mass media—two film clips record his disarmingly deft star turns on 1950s TV talk and quiz shows, with deadpan timing worthy of Jack Benny—speaks to his acute understanding of celebrity culture in this country. Yet for all his serial self-reinventions, Wright never lost sight of his core mission of reshaping architecture into a wholly consistent reflection of democratic American values as he understood them. The care, audacity, and originality with which Wright orchestrated the public presentation of his revolutionary architecture from start to finish—thereby finessing its positive critical reception—is laid out with exceptional thoroughness in Kathryn Smith's *Wright on Exhibit: Frank Lloyd Wright's Architectural Exhibitions* (2017). Despite its apparently circumscribed subject matter, the book widens into an intriguing treatise on career development and is so illuminatingly detailed that it gives a richer portrait of Wright than many full-length biographies. It would be hard, for example, to find a clearer, more concise, and yet poetic summation of Wright's quantum leap at the dawn of the twentieth century than Smith's description of the typical Prairie House and Wright's concomitant introduction of the open plan, a pivotal moment in the history of modern architecture:

A major conceptual breakthrough that he made early on was the realization that mechanical heating made it no longer necessary to close rooms off from each other to conserve heat. This discovery led to the open plan in public spaces—for instance, where the living room opened to the dining room on a diagonal—while maintaining compartmentalized rooms for services. With the hearth no longer used as the major source of heat, Wright was free to use it as a freestanding vertical plane in space.

The other major advance represented by the Prairie House was the rejection of the wall as the traditional solid barrier between inside and outside.... He broke the wall down into a series of elements such as piers, flat planes, and window bands—all geometrically organized by dark wood strips. The wall was now defined as an enclosure of space. Windows were no longer holes punched through a mass, but a light screen filtering sunlight into the interior. The movement out toward the landscape was amplified by the addition of porches, terraces, flower boxes, and planter urns....

The straight line of the horizon became the low sheltering roof, trees and flowers were abstracted as geometric patterns in the art glass windows, and leaves contributed their autumnal palette to the plaster surfaces.

Confirmation of Wright's incomparable and enduring popularity is inescapable when one goes to any of the more than 140 buildings by him open to visitors in the United States and Japan (about one third of his total executed output). In contrast to most modern architectural venues, his buildings attract a broad cross section of nonspecialists who may not even be regular museum visitors. Clearly something about Wright speaks to the general public in a way that the work of no other architect does. Drawing the highest attendance figures of any of the master's buildings is the Solomon R. Guggenheim Museum of 1943–1959 in New York, with 873,402 visitors in 2016.

The most curious publication to appear during his sesquicentennial year was *The Life of Olgivanna Lloyd Wright*, a biography of the architect's third and last wife, whom he married in 1928. It was compiled by Bruce Brooks Pfeiffer, a former Wright apprentice who went on to become the longtime director of the architect's archives, and Maxine Fawcett-Yeske, a musicologist who unearthed a partial and unpublished autobiographical memoir by Mrs. Wright while at Taliesin West researching her musical compositions, an endeavor she took up after her husband's death. To flesh out this incomplete story, Pfeiffer and Fawcett-Yeske augmented it with large excerpts from her several autobiographical books, and the result is most tactfully characterized by the coeditors' own description of it as a "labor of love."

During the dark years of Wright scholarship before Olgivanna Wright's death, Pfeiffer worked valiantly behind the scenes to be of as much help as possible to writers—this one included—without incurring the wrath of the volatile woman he had come to regard as a surrogate mother. Pfeiffer, who died on the very last day of Wright's sesquicentennial year at the age of eighty-seven, arrived at the Taliesin Fellowship as a worshipful nineteen-year-old, and like the outlook of most of the other young people drawn to the master's presence, his was formed by the powerful communal spirit of the organization, which hovered somewhere between that of a supportive extended family, an intrigue-ridden royal court, and a quasi-religious cult. Mrs. Wright vigorously fomented this Byzantine atmosphere, intervened in the sex lives of the Taliesin apprentices as a matter of right, and let no detail of the Fellowship escape her panoptic control.

Much of Olgivanna Wright's reminiscences deal with how she and her husband coped in his very last years with the demands, distractions, and delights of his cultural stardom. Contrary to her dour image as his ferocious protector, the chatelaine of Taliesin was not without humor, some of it unintentional, as is evident in her account of the architect's attempt to persuade Gertrude Stein and Alice B. Toklas to visit the couple at Taliesin after a reading given by Stein in Madison, Wisconsin. Though his northern headquarters was within easy driving distance, the Parisian ladies demurred. Mrs. Wright recalled:

[Stein] smiled while Alice Toklas kept repeating in Steinian style, "No, thank you. Thank you, no. We are flying to Minneapolis tonight. We love to fly to Minneapolis."

Frank still held to his faith and pursued his course: "Taliesin is beautiful," he said. "We have a group of talented young people who will be interested to meet you. They can drive you to Minneapolis."

Miss Toklas answered, "Oh, but we love to fly."

Then Gertrude Stein spoke, "We do really. Really

we do like to fly. We always fly everywhere because we like to fly."

The gorgon-like Olgivanna Wright could not, however, resist one final dig at that odd couple. As she and her husband walked away in defeat she told him, "I knew you were going to fail the minute I laid my eyes on them!" In Lewis Mumford's warmly sympathetic two-part *New Yorker* review of Wright's 1953 Guggenheim retrospective, the critic referred to him as the "Fujiyama of Architecture," an apt metaphor for a master builder who seemed as ubiquitous and eternal as the snowcapped Japanese peak. Yet looking back once again on Wright's achievement and the continued interest he inspires a century and a half after his birth, a more appropriate analogy for him in the natural world might be the giant sequoia. Wright was the hardy evergreen of architecture who towered high above his contemporaries, and although no man can begin to approach the three-and-a-half-millennium lifespan of the oldest giant sequoia, who could doubt that this perennially life-affirming artist is anything but a phenomenon for the ages?

4

JOSEF HOFFMANN AND
THE WIENER WERKSTÄTTE

THE IMAGINATIVE FERVOR that gripped avant-garde master builders and skilled artisans around 1900 in Vienna, the capital of the vast and culturally diverse Austro-Hungarian Empire, epitomized a spirit of change that paralleled an equally intense outpouring of innovation in other creative realms, including the music of Gustav Mahler and Arnold Schoenberg, the painting of Gustav Klimt and Oskar Kokoschka, and the writings of Arthur Schnitzler and Sigmund Freud. Yet the singular contributions to the visual arts that the Viennese made during this epoch have never loomed large enough in general chronicles of Modernism.

The constant rewriting of art history is not solely the province of critics and scholars; cultural institutions exert enormous influence on the way the past is perceived. This has been demonstrated most forcefully by the strong Francophile bias of New York's Museum of Modern Art, whose founding director, Alfred H. Barr Jr., set out a Gallocentric narrative of Modernism—a begat-begat-begat genealogy that began with Cézanne and posited Cubism as the central development of twentieth-century art. Barr's highly selective account deeply affected received opinion for many decades. However, even some loyal supporters of MoMA became aware of how much has been neglected because of Barr's preferences. Among them is Ronald Lauder, the New York cosmetics heir, art collector, and longtime trustee of the Modern, who served as its board chairman from 1995 to 2005 and cofounded the Neue Galerie, a privately funded Manhattan museum devoted to Austrian and German Modernism, in 2001.

The idea for the Neue Galerie began with Serge Sabarsky, a Vienna-born, New York–based dealer in Expressionist art who in 1993 bought a Beaux Arts mansion on the corner of Fifth Avenue and East 86th Street and started a foundation devoted to advancing awareness of that underrepresented work. After Sabarsky's death in 1996, his friend and client Lauder took over the as-yet-unrealized project and created what has become an indispensable part of the city's cultural life, not least because the Neue Galerie's high standards of programming and presentation have almost single-handedly redressed MoMA's systematic overemphasis on the School of Paris. This upstart institution's importance was never more clearly demonstrated than with its 2017 exhibition "Wiener Werkstätte, 1903–1932: The Luxury of Beauty," a comprehensive survey of the applied arts collective founded in Vienna by the architect Josef Hoffmann, the artist Koloman Moser, and the patron and collector Fritz Waerndorfer.

The Wiener Werkstätte (Viennese Workshops) was a direct offshoot of the Vienna Secession, the maverick faction of avant-garde painters, sculptors, and architects established in 1897 by Hoffmann, Klimt, Moser, and the architect Joseph Maria Olbrich, when they seceded from the stultifyingly conservative Union of Austrian Artists in search of more adventurous creative opportunities. (Olbrich designed its Vienna headquarters and exhibition hall, the Secession Building of 1897–1898, a mysteriously windowless structure topped with an openwork dome composed of three thousand gilded bronze laurel leaves, which wags instantly dubbed *das goldene Krauthappel*—the golden cabbage head, in local slang.) This breakaway confraternity in turn led to the establishment of the Wiener Werkstätte six years afterward. And although Hoffmann broke with the Secession in 1905 because of internecine conflicts about exactly how they should pursue their avowed common goal of the *Gesamtkunstwerk* (total work of art), these young revolutionaries all shared values that were at the very heart of the Austrian avantgarde.

The Neue Galerie exhibition made a wholly convincing case for the Wiener Werkstätte's brief efflorescence of incomparably exquisite high-style design, which included furniture, glassware, ceramics, metalwork both precious and base, jewelry, wallpaper, fabrics, graphic design, and the charming artists' postcards with which the art alliance inexpensively propagandized its ambitious agenda. With particularly piquancy it juxtaposed many works by Dagobert Peche

—the Wiener Werkstätte stalwart who might be seen as the organization's id because of his untrammeled and often disruptive inventiveness—with those of Hoffmann, the group's rational superego. And although several scholars have already proposed this notion, the show and its magisterial catalog, now the basic reference on the subject, confirmed that the Wiener Werkstätte was no less than the missing link between Art Nouveau and Art Deco.

Stereotypical notions of the group and its clientele have perpetuated clichés of a decadent imperial society obliviously waltzing on the rim of a political volcano. To be sure, the rarefied objects produced by this decorative-arts consortium now seem characteristic of a pre–Great War culture of plutocratic privilege—in stark contrast to the output of the Bauhaus, which was founded the year after that devastating conflict ended. But because the Wiener Werkstätte managed to persist beyond the downfall of the Austro-Hungarian Empire for more than a decade—a period no less economically difficult for greatly diminished Austria than for its co-combatant Germany—it is incorrect to see it as a cultural hothouse flower.

The Wiener Werkstätte went through several successive phases to survive financially, and if one of its many product lines was not selling, there was no philosophical compunction against coming up with something completely different to please consumers, at least within its expansive stylistic parameters. This noble experiment in radical design was nothing less than a conduit for a richly multicultural, if politically untenable, society that was coming apart at the seams bit by bit. Although there are strong underpinnings of Classicism in many of its designs—such as Hoffmann's famous brass centerpiece (circa 1924), a fluted, footed bowl with extravagant curlicue handles that spiral wildly outward with irresistible insouciance—this tension between tight control and wild abandon gives the Wiener Werkstätte's creations a contradictory quality so much in tune with that time, and ours as well.

Apart from the duality of so many individual Wiener Werkstätte designs—which often juxtaposed urban sophistication and peasant vitality, as in Vally Wieselthier's ceramic sculptures of women who seem equal part jaded showgirl and feckless milkmaid—the group's broad range defies easy definition. In its more folkloristic manifestations one can detect an affinity for the Magyar side of the Austro-Hungarian Empire, while evocations of a far older empire—the Byzantine—are evident in jewelry designs such as Hoffmann's rectilinear brooches, so densely encrusted with multicolored semiprecious stones that they recall the jewels of the empress Theodora as depicted in the Ravenna mosaics. It now seems incredible that one company could turn out both Bertold Löffler's anorexic stoneware bud vases (circa 1906) and then a year later Michael Powolny's chubby ceramic putti representing the four seasons (high-style precursors of the *kitschig* Hummel figurines first made in 1935). Moser's silver-and-niello sugar box of 1903, a cubic form further reinforced by its all-over black-and-silver-checked surface, is as severe as a Donald Judd sculpture. Conversely, Peche's bombastic walnut writing desk of 1922 is so massive and overwrought that it could be best described as Babylonian Baroque. Yet they all bore the superimposed double-W label devised for the firm by Moser (who also came up with distinctive initialed logos for each of its participating artists), and one cannot say that any single aesthetic represents the Wiener Werkstätte, which can only be understood in all its bewildering complexity.

The group faced the same basic problem that bedeviled several of its earlier counterparts in the British Arts and Crafts Movement, including the Century Guild of Artists, established by Arthur Mackmurdo in 1883; the Art Workers' Guild, founded in 1884 by the architect William Lethaby and others; and C. R. Ashbee's Guild and School of Handicraft (1888). Each of them was self-consciously modeled after medieval craftsmen's guilds (though with less emphasis on exclusionary job protection, a central element of those precursors of modern labor unions). They all espoused a return to preindustrial fabrication methods and a commitment to bringing good design to the masses. Yet they wound up producing objects—even those not made from intrinsically precious materials—that were so labor-intensive that they could never compete with machine-made items that the working class could afford, and thus became luxury goods for the rich. Design reform groups that were established along conventional business models fared better financially than their utopian counterparts. William Morris's London-based home furnishings concern, Morris & Co. (as it was renamed in 1875 to capitalize on its mastermind's increasing renown), weathered successive changes in popular taste and lasted until 1940, forced out of business only by the Blitz. Interestingly, it was not the earnest Morris, a crusading socialist, to whom the Vienna avant-garde gravitated among British designers, but rather the Scottish architect Charles Rennie Mackintosh, whose work was darker and more emotionally complex than the heartily straightforward ethos of the Arts and Crafts Movement. Not for nothing was Mackintosh's Glasgow circle called "The Spook School," in response to the wraithlike quality and spiritual subtext of its decorative schemes. Indeed, one of the Wiener Werkstätte's signature motifs—repetitive right-angled grids in wood or metalwork—came directly from Mackintosh, and the group's prime mover was nicknamed "Quadrat-Hoffmann" because of his extreme fondness for square patterns. Mackintosh's designs were extensively published in the new half-tone-illustrated international applied art journals (especially *The Studio*, founded in London in 1893, and *Deutsche Kunst und Dekoration*, established in Darmstadt in 1897) that allowed a rapid and reciprocal exchange of design ideas across great distances. He also met several of his Viennese admirers in 1902 at the First International Exposition of Modern Decorative Arts in Turin, which led the Wiener Werkstätte's greatest early benefactor, Fritz Waerndorfer, to commission a music room for his suburban Vienna villa from Mackintosh despite the abundance of local talent available to him.

This otherworldly environment was completed in 1903, the year that the Wiener Werkstätte opened for business. The economic premise of early design reform groups was always shaky. The Bauhaus was a rare exception, thanks to its being a state-sponsored school (hence its official name, Staatliches Bauhaus) and thus free from the financial pressures of a commercial enterprise. In due course its numerous design patents and licensing agreements (especially the hugely popular Bauhaus wallpaper lines) brought in a steady if not enormous income that, with admirable equity, was parceled out to students who devised the product prototypes in their workshop classes. The Wiener Werkstätte, in contrast, was a money pit from its inception. This has long been known, but the most comprehensive account yet of the group's parlous finances is laid out in disheartening detail by Ernst Ploil in the 2017 Neue Galerie exhibition catalog. Ploil sums up the Wiener Werkstätte's economic dilemma by quoting a letter from Hoffmann to the Belgian engineer and financier Adolphe Stoclet—patron of the architect's *Gesamtkunstwerk* masterpiece, the Palais Stoclet of 1905–1911 in Brussels (see Illustration 4b). As Hoffmann wrote:

> The lady [Miss Wittgenstein] wanted (for months now) two candelabra, each two meters tall, of gilded wood. Finally the drawings were finished and correct, and a cost estimate was drawn up in my absence. That alone is madness, since it is simply impossible to produce a cost estimate for an object you haven't yet made....

Fortunately, Miss Wittgenstein came and said the estimate was too high. And at that moment I already told her that we were freed of any obligation because she did not accept the estimate and that now we will not make the candelabras at any price, because we no longer make unique objects.... "Strange," said Miss Wittgenstein, "and we always thought you were getting extremely rich from these commissions." And I said to her: "You can best see just how much such commissions can enrich us (she wanted to pay eight thousand crowns [equal to more than $100,000 today] for the candelabras) from the fact that now we simply no longer accept such commissions."

Miss Wittgenstein (an unspecified sister of Ludwig's, perhaps the future Margaret Stonborough-Wittgenstein, who was painted by Klimt in 1905) was a member of a steel-manufacturing dynasty that had converted from Judaism to Protestantism and was the second richest in Austria, after the Rothschilds. And as Christian Witt-Dörring explains in the catalog:

The Werkstätte was supported by a small group of artists and primarily Jewish wealthy families that were relatives or friends or were connected by economic interests and backed the project of Vienna's artistic springtime with their commissions. The members of the Jewish families had generally assimilated into Vienna's

Christian culture in the second generation after Austria-Hungary's Jewish population obtained full civil rights from around 1860. Their desire to integrate fit well with ... [the] search for a modern Austrian style ... which gained acceptance in the international market as the "Vienna style," [and] offered the assimilated Jewish population the potential of a feeling of belonging that was not defined in terms of nation.

Another mainstay of the Wiener Werskstätte was the Primavesi family, descended from Italian Jewish bankers who during the eighteenth century emigrated from Lombardy to Moravia (now part of the Czech Republic but ruled by the Austrians from 1809 to 1918). Hoffmann designed two large residential schemes for members of that clan. He carried out a complete interior remodeling of the baronial Primavesi Country House near the Moravian town of Winkelsdorf (1913–1914) for the entrepreneur and parliament member Otto Primavesi. And for Otto's younger cousin and brother-in-law, the banker and industrialist Robert Primavesi, and his wife, Josefine Skywa, he created the neo-Classical Villa Skywa-Primavesi in Vienna (1913–1915), which includes a large formal garden (as does the Palais Stoclet). Otto Primavesi took over Waerndorfer's role as the commercial director of the Wiener Werkstätte in 1915, and he and Robert became its principal underwriters after Waerndorfer's financial collapse.

The idealistic but impractical Waerndorfer came from yet

another rich Jewish family, whose profitable cotton mills allowed him to realize his aesthetic dreams. Yet this true believer's unstinting support of the Wiener Werkstätte soon had disastrous economic consequences. As Witt-Dörring writes, "Waerndorfer's absolute faith in Hoffmann's genius oscillated between the extremes of 'Can I afford it?' and 'I owe it to the world to afford it,'" but the latter attitude invariably won out. This Maecenas's willful lack of caution eventually impoverished him, to the extent that he immigrated to the US, became an artist, and during the Great Depression took up farming in a Philadelphia suburb, where he died a month before the outbreak of World War II.

Josef Franz Maria Hoffmann, the beneficiary of Waerndorfer's unstinting if perhaps foolhardy support, was born in 1870 in a small Moravian town where his father was mayor. The Hoffmanns were Catholic and *Deutschmährer* (German Moravians), an ethnic and linguistic minority (about one third of the predominantly Czech region's population) better known by the 1930s as Sudeten Germans, whom Hitler used as his pretext for breaking up the two-decade-old Czechoslovak Republic when he occupied the German-majority Sudetenland in 1938. Hoffmann first attended a state-sponsored crafts school in Brno, Moravia's largest city, but then moved on to Vienna's far more prestigious Academy of Fine Arts, where he studied under Otto Wagner (and after his graduation in 1895 went to work in his architectural office, where he befriended Olbrich).

Wagner was not only the foremost Austrian master builder

of the period but also a force of such wide-ranging influence that his stature is difficult to appreciate these days, when architects rarely wield such broad cultural power. In our own time Philip Johnson perhaps came closest, although he possessed neither Wagner's high professorial credentials nor critical regard. The so-called *Wagnerschule* (Wagner School) of the master's many disciples dominated Central European architecture for decades; there was never a Johnson School, except perhaps for his eager acolyte Robert A. M. Stern, who patterned his busy but vacuous design career all too closely on the surface-over-substance ethos of his power-broker paragon.

Hoffmann was weirdly secretive, especially as the impresario of a business enterprise so dependent on social interactions. For example, he had an aversion to being touched and refused to eat food prepared by any cook whose hands repelled him. He kept two apartments in Vienna, one where he received people he could not otherwise put off and a second for a wife and child whose existence he kept secret even from his employees. They were later startled to discover that he had a grown son, Wolfgang, who went on to become an architect, though one of little consequence, and immigrated to the US, where he died in 1969.

Even after Hoffmann became preoccupied with the Wiener Werkstätte he pursued an independent architectural career, based mainly on residential commissions, many of them for supporters and clients of his design consortium. But he also received significant institutional commissions, including his Sanatorium Purkersdorf of 1903–1905 (see Illustration 4a), an addition to the Westend Sanatorium in the Lower Austrian *Luftkurort* (air spa) of Purkersdorf. This three-story, rectangular, flat-roofed, bilaterally symmetrical structure was exceptional at the time for its absence of projecting ornament of any sort, with windows set flush into the smooth white stucco walls, a Minimalism that would point to the later, even more severe work of Adolf Loos, the turn-of-the-century Austrian architect now most readily identified with such simplicity. (Loos, who was five days older than Hoffmann, is best remembered for something he never said— "Ornament is a crime"—a distortion of the title of his 1910 book-length essay *Ornament and Crime*, in which he noted a parallel between primitive societies' love of ornament and modern criminals' propensity for tattoos, and argued that "freedom from ornament is a sign of spiritual strength.")

With its comprehensively customized design coordinated down to the smallest detail, the Sanatorium Purkersdorf was every bit as much a *Gesamtkunstwerk* as the Palais Stoclet, although infinitely less opulent, in keeping with the emergent Modernist belief that calm, neutral surroundings were conducive to both physical and mental health. Although this facility specialized in curative baths and physical therapy rather than the treatment of tuberculosis—the focus of such later architectural landmarks as Jan Duiker and Bernard Bijvoet's Sanatorium Zonnestraal in Holland and Alvar Aalto's Paimio Sanatorium in Finland—it signaled that health-care design would become a major focus of the Modern Movement's comprehensive attitude toward social reform.

Throughout the twentieth century, international expositions were important showcases for a nation's cultural identity as expressed through architecture, and it was a sign of Hoffmann's increasing stature in his homeland that he was chosen to design the Austrian pavilion at four of them: the International Fine Arts Exhibition of 1911 in Rome; the Werkbund Exhibition of 1914 in Cologne; the Exposition internationale des arts décoratifs et industriels modernes of 1925 in Paris (which famously gave its name to Art Deco design); and the Venice Biennale of 1934. The first two of these temporary buildings were fairly similar Stripped Classical compositions, replete with stylized pediments, colonnades, and pilasters like the Villa Skywa-Primavesi. An altogether more unusual scheme was his Paris pavilion, one of the fair's architectural highlights and appreciated as such at the time, enough to earn the architect a Légion d'Honneur. Asymmetrical in layout unlike its two predecessors, the 1925 Austrian Pavilion was a further departure from his earlier work thanks to its distinctive stucco exterior, which featured broad horizontal bands that undulated in curving profile like supersized Classical molding, an effect that gave the walls a sensuous rhythm. Inside, one decorative-arts gallery comprised a veritable Wiener Werkstätte showroom. Hoffmann reverted to a symmetrical format in his Venice Biennale pavilion, which is centered by a monumental ground-to-roof portal that bisects the horizontally grooved stucco façade and is wrapped with a glass clerestory strip. This is the only one of his exhibition buildings to survive.

Even before the Wiener Werkstätte went under in 1932, Hoffmann turned to the design of social housing sponsored by the municipal authorities of Austria's capital city, which at the time was termed *das Rote Wien* (Red Vienna) for its far-left sympathies. Avowedly apolitical—"I don't know anything about it," he demurred when questioned about the issues of the day—like countless other Gentiles he apparently felt no compunction about remaining in Austria after Hitler annexed it in March 1938. As Eduard Sekler writes in the standard monograph, *Josef Hoffmann: The Architectural Work* (1985), "Hoffmann welcomed the new regime because it promised economic progress and, above all, revived his architectural practice," despite his close and longstanding connections to Jews who suddenly found themselves in grave danger.

Indeed, he quickly accepted a commission from his country's new rulers. Now that Germany had absorbed Austria, it no longer needed its embassy in Vienna, which Hoffmann was asked to remodel into the headquarters for the occupying armed forces, the Haus der Wehrmacht. Furthermore, he accepted a high bureaucratic appointment from the notorious Baldur von Schirach, the Nazi gauleiter of Vienna who was sentenced at Nuremberg to twenty years in prison. The architect's collaboration seems not to have harmed him greatly during the decade he had left after the war ended, and although during that final phase he built almost nothing, it had more to do with his seeming to be old-fashioned rather than politically tainted. He died in relative obscurity in 1956 at the age of eighty-five.

Another major figure in the Wiener Werkstätte saga was Joseph Urban, the Vienna-born architect who immigrated to the US in 1911 and was instrumental in bringing the group's concepts to the attention of an unprecedentedly large public. Although Urban designed one of Manhattan's early Modernist gems—the crisp gray-brick and strip-windowed New School for Social Research of 1929–1931, as fresh-looking now as the day it was completed—his lucrative and highly publicized career as a stage decorator for the interwar years' quintessential Broadway extravaganza, the Ziegfeld Follies, has overshadowed his other achievements. Much less remembered today is his design work for Cosmopolitan Productions, the movie studio bankrolled by the newspaper magnate William Randolph Hearst, in large part to advance the career of his mistress, Marion Davies, an erstwhile Ziegfeld girl. As the art director on more than thirty Cosmopolitan films and with Hearst's lush budgets at his disposal, Urban created settings that were either directly based on Wiener Werkstätte interiors or incorporated actual pieces made by the design cooperative.

Urban was particularly fond of the assertive designs of Peche, which veritably popped off the screen even in black-and-white, including his boldly patterned white-turquoise-and-black Daphnis wallpaper, which Urban used for E. Mason Hopper's *The Great White Way* (1924). And in

E. H. Griffith's *Unseeing Eyes* (1923), a cameo appearance is made by Peche's silver-gilt and coral jewel box of 1920. Fifteen inches high and topped by a sprightly three-dimensional doe munching on grapes overhead, this bizarre but endearing caprice is now in the permanent collection of the Metropolitan Museum, which has always been far less puritanical than MoMA about what constitutes modern design. Urban's commitment to the Wiener Werkstätte went even further when he decided to establish a New York showroom for the organization in order to help its artists survive during a decade when America was prospering but Austria, like Germany, was mired in the economic depression that followed their defeat. In 1922 he opened a stupendous shop at 581 Fifth Avenue, and America had never seen anything like it, starting with the octagonal, silk-paneled reception room dominated by Gustav Klimt's nearly six-foot-tall canvas *The Dancer*, with a Klimt landscape and an Egon Schiele *Madonna* hung elsewhere on the premises.

But the same impracticalities that had dogged the Wiener Werkstätte for the two preceding decades in Vienna persisted at its Manhattan satellite, where Urban perversely made it as difficult as possible for anyone to actually buy anything. Were they in a private home or a museum rather than a store, even well-disposed visitors wondered? As Urban's daughter, Gretl, reminisced years later, "It was funny to see father upset when one of his favorite pieces was being looked at by a potential purchaser." No wonder the store lasted less than two years. Luxury products bought at the short-lived American outlet often disappeared into well-appointed haut-bourgeois households and lingered there as they slowly morphed from fashionable novelties into historical treasures. The New York Art Deco architect Ely Jacques Kahn, who knew the sociable Urban well, acquired at his friend's Manhattan shop a footed-and-fluted silver bowl designed by Hoffmann in 1917, used it for decades as a dining-table centerpiece in his sprawling Park Avenue apartment, and gave it to the Cooper Hewitt Museum in 1962. And most of the pieces offered at a landmark Wiener Werkstätte show held four years after that at New York's Galerie St. Etienne—the first exhibition of the group's designs in the United States since the Fifth Avenue outpost closed in 1923— came from the Urban family's considerable stock of unsold merchandise.

Interest in the nearly forgotten Wiener Werkstätte grew steadily during the 1960s as part of a widespread Art Nouveau revival. But whereas the more psychedelic aspects of Art Nouveau that so captivated the Sixties counterculture were soon deemed passé, the work of the fin-de-siècle Viennese avant-garde became even more highly prized during the 1980s with the rise of Postmodernism. The proponents of that neotraditional style were eager for a return to pattern and ornament, which had been anathema during the half-century ascendance of the International Style, and they felt a strong kinship with the Wiener Werkstätte's suave melding of Classical and early Modernist elements. Among the younger American architects most beguiled by Hoffmann and his coterie were Richard Meier (who during the 1970s began to collect turn-of-the-century Austrian design objects) and Charles Gwathmey. Both of them created china and metalwork, much of it based on the Wiener Werkstätte's familiar quadratic motifs, for the Swid Powell company, which during the 1980s catered to the new vogue for objects designed by celebrated architects. But the Postmodernist most taken with Hoffmann was Michael Graves, who eagerly turned out furniture, products, and interior designs for numerous clients and modeled his practice after that of the multitalented Viennese master in an attempt to broaden the writ of the architect.

Being able to control all aspects of a large commission had immense appeal for architects who, after the interchangeable-parts ethos of postwar modernism, wanted to achieve a cohesive look that would express a more grounded sense of place and be distinctively different from prevalent taste. Graves envisioned a return to the *Gesamtkunstwerk* as sought by many artists around the turn of twentieth century, including Frank Lloyd Wright, the greatest American exponent of that concept, whose unified approach to all details of a scheme perpetually resonates with the public. But Graves soon faced the same dilemma that thwarted his many predecessors in the design-reform movements: luxury objects, no matter how high the retail markup, are unlikely ever to be as profitable as plentiful machine-made goods. He ultimately concentrated on moderately priced consumer items (for Alessi, Target, and other household product companies), while his architecture came to resemble supersized kitchen gadgets. He got rich on royalties from his bird-topped Alessi teakettle (1.5 million units sold), but grew increasingly embittered as he dropped off the radar of the architectural press. Though he blamed his shift of critical fortune on a prejudice against those who don't focus on buildings, many thought the fault lay in the quality of his work rather than in the genres he pursued.

Another distant echo of the Wiener Werkstätte now spikes the skyline of midtown Manhattan. The real estate mogul Harry Macklowe, the developer of Rafael Viñoly's 432 Park Avenue condominium tower of 2011–2015 (see Illustration 18b), revealed that while the building was under construction, a white-painted gridded-metal wastepaper basket designed by Hoffmann in 1905 served as an "important touchstone" for the design. As Macklowe explained:

> If you look at it very carefully you see a rhythm, you see a pattern, you see what we call push-pull between negative and positive. So that was very inspirational to Rafael Viñoly and I.

In fact, the extremely attenuated proportions of 432 Park —the world's highest residential structure—make it more closely resemble Hoffmann's white-painted metal vases, tall but narrow, which employ the same *Gitterwerk* (latticework) technique. (This design and its numerous variants became one of the Wiener Werkstätte's most notable commercial successes.) But because a $225 reproduction of Hoffman's trash can was at the time on sale in the Neue Galerie's gift shop, few commentators could resist citing it as a source for the $1.3 billion skyscraper. All the same, any object devised for one purpose but grossly transmogrified both in scale (whether bigger or smaller) and function meets the textbook definition of kitsch, even if its aesthetic is minimalist rather than naturalistic.

Further evidence of the Wiener Werkstätte's obsessive perfectionism but hopeless business model could be found in another *Gitterwerk* piece included in the 2017 Neue Galerie show. At first glance, Moser's silver breadbasket of 1904 would seem to be identical to Hoffmann's better-known essays in pierced metalwork. Yet instead of hewing to either a flat or an evenly rounded surface like most of Hoffmann's gridded metal objects, this approximately oval one—ten and a half inches long by two and a half inches high—swells outward in five symmetrical pairs of curving segments, like the ground plan of a Bavarian Rococo pilgrimage chapel, and is a reminder of the playful eighteenth-century impulse that lay beneath so much of the Wiener Werkstätte's output, even early on.

However, when you look more closely at Moser's apparently identical perforations, you begin to realize that although every square seems to be equal, each turns out to be very slightly calibrated to compensate for the billowing curvature. This effortful sleight of hand conveys an impression of uniformity that would not exist without exacting and costly attention to detail. Moser's almost imperceptible and uneconomical deception helps explain why the grand illusion of the Wiener Werkstätte continues to enchant us a century after its frenetic heyday.

5

EDWIN LUTYENS

IN 1970 IT would have seemed preposterous to assert that the two greatest architects of the twentieth century were Le Corbusier and Edwin Lutyens. Although each during his lifetime was considered supreme in his respective sphere—Le Corbusier among modernists, Lutyens among traditionalists—their comparative influence differed tremendously. Whereas Le Corbusier's precepts became the predominant lingua franca of world architecture, Lutyens embodied the final effulgence of Classicism, which the Modern Movement had supposedly rendered irrelevant. Unequal as these antithetical figures may still seem to some, their complementary preeminence was acknowledged as early as the 1920s.

The concurrence during that decade of Lutyens's British imperial capital of New Delhi and Le Corbusier's visionary proposals for drastically rebuilding Paris prompted Indian urbanists to ask both men to devise plans for a new subcontinental city. Lutyens demurred: "With Corbusier I think your friends would be far happier and his flow of language would carry them all." Le Corbusier finally got to build such a city with his Punjabi regional capital at Chandigarh of 1951– 1964. Lutyens was respectful if skeptical of the Swiss-French radical, and in a 1928 review of his *Towards a New Architecture* rightly faulted Le Corbusier's illogical transposition of Mediterranean materials and forms to northern climates.

Today's more inclusive view of the building art makes it easier to contend that although Lutyens was by no means a Modernist, he was most definitely a modern architect, and a very great one at that. While he largely disdained innovative construction methods, he responded to the new needs of the twentieth century with restless imagination, as demonstrated by his up-to-date corporate headquarters, admirable workers' housing, and incomparable memorials to Britain's victims of unprecedented industrialized combat during World War I.

Lutyens worked in four successive but frequently overlapping (and sometimes recurrent) stylistic modes: Arts and Crafts, Art Nouveau, Neo-Georgian, and High Classical. To all of them he brought an unruly vivacity that was his most noteworthy quality. His vernacular version of Arts and Crafts, familiarly known as the Surrey Style, featured traditional regional motifs, including prominent redbrick chimneys, large multiple gables, overhanging red tile roofs, small-paned casement windows, and elevations clad in varying combinations of brick, stucco, tile, clapboard, half-timbering, or sandstone. Asymmetrical massing suggested additions accreted over time, a characteristic of old country houses.

Always attuned to shifts in taste and eager to give clients

what they wanted, Lutyens was more accommodating than his hugely talented contemporaries C. F. A. Voysey and C. R. Ashbee, whose careers foundered as they clung to Arts and Crafts principles long after they'd gone out of fashion. Lutyens next had a brief Art Nouveau phase, seen in houses such as the Bois des Moutiers of 1898 in Normandy, with its exaggeratedly steep roofs and elongated oriel windows in the manner of Charles Rennie Mackintosh. But he was intrinsically wary of the new free style, as he wrote of an extremely stylized Mackintosh tearoom in Glasgow: "The result is gorgeous! and a wee bit vulgar!... All just a little outré, a thing we must avoid, and shall too."

With the demise of Art Nouveau during the new century's first decade, Lutyens reimagined Queen Anne and early Georgian architecture in a series of designs inspired by his idol Christopher Wren, a shift that Lutyens, an inveterate punster, called his "Wrenaissance." Moving on from that phase, his first full-blown essay in Classicism was Heathcote of 1905–1907, an imposing stone villa for a rich Yorkshire businessman. This vigorous symmetrical composition channels the quirky designs of the early-eighteenth-century Mannerist Nicholas Hawksmoor and announces that Lutyens will not be playing Classicism by the cautious Adam Revival rulebook that then predominated. For him Classicism was the absolute summit of the building art. "In architecture Palladio is the game," he wrote. "It is a big game, a high game."

Astoundingly prolific, Lutyens completed some seven hundred commissions, and his range was comprehensive.

His designs included the stage sets for his friend J. M. Barrie's hit plays *Quality Street* (1902) and *Peter Pan* (1904); the sumptuous Queen Mary's Dolls' House (1920–1924), still on view at Windsor Castle; the Hampton Court Bridge (1928) spanning the Thames south of London; and the twin fountains in London's Trafalgar Square (1937–1939). He erected three dramatically sited castles—Lindisfarne (1903), on Holy Island in Northumbria; Lambay (1905–1920), on an island near Dublin; and Drogo (1910–1930), on a Devon hilltop—as well as the thatch-roofed Drum Inn (1934) in the picturesque village of Cockington, also in Devon.

This specialist in country houses (he built some three dozen) also executed several socially conscious schemes, and contrary to his reputation as a spendthrift worked effectively with modest materials and limited budgets. His Arts and Crafts–style building called Goddards of 1898–1899 in Surrey was conceived by its sponsor, a philanthropic tycoon, as a country vacation retreat for low-income women who could not otherwise afford rural holidays (though the patron's less altruistic son later had Lutyens convert it into a home for his own private use). The YWCA Central Club of 1928–1932, a redbrick Neo-Georgian pile in London's Bloomsbury, was commodious enough to be turned into a luxury hotel in 1998. (Lutyens's palatial Midland Bank headquarters of 1924–1939 in the city's financial district reopened in 2017 as a five-star hotel, complete with a member's club called the Ned, the sociable architect's nickname.)

His Page Street and Vincent Street Housing of 1928–1930

in London's Pimlico, for the Westminster City Council, is an unexpected delight in a drab part of the city. The façades of these six-story flat-roofed residential blocks are emblazoned with a striking checkerboard pattern of alternating brown brick and white stucco panels. Set flush to the sidewalk, the apartment buildings surround handsomely landscaped courtyards and are interspersed with shops in Classical pavilions. These low-cost but high-style public dwellings contradict the cliché of soulless modern housing for the masses.

Like other architects with Arts and Crafts roots—especially his two-years-older American counterpart Frank Lloyd Wright—Lutyens preferred to design a building down to its smallest details. He abhorred both Victorian clutter and Edwardian luxe, and instead emulated the rigorously austere interiors of the seventeenth-century Dutch painter Pieter de Hooch. The rooms Lutyens decorated were often short on comfort. He banished overstuffed slipcovered divans in favor of more austere high-backed sofas (based on a seventeenth-century design used at Knole, the stately home of the Sackville family in Kent), reintroduced straight-backed Jacobean oak seating, and instead of wall-to-wall broadloom preferred wooden or black-and-white stone floors scattered with Asian carpets.

Lutyens's horizontally wood-slatted Thakeham garden seat (1902), with the curvaceous outlines of a Chippendale camelback sofa, is the most ubiquitous of his many furniture and lighting designs. It and a number of his other furnishings are still produced by a company his granddaughter runs. The architect's color palette could be startling, demonstrated by his fondness for black-painted drawing-room walls (a marvelous backdrop for pictures) and floors painted an intense shade of green obtained by mixing equal parts chrome yellow and cobalt blue. His strict views on such matters betray his acute class consciousness and anticipate Nancy Mitford's "The English Aristocracy" by several decades. As Jane Ridley relates in her insightful biography, *The Architect and His Wife: A Life of Edwin Lutyens* (2002):

> Ned hated most things about modern middle-class life. His dislikes included: long-stemmed glasses, fish knives, cut flowers, silk lampshades, pile carpets, the seaside, the placing of furniture diagonally, painted nails.

He always had a mathematical bent, and his skillful application of the golden section—a ratio devised by the ancient Greeks to guarantee pleasing proportions—came as second nature. Given Lutyens's spotty education, his mastery of this essential design aid surely drew on innate abilities, for there is no other way to explain his amazing metamorphosis from a callow designer of overgrown country cottages into the most sophisticated manipulator of the Classical vocabulary since John Soane.

Edwin Landseer Lutyens was born in London in 1869 to an eccentric ex-army officer of German descent turned sporting artist, who named him after his mentor, the celebrated animal painter Edwin Landseer, a favorite of Queen Victoria's. Lutyens's Irish Catholic mother became a fervent Protestant Evangelical convert, and her religious preoccupation seems to have left Ned—tenth of her thirteen offspring—emotionally needy of women all his life. His childhood was divided between the family's large house in the capital's arty Onslow Square (Thackeray had once lived nearby, as did the design reformer Henry Cole) and their tumbledown cottage in the Surrey countryside. With the accelerated transformation of that county after the advent of railways into a residential region for nouveau riche Londoners, young Lutyens was among the many antiquarian enthusiasts who scoured the surrounding terrain for quaint buildings to sketch before they vanished.

Although Lutyens later regretted not having gone to public school—more for the aristocratic contacts it would have brought him than for any great love of formal learning—he also liked to boast that he was largely self-taught. "I got the architectural idea about fifteen or so," he recalled, and in 1885 entered London's South Kensington School of Art to study that discipline. After two years he began an apprenticeship with the firm of Ernest George and Harold Peto, called the Eton of architecture for its distinguished and well-connected alumni. Little more than a year later Lutyens decided he'd learned enough and at twenty set up independent practice in London.

In 1889, while working on his first house in Surrey, he

encountered Gertrude Jekyll, a South Kensington alumna more than twenty-five years his senior, whose four hundred garden designs, thousand articles, and dozen popular books helped revolutionize modern horticulture. Jekyll moved prevailing taste away from stiffly regimented Victorian flower beds with garishly colored exotics and toward spontaneous-looking (though carefully composed) drifts of native species deployed like brushwork in an Impressionist painting. Our image of the classic English garden derives directly and almost entirely from her.

What Jekyll needed most was an educable architectural associate—someone to bring structural coherence to large landscape layouts and to build houses that needed her gardens. She found him in Lutyens, and it was a professional match that benefited them both enormously. Together they championed the outdoor room, a roofless geometric space enclosed by masonry walls or hedges of yew or box. Their grandest collaboration, the garden of 1906 at Hestercombe in Somerset, is an Anglicized adaptation of Classical multilevel Italian gardens that completely upstages the adjacent Victorian residence.

Lutyens's much-admired Surrey house for Jekyll's own use, Munstead Wood of 1893–1897 in Godalming, was his first fully mature work (see Illustration 5a). Although it was constructed using age-old techniques and indigenous forms, he adjusted its functions to the needs of a modern working woman (specifying a darkroom, for instance, so she could develop her own photographs, which she used not only for reference but to publicize her services).

Through Jekyll he met his most important client and publicist, Edward Hudson, who founded *Country Life* in 1897. Apart from his designing the paper's London office building of 1904–1906 (a Wrenaissance affair in Covent Garden), and three residences for Hudson (Deanery Garden of 1899–1901 in Sonning, Berkshire; Lindisfarne Castle; and Plumpton Place of 1928–1936 in East Sussex), the architect's work from 1900 onward was regularly published in this bible of the landed gentry and its urban aspirants. Alluringly photographed and uncritically described, Lutyens's houses were presented as the quintessence of English domesticity, and the exposure given him by Hudson brought in client after client.

At twenty-seven, Lutyens met and was instantly infatuated with the twenty-one-year-old Lady Emily Lytton, daughter of the first Earl of Lytton (who had been ennobled after serving as viceroy of India under Disraeli) and granddaughter of Edward Bulwer-Lytton, author of *The Last Days of Pompeii* and other best-selling historical novels. The ambitious architect was likely dazzled by Emily's high status, but despite his ardor and professional prospects, Lutyens's lack of a fortune (even more of an impediment than his comparatively lowly birth) precluded an immediate engagement. After protracted negotiations with her family, he made Emily the beneficiary of a life insurance policy worth the current equivalent of $1.67 million, and they married in 1897. The high premiums for what was tantamount to a reverse dowry drained the architect's resources for years, but his bartered bride remained incorrigibly spoiled. She pulled rank on him constantly and complained that it was impossible to run their London house with fewer than ten servants. Despite their early protestations of everlasting love, Lutyens and Lytton were disastrously mismatched. She worshiped his talent but craved an intimacy undermined by the architect's single-minded devotion to his work. At home he'd immerse himself in endless games of solitaire during which he'd unconsciously puzzle out pending designs. He'd hoped that her aristocratic connections would bring him prestigious jobs, but he received far more referrals from Gertrude Jekyll. Worse yet, she found their sex life unbearable (as detailed in her letters to him and confidences to her daughters), and after she bore five children turned him out of the conjugal bed in 1914.

Emily had meanwhile become a fanatical adept of Theosophy, the Eastern-inflected spiritual cult that held the teenaged Indian mystic Jiddu Krishnamurti to be a messiah. During much of her marriage she made a separate, peripatetic life chasing after Krishnamurti with her husband's money, a rejection particularly painful to Lutyens because it reiterated the emotional neglect of him by his religiously obsessed mother. He found some comfort in an *amitié amoureuse* with the likewise unhappily wed Victoria Sackville-West (mother of Vita), for whom he designed three houses, over which they quarreled to an apparently enjoyable degree. The Lutyenses remained wed until his death from lung cancer at age seventy-four on New Year's Day in 1944.

The architect was painfully shy and nervously inarticulate, serious deficiencies in a field so dependent on personal interaction. He attempted to mask his verbal and social unease with a strenuously jocular demeanor marked by nonstop chatter and a torrent of puns. He averred that "India expects every man to do his dhoti," and observed of a fish course, "This piece of cod passeth understanding." His notion of appropriateness could be astoundingly faulty, as when he told the formidable Queen Mary that the tiny pillows monogrammed MG and GM in the dollhouse he designed for her signified "May George?" and "George May," the latter a play on her private family nickname. She reacted, he reported, like a "frightened mare." Yet many others found his irrepressible bonhomie and boundless sense of fun entrancing, and after Lutyens stopped going about at night with his downer of a wife—to the great relief of countless hostesses who loved him and hated her—he became one of London's most sought-after dinner guests.

Lutyens's expansion into international practice paralleled the British Empire's global reach. He designed his nation's pavilion at expositions in Paris (1900), Rome (1911), and Antwerp (1930) in a succession of different styles—respectively Elizabethan, Classical, and the Mughal-Classical hybrid he devised for New Delhi. After he was awarded the American Institute of Architects' Gold Medal in 1924, the British government returned the compliment and asked him to design its new embassy complex in Washington, his only work in the US. Rather than flaunting Britannic majesty, Lutyens's

Neo-Georgian embassy brings to mind both an English country house and the redbrick Wren Building of 1695–1700 at the College of William and Mary in Williamsburg, Virginia, attributed to Christopher Wren. Because the hilly site near Washington Cathedral had to accommodate both the ambassadorial residence and the chancery, the architect separated the living and working functions and joined the rectangular mansion and the squared-C-shaped office wing with a two-story pedimented bridge that contains the ambassador's study above the main entry arch.

The arrival sequence is thrilling. One gets out of a car under the porte cochere and then ascends a grand stairway with deep treads that slow your pace to a stately gait and increase anticipation. On the piano nobile, a spacious ballroom (used for investitures and other ceremonies) faces three French doors that open onto a two-story stone-columned portico, which in turn leads to the terraced garden. This splendidly orchestrated spatial progression never fails to impress. Architectural jests abound throughout. For example, column capitals are carved with swags and a scallop shell that mimic eyes, nose, and open mouth, while the circular patterns on a curving wrought-iron stairway bannister were inspired by bubbles in a glass of champagne. Lutyens's biographer Jane Ridley perfectly summarizes the overall effect as "light-heartedly subversive, like a Noël Coward lyric."

When the newly crowned King George V and Queen Mary journeyed to India to receive the homage of maharajahs at the Delhi Durbar of 1911, the monarch surprised the assembly by announcing that the capital of the Raj would be moved there from Calcutta. Lutyens's newly minted city-planning credentials—he had laid out the town center for Hampstead Garden Suburb in North London in 1908—won him the commission of a lifetime to design this new British administrative center of India. He immediately comprehended that no one man could act as both urban design chief and project architect for New Delhi's numerous government structures, and thus chose as his collaborator an old colleague from the George and Peto office, Herbert Baker, whose Union Buildings of 1910–1912 in Pretoria, capital of the newly formed Union of South Africa, offered comparable scale and experience no other British architect could match. It was a decision Lutyens would come to regret bitterly.

Although Lutyens's radial city plan for New Delhi followed French Baroque prototypes, including Pierre-Charles L'Enfant's Washington, D.C., there was consensus that the official architecture of the new capital should incorporate Indian references. But Lutyens was at first openly dismissive of historical construction on the subcontinent. "I do not believe there is any real Indian architecture at all, or any great tradition," he declared. Even the universally beloved Taj Mahal he found wanting, and insisted that when viewed from any angle other than the front it was "untidy." His initial contemptuousness of this rich architectural heritage makes it all the more remarkable that in the end he turned New Delhi's centerpiece and his own masterpiece—the Viceroy's House of 1912–1930—into a brilliant fusion of Hindu,

Buddhist, and Mughal motifs seamlessly subsumed and superimposed onto an unapologetically Classical plan. Somewhat larger than the Palace of Versailles, it is crowned by Lutyens's distinctive sandstone dome modeled after a bell-shaped Buddhist stupa, rather than his less felicitous initial plan to reinterpret the cupola of St. Paul's Cathedral by Wren (which was also the prototype for Thomas U. Walter's United States Capitol dome of 1855–1866). The architect's multicultural stylistic synthesis allowed the Viceroy's House to be renamed Rashtrapati Bhavan (President's House) with complete credibility after India won independence from Britain.

Understandably, a two-decade undertaking of this magnitude was fraught with problems, a saga grippingly told in Robert Grant Irving's definitive account, *Indian Summer: Lutyens, Baker, and Imperial Delhi* (1981). Financial strains twice threatened to cancel the project: at the outset during the Great War and again near the end during the Great Depression. Lutyens and Baker were at loggerheads from the very beginning. Their rivalry came to a climax when Baker's mirror-image secretariat buildings—each with an incongruous Italian Baroque dome and tower, flanking King's Way (now Rajpath), the grand central avenue leading to the Viceroy's House—were repositioned, which required altering the upward gradient of the roadway.

An overworked and distracted Lutyens had approved the level change without realizing that his dome would now be obscured during part of the approach. This exacting perfectionist was thenceforth obsessed with correcting his oversight, but regrading the avenue proved too costly. That the dome's brief disappearance and return actually heighten the drama of his conception was immaterial to Lutyens because he had not intended it, unlike the many other architects, even great ones, who are willing to take credit for some serendipitous circumstance and claim it as intentional.

The work that made him a national hero was his Cenotaph of 1919–1920 in London. To give focus to peace celebrations in London, Prime Minister David Lloyd George—a master of public stagecraft who concocted the Prince of Wales's investiture ceremony at Caernarfon Castle in 1911 as a mini-coronation to appeal to his Welsh constituents—commissioned Lutyens to design a temporary commemorative set piece on a traffic island in Whitehall, the thoroughfare that connects Trafalgar Square and the Palace of Westminster. This exquisitely proportioned but severely restrained plywood structure—in the implicit form of a sarcophagus raised thirty-five feet above street level atop a narrow plinth—immediately struck such a responsive chord with the public that the architect was asked to render it permanent in stone as Britain's principal war memorial.

This deceptively simple scheme is in fact extraordinarily complex, a quality typical of Lutyens at his best. What seem like straight lines are actually very subtle arcs in the Greek tradition of entasis, a slight narrowing of verticals to prevent an upright structure from appearing to bulge at the top. Even more than its Classical references, the Cenotaph (the Greek word for an empty tomb) atavistically connects with prehistoric monoliths that remain unsurpassed as cynosures of collective memory. Moreover, the exceptional level of abstraction Lutyens achieves here allows viewers to project their own emotions onto a design unencumbered by intrusive representational elements, a condition that makes Maya Lin's Vietnam Veterans Memorial in Washington, D.C., and Michael Arad's National September 11 Memorial in New York City commensurately powerful.

Even before hostilities ended, Lutyens was asked to serve, along with Baker and Reginald Blomfield, as an architectural adviser to the newly organized Imperial War Graves Commission (IWGC) for planning military cemeteries in France and Belgium. The war's horrendous death toll—about one million British Empire soldiers were killed—resulted in 967 cemeteries. Lutyens designed 140 of them, ranging in size from 25 to 10,773 graves. His first major contribution was to propose that each burial field contain a War Stone, a twelve-foot-long horizontal monolith reminiscent of both an altar and a sarcophagus but devoid of overt religious symbols. Rudyard Kipling, whose words THE GLORIOUS DEAD are inscribed on the Cenotaph, also composed the epitaph for the War Stones: THEIR NAME LIVETH FOR EVERMORE. His only son had died in action in France in 1915, aged eighteen.

Although more than a dozen other architects took part in this immense project (including many who had served in the war), certain organizing principles were followed by all of them in order to confer visual unity and comradely equality on the entire effort. Yet the general outlines also allowed for individual responses to specific locales and differing historical circumstances. However, even a cursory overview of the program makes clear that Lutyens's cemeteries are the commission's finest. His experience with Gertrude Jekyll afforded him a firm grasp in siting and landscaping each graveyard. The small shelters he designed to give visitors a place to sit or take refuge from the elements, as well as to enshrine a register inscribed with the names of all those interred there, are at once as dignified as Classical temples and as inviting as English garden gazebos. Planted with trees, shrubs, and flowers reminiscent of a Home County garden, the graveyards—which to this day are impeccably maintained thanks to the vigilance of grateful British, French, and Belgian governments as well as private volunteers—fulfill Rupert Brooke's famous vision of "a foreign field / That is for ever England."

But unquestionably Lutyens's most affecting military monument is his Memorial to the Missing of the Somme of 1927–1932 at Thiepval, France (see Illustration 5b). Rising the equivalent of fourteen stories over open countryside near the site of one of the Great War's bloodiest massacres, this brick-and-stone structure is composed of a series of intersecting arches set at right angles to each other. They increase in height as they move inward from the periphery and culminate in the tallest, central arch, an arrangement that creates sufficient wall space for the engraved names of the 73,357 British Empire soldiers who went missing there in 1916.

As one moves around this enigmatic construct—part

cathedral, part watchtower, part sphinx—its apparent massiveness is continually subverted by the many apertures cut straight through it. The age-old triumphal arch motif has never felt more hollow, the void left by death never more gaping. While paying all honor to the fallen, this masterpiece of funereal art does not console, and in its realistic address of the horrors that prompted it reveals the life-enhancing genius of Edwin Lutyens at its most urgent and timeless.

6

JAN DUIKER

THE EXCEPTIONAL LONGEVITY of many modern architects would seem to indicate that master builders are an uncommonly hardy lot, if we consider such celebrated centenarians as Oscar Niemeyer, I. M. Pei, and Margarete Schütte-Lihotzky; nonagenarians, including Philip Johnson and Frank Lloyd Wright; to say nothing of octogenarians far too numerous to mention. Apart from the steady extension of the human lifespan in developed countries during the twentieth century, one wonders if so many architects reach an advanced age because so few of them begin to receive major commissions before they turn forty, and often not until they are in their fifties. Perhaps there is some unknowable process of occupational self-selection involved, similar to that among symphony orchestra conductors, another unusually superannuated demographic.

The pursuit of architecture on a high level can be an agonizingly slow climb for the ambitious. After the thunderous acclaim that greeted the opening of Frank Gehry's Guggenheim

Museum Bilbao in 1997, the architect mordantly remarked that it took him until he was almost seventy to become an overnight global sensation. At the opposite end of the actuarial tables are the highly talented architects whose lives were so much shorter than average that their achievements seem all the more miraculous in retrospect. Among major twentieth-century practitioners this was especially true of Eero Saarinen, who succumbed to a brain tumor that ended his decade-long independent career—a nonstop succession of dramatically styled, much-publicized designs for high-profile corporate, educational, and governmental clients— just days after his fifty-first birthday. But he was able to achieve so much in so little time because this uncommonly precocious talent began working at age fifteen on small decorative design tasks for his Finnish émigré father Eliel (who was then building the Cranbrook Academy of Art in Michigan) and thanks to the long-established reputation of the family firm had a rapid solo ascent after the elder Saarinen's death in 1950.

The unanswerable question of what might have been hovers over the memory of all artists who die at an early age. But how they are perceived in the long view of history has more to do with the quality, not the quantity, of what they leave behind. The hugely prolific Austrian-born German-based architect and industrial designer Joseph Maria Olbrich (1867–1908)—whose work had a direct influence on Frank Lloyd Wright that remained unacknowledged by the proudly independent American—left such a considerable artistic legacy that his premature demise from leukemia at forty is now little remembered. The all-too-youthful victims of war, accident, or epidemic are exemplified by the Italian architect Antonio Sant'Elia, who was killed in action at twenty-eight during the Great War, before he had a chance to build much of anything, but who produced visionary schemes of such inventive audacity that he remains a staple of survey histories. Matthew Nowicki, a socially conscious Polish architect whose career had been stalled by World War II, soon afterward won one of the major planning commissions of the period: the design of Chandigarh, the new capital city of the Punjab. But he died at forty when his plane crashed in Egypt on his way home from India in 1950 (whereupon that dream job passed to Le Corbusier). And the death from AIDS in 1996 of the hugely promising Los Angeles architect Franklin D. Israel—whose contemporaries include such now major figures as Rem Koolhaas, Thom Mayne, Tod Williams, and Billie Tsien—reminds us of the wide swath that plague cut through the arts during the twentieth century's two concluding decades.

To this twentieth-century necrology must be added one of the most unjustly neglected figures in modern architecture, Jan Duiker, who died at forty-four and whose posthumous reputation is now overshadowed by his better-known Dutch contemporaries J. J. P. Oud and Gerrit Rietveld (both of whom lived three decades longer than he did). Despite its small size, the Netherlands between the two world wars encompassed some of the most densely settled areas in Europe, with a population of around seven million and a lively but highly factionalized architecture scene. During those years the Netherlands witnessed an extraordinary outpouring of architectural excellence, in three successive waves. Most conspicuous was the so-called Amsterdam School, a circle of like-minded urbanists that included Michel de Klerk, Piet Kramer, and Joan van der Mey—all of whom produced free-wheeling reinterpretations of traditional Dutch building forms with an Expressionistic edge (as did Duiker himself at the outset of his career).

Because Holland was a noncombatant in World War I, civic construction sponsored both by municipal governments and by nonprofit private building societies proceeded apace throughout the 1910s. Dutch authorities put strong emphasis on urban planning, social welfare projects, and public housing, which would exert a wide influence on new architecture across Europe during the years of widespread rebuilding that followed the end of hostilities, particularly in Germany. The concentrated activity of the Amsterdam School, which continued into the mid-1920s, made it one of the most significant architectural reform movements of the early twentieth century.

Earlier in that decade, avant-garde developments elsewhere in Europe inspired an emergent generation of Dutch architects to turn from the predominant redbrick mode of their homeland and adopt the minimalist machine aesthetic now commonly—if inaccurately—known as the Bauhaus style. In Holland the equivalent tendency was dubbed De

Stijl (the style), which placed a particular emphasis on aesthetically pleasing surface compositions that Duiker deemed too superficial to be the basis for an architectural philosophy. His opinion was shared by Le Corbusier, who dismissed the De Stijl exhibition held at the Paris gallery L'Effort Moderne in 1923. Duiker's published criticisms of De Stijl—a circle that included, among others, Oud, Rietveld, and the architect Robert van 't Hoff, as well as the painters Piet Mondrian and Theo van Doesburg—understandably aroused their enmity. Van Doesburg, who published *De Stijl*, the group's hugely influential journal (now considered an essential document of early Modernism), effectively banned Duiker's work from its pages, a major reason why his posthumous reputation has languished. Yet there was even dissent among De Stijl members, evident in 1926 when Oud declared that van Doesburg lacked even "the slightest notion of building."

Duiker instead aligned himself with yet another progressive Dutch faction, De 8, which was founded in 1927 by six young architects (now known only among architectural experts) who believed in a more pragmatic, structurally based approach than the De Stijl group. The name De 8 did not derive from the number of founders but instead came from the Dutch word *acht*, a homonym that can mean either "attention" or "eight." One of the group's participants who had served in the army recalled the command *geef acht* (pay attention) and deemed it a fitting call to architectural action. Duiker joined the half-dozen originators in 1928, became De 8's president five years later, and presided over its merger with yet another architectural coterie, Opbouw (construction), headed by the architect and tubular-steel furniture pioneer Mart Stam, who edited the conjoined organization's magazine, *De 8 en Opbouw.*

Johannes Duiker—more familiarly known as Jan—was born in The Hague in 1890, where his father was a school principal and his mother a teacher. He studied architecture at the Netherlands' foremost institution for the profession, the Delft University of Technology, where he met a fellow student, Bernard Bijvoet, who would become his principal architectural collaborator. After Duiker and Bijvoet received their diplomas in 1913, they began working in the architectural firm of their main professor, Henri Evers, who was then designing Rotterdam's neotraditional city hall of 1914–1920.

In 1916 they set up their own practice in Zandvoort, a coastal town west of Amsterdam. Among the pair's early commissions was the Karenhuis of 1916–1920 in Alkmaar, a low-rise old age home that fits seamlessly into the redbrick vernacular of that charming cheese-market town and is now designated a national monument. The partners won the competition for this scheme because they provided more individual housing units than any of the other entrants. But this symmetrical four-winged building, sheltered by a massive attic roof, brings to mind the comforting solidity of the British Arts and Crafts Movement even as its clean lines, strong horizontal fenestration, and lack of fussy detailing look forward to the startling new directions advanced Dutch architecture was about to take.

The predominant architectural influence in early-twentieth-century Holland was Hendrik Petrus Berlage (1856–1934), a generational father figure akin to his older Viennese contemporary Otto Wagner in his powerful influence on countless followers. Berlage's vigorous redbrick structures conveyed much the same strength and gravitas as those of his older America counterpart H. H. Richardson. But when young Dutch architects of the early twentieth century looked abroad for inspiration, they were particularly responsive to the works of Frank Lloyd Wright, who might be called Richardson's spiritual grandson because his early mentor Louis Sullivan in his own youth worked for and was influenced by Richardson.

Wright's particular popularity among Dutch architects was due in large part to to the spirited advocacy of his foremost champion in Europe, Hendrikus Theodorus Wijdeveld (1885–1989), yet another very long-lived architect, who founded the influential arts magazine *Wendingen* (turnings) in 1918 and edited it until it folded during the Great Depression in 1931. Six years before that Wijdeveld devoted an entire issue of his periodical to that American master and reissued the contents in book form as *The Life-Work of the American Architect Frank Lloyd Wright*. It served as the basic reference for the decade and a half until publication of Henry-Russell Hitchcock's *In the Nature of Materials 1887–1941: The Buildings of Frank Lloyd Wright*. Appearing as it did at a particularly low point in Wright's wildly fluctuating fortunes, Wijdeveld's richly illustrated encomium helped bolster his subject's international reputation at a time when this middle-aged has-been could barely find work in the US.

The impact of Wright's designs in the Netherlands and its foreign possessions was widespread, as seen, for example, in adaptations of his characteristic overhanging roofs by Willem Marinus Dudok for several of his remarkable schools in Hilversum during the 1920s, as well as in his flat-roofed Hilversum Town Hall of 1928–1931, with its lingering echoes of Wright's Unity Temple. Duiker and Bijvoet channeled Wright in their closely clustered group of fourteen seaside villas of 1921–1923 in the Hague beach community of Kijkduin. These transposed Prairie Houses, several of them semidetached, are demonstrably Wrightian in their combination of redbrick, horizontal wood siding, and stucco, with ground-hugging profiles and deep eaves, as well as porte cocheres, verandas, and planters that extend out to embrace the sandy seaside landscape. Some of their interiors are even embellished with leaded-glass windows in abstract geometric patterns, much like those in Wright's revolutionary Prairie Houses of 1900–1914.

The worldwide transmission of Wright's ideas through his admirers in Holland can likewise be seen in the Dutch colonial architect Charles Prosper Wolff Schoemaker's Preanger Hotel of 1929 in Bandung, Java. This exotic structure's strong horizontality and distinctive Mayan-inspired stone ornamentation closely resemble Wright's Imperial Hotel of

1914–1923 in Tokyo, which is nearer to the erstwhile Dutch East Indies than Amsterdam. Though Schoemaker's sobriquet of "the Frank Lloyd Wright of Indonesia" seems a bit overreaching, there can be little doubt that he too was looking closely at the output of this American innovator. Later on, Duiker and his cohort paid closer attention to Russian Constructivism, which emerged well before the October Revolution but quickly became the built embodiment of the radical new regime that promised a complete reshaping of society in all its aspects, not least architecturally (until the new style fell out of favor with Communist Party functionaries in the early 1930s and was superseded by the sub-Classicism preferred by Stalin). Constructivism stressed its departure from conventional approaches to building through its emphasis not just on the frank exposure of a building's function but also its actual structure, based on a belief that it was dishonest to hide the inner workings of architecture beneath an opaque exterior. What better conjunction of theory and practice in this regard than to apply this idea to the healing powers of modern medicine?

The life and death of buildings is more than mere metaphor when it comes to one category of architecture closely identified with the Modern Movement: the sanatorium. These facilities for the treatment of tuberculosis have been as emblematic of changing attitudes toward architecture as of shifting views on contagion. Whereas Romantics saw consumption (as TB was long popularly known) as an expression of personal tragedy—exemplified by Alexandre Dumas's

La Dame aux camélias—Thomas Mann signaled a wider shift in societal perceptions by drawing an analogy between tuberculosis and the ills of the modern world; two of his most memorable works (*Tristan* and *The Magic Mountain*) are set in Alpine sanatoriums.

The design of European health-care facilities in the twentieth century got off to a strong start with Josef Hoffmann's Sanatorium Purkersdorf of 1903–1905 in Austria, whose severely simple exterior—flat-roofed and devoid of projecting ornament—anticipated the flat surfaces of the International Style by two decades (see Illustration 4a). But the modern clinic attained transcendent qualities with Duiker and Bijvoet's Sanatorium Zonnestraal of 1926–1931 near Hilversum (see Illustration 6a). Built on a hillside in an idyllic country setting, this white-framed assemblage of low-slung, flat-roofed pavilions seems to be (as is famously said of the Elizabethan stately home Hardwick Hall) "more glass than wall," and exemplifies the most daring structural advances of Modernism. Yet its sleek efficiency and lack of sentimentality did not inhibit a comforting aura, and the facility conveyed a feeling far different from the antiseptic anonymity of conventional hospitals. As the architectural historian Barry Bergdoll writes in the monograph *Sanatorium Zonnestraal: History and Restoration of a Modern Monument*, this pathbreaking scheme elided "the hopes for restoring tuberculosis victims through sun and ventilation and the utopian hopes of the modern movement that architecture might be socially transformative."

This new approach, rationalized and reductive, was ideally suited to the requirements of sanatoriums. The nearly invisible window-walls of this revolutionary building format, taken to an unprecedented extreme by Duiker and Bijvoet, provided generous access to sunlight and fresh air, believed to be cures for tuberculosis. The International Style's proscription against applied ornament and dust-catching decorative details further served the sanatorium's requirements for the hygienic easy-to-clean surfaces deemed essential to the containment of this highly contagious ailment. These ideas caught on quickly, as evidenced by Alvar Aalto's Paimio Sanatorium of 1929–1932 in southern Finland, an International Style high-rise that took several organizational cues from Duiker and Bijvoet's scheme.

Zonnestraal ("sunbeam" in Dutch) began as a commission from an Amsterdam diamond workers' health-care cooperative in 1919, in response to the alarming rate of tuberculosis among cutters and polishers who could not help but inhale dangerous amounts of diamond dust. Because sanatoriums were usually sited in rural areas with low air pollution levels, Zonnestraal's sponsors bought a 286-acre estate—a varied terrain of woodland and heath—on the outskirts of Hilversum (which would soon become the center of Holland's radio broadcasting industry).

But funding for the sanatorium stalled and the design partners drifted apart. In 1925 Bijvoet relocated to Paris, where he worked with Pierre Chareau on the celebrated Maison de Verre of 1928–1932, a glass-walled private house–cum–medical office on the Left Bank that ingeniously combined both functions through a host of inventive structural strategies. When Dutch government subsidies at last allowed final plans for Zonnestraal to be drawn up in 1926, Duiker was primarily responsible, with considerable help from the structural engineer Jan Wiebenga, whose technical expertise is reflected in the building's poured-concrete framework.

The unusually lightweight, almost immaterial feeling Duiker and Wiebenga gave to this sprawling, two-story complex—attributable to a cantilever-support system that enabled floor and ceiling slabs to be extended far beyond the core and obviated the need for solid outer walls—was likened by one Dutch critic to "a small town in Japan, or... white-painted ocean-liners with tall smokestacks, bridges, and crow's nests." Such nautical imagery was apt. In his revolutionary manifesto *Vers une architecture* (1923), Le Corbusier cited the no-nonsense functionalism of modern transatlantic ships as a major source for his Purist aesthetic, which was quickly adopted by his admirers in Holland's Nieuwe Bouwen (new building) movement, a catchall term for the many Dutch avant-garde factions working toward the same general goals.

Duiker's spacious arrangement of Zonnestraal's five freestanding structures—a central administration building at the north end, with four long, narrow residential wings splayed in pairs below it to maximize southern exposure—approximated the outline of a butterfly. Furthermore, the grouping seems to hover above the ground, a floating quality enhanced by continuous rows of deep balconies outside each patient's room, where beds could be moved into the open air as weather permitted. The sanatorium's clientele was at first intended to be all male, limited to low-wage diamond cutters, with a special emphasis on occupational therapy to get those family breadwinners back on their feet financially as well as physically. But when public funds were needed to bring the faltering scheme to completion at the onset of the Great Depression, government officials insisted that the facility treat patients of all backgrounds, and individual dormitories were dedicated to men, women, and children.

Though Zonnestraal was hailed internationally upon completion, it lacked classic (and collectable) furniture made specifically for the project, as opposed to Hoffmann's reclining Purkersdorf *Sitzmaschine* or Aalto's bent-plywood Paimio armchair, and in time the Hilversum complex slipped from the canon. That decline paralleled the abatement of the "white plague" after the advent of antibiotics in the 1940s, which led to the virtual eradication of tuberculosis; by 1970 Zonnestraal was abandoned and demolition loomed. Luckily, enlightened municipal authorities of Hilversum, which arguably has more distinguished early Modern architecture than almost any other comparably sized European community, wisely forestalled the decrepit sanatorium's destruction. After numerous feasibility studies, a full-scale restoration was begun in 2001 by Hubert-Jan Henket and Wessel de Jonge, best known as the founders of Docomomo, the Modernist historic preservation society they launched in 1988.

Henket and de Jonge (who won the 2010 World Monuments Fund/Knoll Modernism Prize for their work on Zonnestraal) here set new standards of authenticity in recreating details and finishes in accord with period techniques. To make a self-financing enterprise out of the former sanatorium, the architects designed a four-building assisted-living facility for the property in an appropriately neo-Corbusian mode and placed it at a respectful remove from the landmark ensemble. The sanatorium itself has been adapted for present-day health issues by including obesity and sports-injury clinics, and can be visited at times that do not interfere with its operations. (The former administration building can now be rented for weddings and other parties.)

In 1928, Christian Zervos, the influential publisher of *Cahiers d'Art* and now best remembered for his multivolume catalogue raisonné on the works of Picasso, faulted Zonnestraal for its lack of "either monumentality or charm." But in its happily restored state, this structurally ingenious, gracefully composed, playfully turreted scheme fairly radiates a charisma equal to any of the finest architecture of the interwar years. Zonnestraal's embracing intimacy and palpable humility make the postmillennial resurrection of Duiker and Bijvoet's architectural gem no less than a modern miracle.

Duiker's most conspicuous post-Zonnestraal design was for the Openlucht school of 1929–1930 in Amsterdam, which embodied one of the period's prevalent notions of education reform—that children would learn better if they were not cooped up in conventional classrooms but afforded the physically and mentally bracing effects of fresh air (see Illustration 6b). To be sure, the chronic inattentiveness of primary and secondary school students has plagued educators for centuries, but the fairly recent realization that adequate sleep and proper diet might have more to do with pupils' concentration than brisk ventilation seems not to have been a priority among proponents of the fresh-air theory, and a vogue for outdoor education swept Europe during the early twentieth century.

This commission suited Duiker's specific architectural aims perfectly. Buildings generally stand up in one of two ways: either through the support of load-bearing exterior walls (such as Duiker used for the massive brick exterior of the Karenhuis in Alkmaar) or through an inner structure that carries the weight of floors from within. The higher a load-bearing-wall building, the thicker its periphery needs to be at its base; the tallest structure of this kind ever erected, Daniel Burnham and John Wellborn Root's seventeen-story Monadnock Block of 1891–1893 in Chicago, has six-foot-thick ground-floor masonry to support it, more like a fortified Florentine Renaissance palazzo than a modern office building.

But this wasteful use of materials was recognized as unnecessary once the economy and adaptability of reinforced concrete skeletons were fully understood by architects, engineers, and their clients as the twentieth century progressed. Duiker exploited his rapidly expanding technical know-how to free the exterior of the four-story Openlucht school (on which Bijvoet came back to consult as well) so that its outer walls could be composed of sliding floor-to-ceiling planes of glass that roll back to create a veritable outdoor environment for the pupils inside. Though this was not always a feasible option in the North Sea climate of Holland, Duiker went on to use the same structural format in his Nirwana apartment house of 1930 in The Hague, a block of luxury apartments that differed from the Amsterdam prototype in that its periphery was not entirely retractable.

The Duiker building that most clearly displays the influence of Russian Constructivism is the Handelsblad Cineac Cinema of 1934, a small screening room on a busy central Amsterdam commercial street. It stands directly across from the city's most flamboyant interwar movie palace, Hijman Louis de Jong's Theater Tuschinski of 1919–1921, a vibrant mash-up of late Art Nouveau, early Art Deco, and Amsterdam School stylistic motifs. In contrast to this sumptuous showcase for first-run commercial films, the Cineac Cinema (owned by the Dutch business newspaper *NRC Handelsblad*) was conceived as a self-consciously utilitarian outlet for the nonstop presentation of newsreels, a relatively recent development in mass communications. Duiker felt that the immediacy of such documentary films demanded a more forthright aesthetic than the seductive showbiz glitz epitomized by the escapist fantasy of the Tushcinski.

A basic concern for Duiker was how to make his little theater visible amid its cluttered surroundings. Apart from his disinterest in lush ornamentation of the sort that distinguishes the Tuschinski's elaborately articulated terra-cotta façade, he was given a tight budget. Newsreels were a new form of entertainment whose profitability was far from guaranteed, but as it turned out the fast-moving political and social developments of the 1930s made it a medium very much in touch with the hectic tenor of those unsettled times, well before television became widely available. In order to make the Cineac Cinema stand out among its neighbors, the architect reduced it to a billboard-like essence, with a diagonally angled rooftop framework that displays the theater's name spelled out in large neon letters and repeated on a vertical banner perpendicular to the street for maximum legibility from near and afar.

Duiker was clearly taking major cues from one of the Russian Constructivists' hallmark inventions, the propaganda kiosk for dissemination of news in various formats. This might be either a fixed installation or even a vehicle such as a truck or railroad car that was retrofitted to its new function and transported to outlying destinations to inform local inhabitants of the revolution's latest developments. Propaganda kiosks were akin to three-dimensional billboards in their bold graphic legibility, and they often incorporated electronic sound amplification to attract further attention from passersby; some even enclosed small screening rooms for the projection of short film clips. Further characteristic of the Constructivist ethos, Duiker designed the façade of the Cineac with a transparent strip window that allowed the workings of its projection room to be seen from the street, a veritable teaser for what was going on inside. (This same basic idea was expressed by Diller Scofidio + Renfro with their 2003–2010 remodeling of New York's Juilliard School of Music, in which they revealed the institution's dance studios to the full view of passersby on Broadway.)

Commercial buildings of great architectural distinction are often more prone to destruction than other landmarks, for once they cease to make money for their owners they are frequently demolished unless a new function can be found for them—the reason why so many of the grand cinema palaces of the interwar years have disappeared. When film newsreels were made obsolete by the wider availability of television news in the 1960s, the Cineac became a grindhouse for second-run movies, and the rise of home video put an end even to that reprieve in 1995. Thereafter Duiker's hardy little survivor briefly became a Planet Hollywood theme restaurant, but when that venture failed the structure was carved up into apartments with yet another restaurant space on the street front. Through all these changes the exterior has remained remarkably intact, including the all-important Cineac signage. Duiker himself lived for only a few months after his final small masterwork was finished. His far too early death, from leukemia, was an ironic end for a man who set so much store in the healing powers—both physical and psychic—of the new form of architecture he did so much to advance.

7

ALBERT SPEER / GERDY TROOST

AMONG THE ODDER conceits of the Romantic movement was the vogue for rendering new buildings as ruins. Inspired by Piranesi's moody *vedute* of noble Roman monuments in picturesque decay, late-eighteenth- and early-nineteenth-century architects such as John Soane had their latest works depicted as they might look millennia in the future—bare ruin'd choirs and whited sepulchres that spoke of vanished glory and implied emotional depth. This bizarre practice was revived by Albert Speer, Adolf Hitler's master builder, who appealed to his patron's apocalyptic instincts by urging him to anticipate their projects' *Ruinenwert* (ruin value) and thereby approve extra expenditures to guarantee that the Thousand-Year Reich would leave architectural remains equal to those of the ancients. Speer's vision was fulfilled much sooner than he expected, and among the more popular picture postcards that Allied soldiers sent back home from Germany in 1945 were images of the architect's Reich Chancellery of 1936–1939 in Berlin as a blasted shambles and

Hitler's country house of 1935–1937 in Berchtesgaden as a hollowed-out wreck.

Yet several major examples of Nazi architecture—a twelve-year outpouring of publicly financed construction that encompassed everything from the Autobahn system of 1933 onward and the 1936 Berlin Olympic Stadium to officer-training schools and extermination camps—were so solidly crafted that even Allied saturation bombing could not reduce them to rubble. Some have served several successive German governments, such as Ernst Sagebiel's sprawling, stone-clad Aviation Ministry of 1934–1935 in Berlin, which was first recycled by the Communist East Germans as the House of Ministries, then after reunification was used by the government's restitution agency, and now houses the nation's Finance Ministry.

Two decades after the war, the still-vexing question of how and even whether to deal with this long-taboo chapter in twentieth-century culture was finally addressed at the Modern Architecture Symposia (MAS), three biennial conferences held at Columbia University in 1962, 1964, and 1966 to define and codify the Modern Movement for the first time as a historical development. Participants included many of the period's leading architecture and art scholars—including Alfred H. Barr Jr., Vincent Scully Jr., and Rudolf Wittkower—but transcripts of most of these fascinating proceedings remained unavailable until the publication in 2014 of a new critical compendium of highlights edited by Joan Ockman and my wife, Rosemarie Haag Bletter, with Nancy Eklund Later.

For the second of the three symposia, which dealt with the 1930s, the historians Henry-Russell Hitchcock and George R. Collins invited the principal benefactor of the series, Philip Johnson, to discuss Nazi architecture, a logical enough choice because of his fascist sympathies during the period under discussion and the throwback Stripped Classicism of his most recent buildings. But Johnson demurred, doubtless worried that his shameful political past would harm his blossoming architectural practice. Instead, this still-touchy subject was handled, albeit somewhat obliquely, by the Vienna-born Harvard historian Eduard Sekler, who examined architectural reactions to Hitler in their native Austria, rather than the main manifestations of Nazi construction in Germany. With perhaps an excess of Viennese evasiveness, Sekler admitted that until then he'd considered Nazi design merely "a rather distasteful interval." More pointedly, a Columbia graduate student (and later Cornell architectural history professor), Christian F. Otto, delivered a short, sharp overview of the ideological roots of urbanism in the Third Reich, which he characterized as "a perversion of the traditions of German architectural and planning theory" with one goal: "the absolute control of the leader over the led."

The MAS discussions did not address the lack of women in the profession—an issue that would not fully emerge until the 1970s—but even if they had it was unlikely that much attention would have been accorded Gerdy Troost, who figures prominently in *Hitler at Home* (2015), by the architectural historian Despina Stratigakos. Although a book about the Führer's taste in interior decoration might seem like a Mel Brooks joke, the crucial part that aesthetics played in advancing the National Socialist agenda was no laughing matter. The Nazis' far-reaching visual propaganda program —which in addition to Speer's architecture included the films of Leni Riefenstahl, the photography of Heinrich Hoffmann, the sculpture of Arno Breker, and, as Stratigakos firmly established, the designs of Gerdy Troost—did much to support authoritarian power through a consistent artistic projection of strength, order, and unity. No aspect of the man-made environment escaped the dictator's obsessive attention, down to his table settings and stationery, not surprising for this failed artist and thwarted architect. Indeed, even as his short-lived empire collapsed around him, one of his favorite distractions in the Berlin Chancellery bunker was the architect Hermann Giesler's 1945 scale model of the Austrian city of Linz reconceived as a new pan-Germanic cultural capital, which the patron would pore over for hours at a time.

Though the Modern Movement in architecture reflected many advanced ideals of social-reform groups, its attitudes toward women were often stubbornly retrograde. Female students at otherwise progressive art and design schools, including the Bauhaus, were routinely steered away from architecture—traditionally deemed a "masculine" pursuit—and toward weaving, embroidery, ceramics, interior decoration, and other more "feminine" occupations. Nonetheless, several strong-minded young women resisted gender stereotyping and became architect-designers of great distinction, including Margarete Schütte-Lihotzky and Charlotte Perriand, whose singular contributions were long attributed to the more famous men they collaborated with (Ernst May and Le Corbusier, respectively). Yet another member of this penumbral sisterhood was Gerdy Troost, born Sophie Gerhardine Wilhelmine Andresen in Stuttgart in 1904. Her father owned the German Woodcraft Studios, which executed high-end furniture and paneled rooms for institutional and private clients. She completed high school and worked in the family firm, where at nineteen she met the architect Paul Troost, twenty-six years her senior, whose furniture designs were fabricated there. His 1920s schemes for North German Lloyd ocean liners, including the much-admired SS *Europa*, exemplified the *Dampferstil* (steamship style) of substantial, sober, quietly luxurious Stripped Classical decor that became fashionable among those who abhorred both the most advanced Modernism—what we now call Bauhaus design—and kitschy historical revivalism, but still wanted an up-to-date look. The two married in 1925, and Gerdy, who had no formal architectural training, later maintained that they were full artistic partners. In a characteristic division of labor—like that between Ludwig Mies van der Rohe and his longtime collaborator (and mistress) Lilly Reich—Paul Troost concentrated on architectural design and construction while his wife attended to interiors.

Admirers of Paul Troost's costly domestic furniture included the author of *Mein Kampf*. Newly flush with royalties from his runaway best seller—which by 1933 earned him 1.2 million reichsmarks (the current equivalent of about $4.7 million)—Hitler outfitted the 4,300-square-foot, full-floor Munich apartment he moved into in 1929 with several of the architect's pieces, including a huge desk its designer made for himself but relinquished to the rising politician after repeated requests. This was a shrewd move, for although Troost still had few buildings to his credit, Hitler felt he'd discovered the greatest architect of the age, a veritable modern-day Schinkel. The Troosts were reciprocally enchanted by the Nazi chief, who, Gerdy wrote, "behaves like a truly splendid, serious, cultivated, modest chap. Really touching. And with so much feeling and sensitivity for architecture." In 1930 he asked Paul Troost to refurbish the Nazi Party headquarters in Munich, and five years later had Atelier Troost redo his nearby apartment, which cost the equivalent of $5.2 million today (nearly as much as Hitler later would pay for the entire building).

Oddly enough for a country punctilious about educational credentials, few questioned Gerdy Troost's lack of professional qualifications, least of all herself or Hitler, who awarded her the title of Professor, highly prestigious in Germany. She eventually wielded such influence with the Führer that even Speer, a consummate political operator, knew better than to tangle with her. His cautiousness was borne out by how, in a single stroke, she effectively ended the career of the archconservative architect Paul Schultze-Naumburg, a leading theoretician and propagandist of the nativist right-wing *Blut und Boden* (blood and soil) movement, which stressed a connection between German vernacular culture and Aryan supremacy, and stigmatized Modernist architecture as an attempt to undermine traditional *Völkisch* (nativist and populist) values. Schultze-Naumburg's poisonous 1928 book *Kunst und Rasse* (Art and Race) was a foundational text in Hitler's view that Modern art and architecture were degenerate and by implication Jewish. Schultze-Naumburg had fully expected to prosper as his idol's star ascended, but he did not reckon that he would have to contend with the interference of Frau Professor Troost.

When Paul Troost died unexpectedly at fifty-five in 1934, a year after Hitler took power, his widow had no intention of closing their office. Big commissions were just beginning to come in, most notably for the House of German Art in Munich, which she completed in 1937 to her late husband's designs, helped by his chief architectural associate. (Bavarian wags dubbed this flat-roofed Stripped Classical structure *der Weisswursttempel* because its extruded façade of twenty-two monumental limestone columns resembles an upright phalanx of veal sausages, a Bavarian delicacy.) As a woman alone in a male-dominated profession, she became increasingly aggressive toward competitors. When, after Paul Troost's death, Schultze-Naumburg heard that the architect's widow was forging ahead with the Munich job he cracked, "Oh please, I would not let a surgeon's widow operate on my appendicitis." This got back to her, and when she accompanied Hitler to inspect Schultze-Naumburg's remodeling of the

Nuremberg Opera House she exacted her revenge. During the walkthrough, Troost whispered to the dictator, who, as Stratigakos writes,

> erupted in a tirade of criticism, berating the architect in front of everyone. He ordered Schultze-Naumburg to share oversight of the construction with Troost, at which point the aggrieved architect withdrew from the project... [and] had little further contact with Hitler or the Nazi Party.

Decades later, Troost disingenuously claimed she'd simply offered her professional opinion and told Hitler that the auditorium had been "very well renovated. What I found excessive was that Schultze-Naumburg had installed the swastika in very large—far too large—emblems in front of the box seats," a detail unlikely to have enraged a megalomaniac for whom overscaled Nazi symbolism knew no limits.

Gerdy Troost's place in Hitler's inner circle was cemented by her interior decoration of his Alpine retreat near the village of Berchtesgaden in the Obersalzberg region of southern Bavaria. In 1928 he began renting a modest two-story hillside chalet there, named Haus Wachenfeld for its views over fields. As his fame (and literary income) grew, he found it inadequate for entertaining on a scale commensurate with his new status, to say nothing of his desire to link himself in the public imagination with a stunning scenic setting framed by photogenic snowcapped peaks as towering as his ambitions.

ALBERT SPEER / GERDY TROOST

A few months after he became chancellor in 1933 he bought the place and immediately embarked on the first of two major expansions. Hitler, an art school reject and would-be master builder, sketched rough plans that were smoothed out by a Munich architect. Not surprisingly, he quickly found his enlarged residence inadequate and proceeded to make it even bigger. He renamed the resultant maxi-chalet the Berghof, which can be translated either as "mountain farm" or "mountain court," a combination of Marie Antoinette faux rusticity and stealth grandeur akin to a Thurn und Taxis princess decked out in a haute-couture dirndl.

Numerous illustrated articles about the Berghof were published in Germany and abroad, including a rapturous feature in *The New York Times Magazine* entitled "Herr Hitler at Home in the Clouds," which was published in August 1939, twelve days before he invaded Poland and the war began. Such publicity aroused intense interest in the way Hitler arranged his personal spaces, which he exploited to soften perceptions of himself as a warmonger seeking world domination.

The centerpiece of the aggrandized house was the forty-two-by-seventy-four-foot Great Hall, a bi-level, eighteen-foot-high reception-cum-living room with two hallmarks of the Hitler look: a low round table surrounded by a herd of vast upholstered armchairs and a wall hung with a huge antique Gobelin tapestry. Another wall was dominated by a twelve-by-twenty-eight-foot panoramic window that overlooked Austria and the fabled Untersberg, the massif within which it was said that Charlemagne (or, according to another legend, Frederick Barbarossa) awaited resurrection to found a German Reich not unlike Hitler's (see Illustration 7b). "You see the Untersberg over there," the owner portentously pointed out to Speer. "It is no accident that I have my residence opposite it."

Thanks to a mechanism similar to one that Mies van der Rohe devised for his Tugendhat house of 1928–1930 in Brno, Czechoslovakia (built for a wealthy Jewish family), this immense window could be cranked into a recess in the floor, an effect that invariably thrilled visitors. As the Nazi acolyte Unity Mitford rhapsodized to her sister Diana, wife of the British fascist leader Oswald Mosley:

> The window—the largest piece of glass ever made—can be wound down...leaving it quite open. Through it one just sees this huge chain of mountains, and it looks more like an enormous cinema screen than like reality. Needless to say the génial idea was the Führer's own, & he said Frau Troost wanted to insist on having *three* windows.

The rest of the Berghof was much less dramatic. Troost's decor included such folksy touches as a knotty-pine dining room, tile-clad corner stoves, and wooden Bavarian-style chairs with heart-shaped cutouts, *gemütlich* to a chilling degree considering the activities that transpired there.

Troost's firm received no further large-scale architectural commissions from the Nazis after the Munich art gallery, but Hitler continued to use her for personal commissions, including the design of a Nymphenburg porcelain dinner service, Zwiesel glassware, and silver cutlery bearing his AH monogram, an eagle, and a swastika. Her lavishly illustrated 1938 survey of Nazi architecture, *Das Bauen im Neuen Reich* (Building in the New Reich), which gave pride of place to her late husband's works, was reprinted in multiple editions. During the war she designed military commendation certificates as well as medals inlaid with diamonds looted from Dutch Jews. And though she saved a number of Jewish acquaintances from deportation, Troost insisted that neither she nor Hitler himself knew anything about the genocide. Not surprisingly, her denazification trial went badly. One German official recorded that "she is and remains a fanatical Nazi follower," and when put under house arrest she bridled at the indignity of being guarded by *US-Negern*—African-American soldiers. The repellent Gerdy, who endlessly invoked Brahms, Kant, and other touchstones of German high culture, went to her grave unrepentant in 2003, less than two years shy of her centenary.

But Gerdy Troost's culpability pales in comparison to that of Albert Speer, who spent twenty years in prison for crimes against humanity. This Alberich of architecture published three books unsurpassed in their dissembling, distortion, and deviousness. His *Erinnerungen* (1969) was issued in the US as *Inside the Third Reich* and spent thirty weeks on the *New York Times* best-seller list. *Spandauer Tagebücher* (1975), translated as *Spandau: The Secret Diaries*, became another best seller. And *Der Sklavenstaat: Meine Ausein-andersetzungen mit der SS* (1981) appeared in English as *The Slave State: Heinrich Himmler's Masterplan for SS Supremacy.* As Speer assiduously tried to recast his public image —from heinous war criminal to overambitious architect who couldn't resist the temptation of building on an un-precedented scale—he found an avid coprofessional advo-cate in Léon Krier, the Luxembourg-born Classical-revival architect best known for designing Poundbury, the neo-traditional new town in Dorset begun in 1988 by Prince Charles. In 1985 Krier caused a stir by publishing *Albert Speer: Architecture, 1932–1942,* a deluxe monograph in which he asserts that his subject would have been esteemed as one of the twentieth century's greatest architects and ur-ban planners were it not for his regrettable political associa-tions—a notion as aesthetically preposterous as it is morally indefensible.

Apart from Krier's fellow ultraconservative contrarians, few have endorsed his revisionist reassessment. A more kindly view of Speer's accomplishments is unlikely ever to prevail thanks to the British-Canadian historian Martin Kitchen's brilliant and devastating biography of this manip-ulative monster, *Speer: Hitler's Architect* (2015). With a mountain of new research gleaned from sources previously unavailable, overlooked, or disregarded, Kitchen lays out a case so airtight that one marvels anew how Speer survived the Nuremberg trials with his neck intact, given that ten of his codefendants were hanged for their misdeeds (some arguably on a smaller scale than his own).

Instead, during his incarceration in the Spandau fortress he gardened for up to six hours a day and inveigled employees to smuggle in rare Bordeaux, foie gras, and caviar, and smuggle out manuscripts and directives to his best friend and business manager. In 1966 he exited a rich man, his war-profiteering fortune amazingly intact thanks to shrewd concealment and canny investments. As an international celebrity author he further cashed in on his notoriety during the remaining fifteen years of freedom he highly enjoyed. This Faustian figure died in London, where he had gone for a BBC-TV interview, of a stroke at seventy-six after a midday rendezvous at his Bayswater hotel with a beautiful young woman.

Berthold Konrad Hermann Albert Speer was born in Mannheim in 1905, the son of an architect who made no pretense of his love for money and a grasping, social-climbing mother. It is indicative of Kitchen's painstaking scholarship that he accepts nothing his tenaciously mendacious subject said at face value, not even Speer's account of his own birth. Although he claimed it took place amid the dramatic conjunction of a thunderstorm and noonday bells pealing from an adjacent church, his biographer found that the sanctuary in question was not built until the boy was six, and furthermore that it rained in Mannheim that day only later in the afternoon. Thereafter Kitchen catches him in dozens of lies, big and small, throughout this harrowing account.

Speer studied architecture at what is now the Technical

University in Berlin under Heinrich Tessenow, whose architecture was characterized by what Eduard Sekler called an "unassuming, rather charming simplicity...[that] had its roots in the same soil where folklore and classicism grew side by side." Tempting as it may be to see Speer's Third Reich fever dreams as inflated versions of Tessenow's pared-down Classicism, he utterly lacked his teacher's delicate touch, gift for faultless proportions, and sense of humane scale. An architectural third-rater by any measure, Speer would have languished at some back-office drafting table had he not joined the Nazi Party in 1931. Such were his networking skills that a year later he was asked to refurbish the party's Berlin headquarters.

Within months of Hitler's takeover he improvised a stunning scheme that secured his place in the Nazi hierarchy. The annual National Socialist convocation in Nuremberg, held on campgrounds outside the city, took on added importance once Hitler gained political legitimacy. But before Speer was able to execute his Brobdingnagian stadium of 1935–1937, he had to come up with a suitably impressive interim solution. In 1933 he requisitioned 152 antiaircraft searchlights from the Luftwaffe, placed them around the perimeter of the assembly grounds, pointed them upward, and after nightfall created the *Lichtdom* (cathedral of light), a mesmerizing spectacle in which columns of icy illumination seemed to rise into infinity, or, alternatively, formed the bars of a gargantuan virtual cage. This coup de théâtre was such a triumph that the kliegs remained after the stadium was completed.

(New York City's Tribute in Light, the yearly commemora-
tion of the 2001 attack on the Twin Towers, has employed
beacons trained skyward in an identical manner, though few
have emphasized the concept's unfortunate provenance.)

Speer first attracted international attention with his German pavilion at the 1937 World's Fair in Paris, where the
exposition's officials limited the height of his building—a
granite shoebox with a squared-off frontal tower—at 177
feet so as not to overpower the USSR pavilion, designed by
Stalin's favorite architect, Boris Iofan, directly across the exposition's central esplanade (see rear endpapers). Not to be
outdone by the Bolsheviks, Speer added a thirty-foot-high
gilded eagle atop his composition, which, juxtaposed against
the Soviet building's seventy-eight-foot-high stainless-steel
roof sculpture of workers brandishing a hammer and a
sickle, presented a prophetic architectural preview of the
coming world cataclysm.

Hitler planned to rename Berlin "Germania" after he
won the war and wanted, by 1950, to carry out Speer's mammoth design to transform the city and make it the capital not
only of the Third Reich but of the world itself. Any doubts
about the architect's irredeemable vileness are countered by
Kitchen's methodical exposition of precisely how Speer persisted with this insane project even after the war started. The
quick prosecution of the blitzkrieg against Norway, Den-
mark, the Low Countries, and France prompted euphoric
Nazi expectations that this would be a short campaign,
whereupon Speer began Germania in earnest. He would

brook no opposition, and when the subordinates of a top Hitler henchman annoyed him he threatened, "If your three protégés can't shut their traps, I'll order their houses to be demolished," hardly the harshest punishment he meted out. Previously Speer had been constrained by law from evicting tenants in Berlin apartment houses that would have to be torn down to make way for his grand axes of triumphal avenues terminating at his colossal Great Hall, which if built would have been the world's largest domed structure, equal to a seventy-two-story skyscraper (see Illustration 7a). (Krier, in one of his most astounding passages, writes of this monstrosity that "a dome, however large, is never oppressive; it has something of the archetypally benevolent. Speer's Great Hall would have been a monument of promise, not of oppression.")

Legal niceties were now dispensed with, despite objections from a few brave civic officials, and as Kitchen documents, Jews were evicted from their homes and sent to concentration camps specifically to free real estate for Speer's requirements, a process entrusted to Adolf Eichmann before he hit his fully murderous stride elsewhere. Furthermore, so insatiable was Speer's need for gigatons of stone to encase Germania's new buildings that he abetted the enslavement of Jews and foreign captives to mine quarries until they dropped. When Speer was confronted by those brave enough to speak up about the cruelty of this and other deadly servitude, he breezily replied, "The Yids got used to making bricks while in Egyptian captivity."

As the war went on, Speer was given huge responsibilities

for supervising the German war machine, for which he astonishingly evaded responsibility at Nuremberg. Kitchen writes:

> He was very fortunate that it was not brought to the court's attention that Mittelbau-Dora, the notorious underground factory where the V2 rockets were built and where thousands died due to the appalling conditions, was part of Speer's armaments empire. Nor was any mention made of his complicity with Himmler's policy of deliberately working prisoners to death.

The fiasco of Operation Barbarossa—the disastrous German invasion of the Soviet Union named after the conqueror supposedly waiting to be awakened within view of Hitler's Berchtesgaden picture window—forced Speer to abandon his work on Germania and redirect his organizational talents as minister of armaments and war production, a position that allowed him to prosper obscenely through all sorts of corrupt schemes. At the Nuremberg trials, one of the rare officials not taken in by his insidious charm and ersatz penitence was a British army major, Airey Neave, who on reflection deemed Speer "more beguiling and dangerous than Hitler."

Behind the Führer's desk in the ridiculously bloated Berlin Chancellery office designed by Speer—where the dictator was never photographed because its stupendous scale would have made him look like a dwarf—hung a partly unsheathed sword. He gleefully said it reminded him of a line from

Wagner's music drama *Siegfried*: "*Hier soll ich das Fürchten lernen?*" (Is this where I should learn fear?) Even before visitors reached this chamber they were subjected to an angst-inducing march along extended corridors paved with intentionally slippery marble to put them off balance. At its dark heart, the architecture of Albert Speer—and by extension that of Nazi construction in general—promoted control through intimidation. This was the explicit purpose, not a random by-product, of official design in the Third Reich. The direct reflection of a society's values in what it builds, always a fundamental aspect of architecture, has never been clearer or more loathsome in the entire history of this art form.

8

THE LEVITT BROTHERS

ALTHOUGH THE GREAT RECESSION of 2007–2009 was set off when the United States housing bubble burst, not long afterward amnesiac Americans again began speculating in domestic real estate. The steep rise in residential property values during the final two decades of the twentieth century still lingered in many people's minds, as did the widespread memory among the baby-boom generation that the family house was the best investment their parents ever made. People in this country seemingly cannot resist the temptation to "flip" real estate—that is, buying and reselling in the short term to make a quick profit.

Midway through the millennium's second decade, recovery in the national housing market remained spotty—in 2015, 7.4 million home mortgages were seriously "underwater" (i.e., the balance of the loan was more than 25 percent higher than the property's current assessed value)—but a healthy local economy could still support flipping even modest residences, though perhaps not as profitably as a few years earlier. Several cable TV channels broadcast series that followed this process, including *Flip This House*, *Flipping Virgins*, *Rehab Addict*, and my personal favorite, *Flip or Flop*. This program starred a telegenic young Southern California couple who took down-at-the-heels Orange County tract houses, remodeled them to suit contemporary tastes—with loftlike "open concept" floor plans, spa-inspired bathrooms, and obligatory granite kitchen countertops—and often made a five-figure return on their investment, although some of their cost estimates seemed suspiciously low and their completion schedules improbably speedy to anyone who has ever done home improvements. *Flip or Flop* (which ended in 2017 after four years when the co-stars divorced) and other examples of what has been called real estate porn remind us that there is a huge inventory of postwar suburban housing stock all around the country, much of it in the style we now call midcentury modern, although more exists in hybrid modes that mix traditional and contemporary elements. Millions of detached single-family houses were erected on the outskirts of American cities between the end of wartime building material restrictions in 1947 and the onset of the oil embargo recession in 1973.

In his study *Detached America* (2015), James A. Jacobs states that during the quarter-century after the war "private builders and building companies constructed about 35,500,000 housing units...[of which] the overwhelming majority...were the detached single-family houses that define suburbia." The mass migration at midcentury—by 1950 more Americans lived in suburbs than in cities—represented a thoroughgoing reformulation of our domestic landscape and a colossal demographic upheaval. This immense shift grew out of the pent-up demand created by nearly two decades of severely curtailed construction during the Great Depression and World War II. An acute housing shortage was exacerbated by a sharp increase in postwar birth rates, which resulted in a whirlwind of suburban residential development that had been anticipated but delayed for some time. For if planners could not have predicted the back-to-back economic and military traumas of the 1930s and 1940s, housing reformers had long foreseen a looming crisis in the uncontrolled growth of older urban centers.

The proliferation of automobile ownership during the century's second and third decades gave new if short-lived impetus to the Garden City Movement, founded in 1898 by the British planning theorist Ebenezer Howard, who opposed unlimited urban growth in favor of multiple, moderate-sized "conurbations" with dwellings and workplaces in convenient proximity. Such medium-density centers would ideally be surrounded by undeveloped greenbelts for recreation and as barriers against pollution. Yet this congenial middle ground between urban overcrowding and rural isolation made little headway in the US, despite the spirited advocacy of the critic Lewis Mumford and his fellow members of the Regional Planning Association of America, which was organized in 1923 by the architect and planner Clarence Stein to promote New Towns in America.

A rare application of Garden City principles in this country was Stein and Wright's Radburn, New Jersey, of 1928–1930, the only partially realized but nonetheless internationally influential "New Town for the Motor Age." Yet however intelligently Radburn accommodated the burgeoning car culture, it did not incorporate businesses (beyond a few shops for local residents)—a crucial component of British New Towns, which sought to integrate the domestic and professional spheres of life more intimately—and it became by default a commuter suburb, albeit a very fine one, for people with jobs in nearby cities, especially Newark and New York. Importantly, Radburn was predicated on the radical belief of the nineteenth-century political economist Henry George that "we must make land common property." Thus, although Radburn's homeowners hold title to their dwellings, the ground beneath them is retained in trust for all by a cooperative association. This egalitarian principle removed a major financial incentive that typically drives developers and investors who can make money from the sale of unbuilt plots (usually at steadily increasing prices) if a community thrives, as was done with Seaside, Florida, founded in 1981 and a paradigm of the neotraditional New Urbanism Movement in the United States. For this and other reasons, the wholly noncommercial Radburn idea never caught on in the States.

The great unanswered question about the suburbanization of mid-twentieth-century America is this: Could it have been done better? A more intelligent approach to design was certainly shown by the Case Study House Program—the loose association of like-minded Modernist architects organized in 1945 by John Entenza, the editor of the California-based *Arts and Architecture* magazine, who solicited superior prototypes for residential living from some of the period's most imaginative designers. However, their plans were neither conceived for mass production nor geared to providing the cheapest possible dwelling per square foot. In contrast, affordability, not design distinction, was the overriding motivation for the best-known postwar tract-house manufacturers, the Levitt brothers—William, who headed the company (established in 1929 by their father, Abraham, the son of a Russian rabbi), and Alfred, its chief architectural designer and planner.

William Jaird Levitt and Alfred Stuart Levitt were born in Brooklyn in 1907 and 1912, respectively, and although both studied at New York University, neither of them took a degree. Their father was a real estate lawyer who in the mid-1920s accepted vacant real estate plots in Rockville Center, a Long Island suburb, from a bankrupt client in lieu of cash payment. When builders with whom he had joined in a speculative project to erect forty houses on the property defaulted, he asked his sons to complete the job, which they successfully did shortly before the stock market crash.

The brash, outgoing Bill Levitt was a born salesman and perfect front man for the family-owned operation, whereas the retiring Al was artistically inclined. The pragmatic Abe Levitt once said of his younger son, "Alfred loved to draw, but he didn't know what a two-by-four was." Oddly, despite the aspiring master builder's obvious knack for creating houses from an early age, he never had any formal design education nor did he ever receive an architecture license, and thus always needed a registered architect to sign and seal his plans.

The Great Depression notwithstanding, the Levitt firm went on to construct small groups of high-end houses on Long Island before World War II. But when the Levitt brothers were drafted into the military they observed a number of industrialized engineering and fabrication techniques that could be profitably applied to the mass production of lower-priced dwellings for returning servicemen, the postwar period's most obvious growth market. They were only two of many servicemen with some prior connection to architecture or the construction industry who discovered transformative ideas for improving building methods and materials thanks to the necessarily improvisatory and innovative atmosphere stimulated in the armed forces by the all-out war effort.

To cut expenses on the very different kind of houses they decided to build when peace came, the Levitts' no-frills, wood-frame structures did not have an excavated basement, but instead were erected atop a concrete slab poured directly onto the ground and inlaid with radiant heating (a method Frank Lloyd Wright pioneered in his low-cost Usonian houses of the 1930s onward, which featured several other concepts that Alfred Levitt proudly admitted he'd swiped from the grand old master). Although it is often assumed that Levitt houses were prefabricated, they were merely standardized, with interchangeable components and simplified assembly strategies that resulted in considerable economies. Therefore the company could deliver compact, freestanding "minimum houses"—a term that originated in Weimar Germany's social-housing movement as *das Existenzminimum* (the minimum required dwelling area)—that war veterans could buy for less per month in total carrying charges than the going rental rates for many city apartments. The Levitt company required no down payment, and the low-interest, thirty-year mortgages provided to vets by the Federal Housing Administration put these houses within easy reach of even those with moderate incomes. Who could resist owning a brand-new homestead in the countryside with the last word in kitchens and bathrooms, instead of leasing an old inner-city apartment with a claw-foot tub and no backyard?

The first houses offered by the Levitts in their now famous development in Hempstead, New York, thirty-seven miles east of Manhattan—initially called Island Trees but renamed Levittown after marketers discovered that the family name signified quality to consumers—were completed in 1947 (see Illustration 8a). (They were initially for rent only, with an option to buy after one year, but became available for outright purchase in 1949.) The 750-square-foot floor plan comprised a living room, kitchen, two bedrooms, and one bathroom, with an unfinished partial attic space suitable for future expansion. This tidy Cape Cod cottage sold for $6,990 (more than $78,000 in current value), but the brothers soon found that buyers would willingly pay somewhat more for upgrades, and in 1949 they introduced an equally successful 800-square-foot ranch-style version for $7,990 (equivalent to nearly $84,000 today). Though the dimensions of these initial Levittown houses seem minuscule by current standards—the median size of new single-family American houses is 2,521 square feet, more than three times larger than the Levitts' first offerings—they were considered capacious enough by a generation long inured to overcrowding at home during the deprivation of the Depression and the housing shortage of the war years, when separate bedrooms for each child and multiple bathrooms were unheard of except among the rich.

The Levitt brothers' venture into mass production was backed up by the bountiful provision of home-financing benefits through the Servicemen's Readjustment Act of 1944. Commonly called the GI Bill, it contrasted dramatically with the disgraceful treatment of World War I veterans at the onset of the Great Depression, when the 1932 Bonus Army March on Washington was violently suppressed. Along with generous tuition subsidies for former servicemen—this country's most extensive foray into socialized higher education—the 67,000 mortgages guaranteed through the GI Bill made home ownership possible for more citizens than ever before (except nonwhites, who received fewer than one hundred of those loans). To take advantage of this bonanza in government-guaranteed home ownership—a key component of encouraging a large, stable, taxpaying middle class—astute entrepreneurs across the country quickly copied the Levitts' cost-efficient formula.

In her book *Houses for a New World* (2015), the architectural historian Barbara Miller Lane investigated the output of a dozen lesser-known tract-house developers in four diverse regions—New England, the mid-Atlantic, the Midwest, and Southern California—and analyzed the period's typical Cape Cods, ranches, and split-levels with the serious formal analysis once reserved for high-style architecture. Her tour de force of research is all the more impressive because she assembled documentation akin to that previously available on the residential work of important postwar figures such as Richard Neutra, William Wurster, and Marcel Breuer but largely overlooked for builders other than the Levitts. Her vivid evocation of the postwar suburban building boom recalls a hopeful time when a popular American middle-class weekend pastime was to pile the kids and in-laws into the family car and drive around looking at model houses, whether or not you were actively shopping for a new place.

Lane found newspaper advertisements and promotional materials for subdivisions that were clearly aimed at wives (who wielded huge influence about housing decisions even though their husbands were the breadwinners) and stressed the transformational nature of life in these up-to-the-minute dwellings. A revealing example of that direct emotional appeal to women can be found in a 1955–1957 sales brochure for Cinderella Homes, a new Anaheim, California, subdivision not far from the recently completed Disneyland. This booklet depicts a princess-like figure and regal coach next to a rendering of a sprawling ranch-style house and the words "your every wish for a home ... come gloriously true." The Disneyesque iconography chimes perfectly with the opening lines of "Young at Heart," Johnny Richards and Carolyn Leigh's 1953 hit song for Frank Sinatra: "Fairy tales can come true / It can happen to you...."

A phenomenon as pervasive as this vast population redistribution could not have gone unnoticed by commentators in various disciplines, and an extensive literature on the new suburbanization quickly developed. Critical responses tended to be negative from the outset, typified by such debunking books as the newspaperman John Keats's *The Crack in the Picture Window* (1956) and a dubious pop psychological report by the physician Richard E. Gordon, his wife Katherine K. Gordon, and the journalist Max Gunther titled *The Split-Level Trap* (1960), which claimed that the new suburbs made people physically and mentally ill. In due course several methodologically sound (and now classic) studies—led by the sociologist Herbert Gans's *The Levittowners: Ways of Life and Politics in a New Suburban Community* (1967) and the urban historian Kenneth Jackson's *Crabgrass Frontier: The Suburbanization of the United States* (1985)—presented more nuanced interpretations. So did *The Suburban Myth* (1969) by the historian (and future literary biographer) Scott Donaldson, who argued that mass-produced postwar housing had less to do with the malaise of corporate conformity than the persistence of the Jeffersonian ideal ("the champion American myth of all time"), which a century and a half earlier established patterns of individual exurban living that worked against the development of cohesive communities.

Lane attempts to make a case for the architectural virtues of midcentury tract houses, and traces the origins of their organizational formats to specific parts of the country where they originated before spreading nationwide. Thus we learn that the once-trendy split-level, which typically combined three strata within a two-story shell—

> a basement level on a slab, containing the garage, a utility enclosure, and sometimes a small "den"; then, half a level up, the living room and kitchen; then, another half level up, the bedrooms and bath (usually over the garage)

—emerged in hilly areas where the semi-submerged garage could be dug into a sloping site, and were particularly suited to the terrain of New Jersey. She also points out that because the interior volumes of the split-level were stacked, the "footprint" could be half as large as that needed for a single-story ranch, which saved on land costs.

Furthermore, Lane minimizes the damage caused by racial segregation, which systematically banned blacks from buying into new suburban developments for two decades. She writes:

There was a very significant melting-pot experience in the new postwar communities. Italians, Jews, Catholics, Irish, Polish, and others who had been segregated in American cities and excluded from earlier American suburbs now mingled freely, forming new kinds of communities that they valued intensely. I think that this experience may have helped Americans to become more accepting of diversity, even where color lines were initially maintained. In fact, suburbs became integrated more quickly than cities: by the 1970s, barriers were broken down nearly everywhere.

However, an entire generation of African-Americans was unable to participate in the grand social experiment of postwar suburbanization. As James Jacobs writes in *Detached America*, this gross injustice was committed by the federal government:

The FHA did not, as is commonly held, develop racially neutral policies that were then applied in a racist manner. Rather, FHA policy itself was purposefully written in a way to exclude nonwhite Americans, using the abstract notion of "market demands" as blanket justification for discrimination in sales. A prejudiced appraisal system for mortgages passed over existing houses that were believed by officials to pose a risk for devaluation—those in mixed-race subdivisions, for example, or properties in older urban neighborhoods—which further reduced access to the financial windfall that became available to white veterans and their families.

To be sure, many blacks did make it to suburbia, though not easily. By 1960 there were an estimated 2.5 million African-Americans living in suburbs; a decade later, after passage of the Fair Housing Act of 1968, that number almost doubled, to 4.6 million. But Jacobs observes that blacks moved into older inner-ring suburbs vacated by cynically manipulated "white flight":

> Such neighborhoods frequently became available for black ownership through blockbusting, a process structured by the purposeful use of racial anxiety and panic to undermine the residential housing market, ultimately for the profit of real estate brokers. These agents convinced white residents that they should sell their properties at below-market values because blacks were beginning to buy in the neighborhood, and their property values were bound to fall even more. Agents then turned around and sold the properties to black buyers at inflated prices . . . [and] departing white families often ended up in a new house on the suburban periphery.

There were hardly any mid-twentieth-century equivalents in design quality of the exemplary Greek Revival house plans that were widely disseminated through carpenters' pattern

MAKERS OF MODERN ARCHITECTURE, VOLUME III

books for many decades after the American Revolution—the main reason vernacular construction in this country maintained such a high general standard, even in rural regions, until the Civil War. Instead, the semi-modern yet quasi-traditional forms devised by most 1950s and 1960s American developers were fundamentally derivative and debased, no matter how evocative they may now seem of their period. None of the houses documented by Lane, for example, displays the nearly faultless proportional logic—especially the pleasing relation of the part to the whole—that distinguished even run-of-the-mill construction by itinerant early-nineteenth-century craftsmen in this country.

Thus the New Urbanists—revisionist planners who since the 1980s have promoted American housing developments with a stronger sense of community values, which they feel can be fostered by traditional design elements, including front porches and sidewalks—have looked not to postwar suburbia but to premodern prototypes, including pattern book designs. Yet the higher density of dwellings espoused by the New Urbanists is not in itself a solution, especially since few such enclaves have effectively addressed the continually vexing place of the automobile in a society slow to pursue more ecologically responsible transportation options.

Because midcentury tract houses tended to be built very close together (units were usually no more than twenty-five feet apart), their side elevations were often left as windowless blanks. Another accommodation to privacy was the strip window, inserted high on bedroom walls to admit light but prevent neighbors from looking in. This lack of direct visual connection with the outdoors could recall a jail cell, and although tract houses were physically proximate, they often felt emotionally isolated. Another problem with postwar suburban developments was their dull uniformity, determined by lot lines more than any other factor. Though some builders tried to vary streetscapes by shifting and flipping similar layouts this way and that, there were limits to what could be achieved in such tightly packed settings. The major problem was that these designs were insufficiently conceived in all three dimensions. The backs of even architect-designed houses can sometimes seem like afterthoughts, but the minimally detailed rear elevations of typical 1950s and 1960s American subdivision schemes were perfunctory in the extreme, and presented a bleak aspect until landscaping could soften their stark appearance, though most suburban backyards typically contained an unsightly jumble of recreational paraphernalia.

Developers focused almost solely on the street façade to make an arresting first impression on prospective buyers, a quality known in the real estate trade as "curb appeal." Thus onto the front of these generic boxes they added an array of more-or-less traditional appliqués—touches of brick or fieldstone to give greater heft to the predominant asbestos shingles or wood (and occasionally aluminum) siding; nonfunctioning window shutters; wrought-iron railings and Colonial-inspired lighting fixtures; and that ubiquitous symbol of the postwar suburban home, the picture window. But because such flourishes were typically treated as marketing devices rather than emanations of an integrated design, detailing tended to have a tacked-on quality that inadvertently underscored the thin character of mass-produced construction. There were some notable exceptions to this lack of architectural distinction, particularly on the West Coast, where the public was more receptive to popularized forms of modern architecture and eagerly embraced the prevailing new style—updated reinterpretations of the traditional California ranch house. One of its most vigorous champions was the architect/builder Cliff May (1909–1989), whose flair for self-promotion—evident in such best-selling books as his *Western Ranch Houses* (1956)—was equaled by strong design skills that have made his sprawling, light-filled, well-crafted structures a byword for pleasurable, informal indoor-outdoor living and desirable properties on the resale market to this day. The same is true of the developer Joseph Eichler (1900–1974), whose houses (mostly in the San Francisco Bay Area) were more fully informed by High Modernism than May's but now are similarly prized as among the best of their kind.

Interesting though it is to see midcentury tract houses treated with scholarly gravitas, for the most part these are not designs particularly worthy of preservation or emulation. They paid little attention to sustainability or energy conservation, were predicated on a restrictively traditional model of family life that seems outdated if not oppressive to many Americans today, and few of these structures were so solidly built that they can do without substantial retrofitting as they enter their sixth or seventh decades. They now seem more important in sociological than architectural terms. In 1940, only about 40 percent of Americans were homeowners; by 1965 that figure had soared to almost 63 percent. The extraordinary social mobility indicated by these numbers seems all the more poignant when one considers a reverse development in the United States recently. In 2007–2009, before the full impact of the Great Recession was felt, 66.4 percent of housing units were owned by their occupants. By 2014 that figure had dropped to 64.7 percent, the lowest since 1995.

Rather than glamorizing the white-bread world of Eisenhower-era cookie-cutter suburbia, I prefer to think of more socially admirable efforts such as Reston, Virginia, twenty miles west of Washington, D.C., which was founded in 1964 by the developer Robert E. Simon. (His initials formed the first three letters of this start-from-scratch community's name.) With its sensible and salable mix of housing formats, including clustered town houses and high-rise condominiums, and encouragement of businesses that provided jobs for its residents, Reston more closely resembled European New Towns than postwar American suburbs. As Simon's 2015 *New York Times* obituary noted:

> He laid out a town of open spaces, homes and apartments that would be affordable to almost anyone, racially integrated, economically self-sustaining, pollution-free and rich in cultural and educational opportunities.

That is something to be nostalgic about. You'd have to look very hard in the suburbs of America today to find a single builder following his high example.

As for the Levitt brothers, their central part in making affordable single-family houses more widely available than ever before in our country's history seems attributable to a conjunction of circumstances unlikely to ever occur again here, most importantly a huge demographic demand supported by generous government subsidies, the very opposite of the inequality in income and social advancement that has become a hallmark of postmillennial America. Thus it was perhaps not entirely surprising when in a 2017 speech at, of all things, a Boy Scout summer jamboree, President Donald Trump delivered a bizarre denunciation of William Levitt, a real estate developer of far greater import than either himself or his father. Although Trump began by citing Levitt's "unbelievable success," he went on to claim:

> In the end he failed and he failed badly. Lost all of his money. He went personally bankrupt. And he was now much older. And I saw him at a cocktail party. And it was very sad because the hottest people in New York were at this party....
>
> And I see, sitting in the corner, was a little old man who was all by himself. Nobody was talking to him. I immediately recognized that that man was the once-great William Levitt of Levittown.

According to *The New York Times*, "After asking Mr. Levitt what went wrong with his business, Mr. Trump recalled his response: 'Donald, I lost my momentum. I lost my momentum.'" James Levitt, a son of the legendary builder, reacted with justifiable anger:

> I find that Donald Trump's use of a story regarding my dad in a somewhat negative light is, at best, pure hypocrisy. Donald Trump couldn't hold a candle to my dad's achievements. My dad worked very hard to earn his money. He paid his contractors and suppliers for their work and efforts. He believed in integrity as a business ethic....
>
> Trump may have chosen that word [momentum] to use as an inadvertent admission that he too has lost momentum on both the political and business fronts. In his comments, Trump uses the word...then acknowledges that it can be lost. Perhaps he's telegraphing his own feelings.

Indeed, as one resident of Levittown pointed out to a *Times* reporter, "How many times has Trump declared bankruptcy?"

9

THE NEW BRUTALISTS

LITERATURE THAT TAKES a wistful backward glance at the outmoded manners and mores of the previous forty or fifty years—most famously Proust's *À la recherche du temps perdu*—has a direct parallel in architecture. Time and again we have seen reawakened interest in the disdained buildings of two generations earlier, a span still within living memory but not quite yet history. For example, Oxford aesthetes of the 1920s (a coterie that included John Betjeman, Osbert Lancaster, and Evelyn Waugh) discovered new charm in ornate Victorian monuments that their parents' contemporaries dismissed as eyesores. The bizarre, proto-psychedelic fantasies of the Catalan outlier Antoni Gaudí emerged from a half-century of oblivion in the 1960s and enthralled an international counterculture. And the 1970s saw a new vogue for the jazzy modernistic riffs of Art Deco, which four decades earlier was banned from the new Museum of Modern Art by its mandarin tastemakers Alfred H. Barr Jr. and Philip Johnson as populist kitsch.

With almost clockwork inevitability, a sudden concatenation of postmillennial books indicated that the rehabilitation of yet another once-reviled phase in the building art was underway. The architecture in question is an industrial aesthetic that arose in postwar Britain and was dubbed New Brutalism, a semi-ironic, quasi-pejorative label on the order of Gothic (which implied the barbarism of the Goths) and Baroque (from the Portuguese word for a misshapen pearl). The Swedish architect Hans Asplund coined the term *nybrutalism* in 1949, and four years later its English translation was used for the first time in the British journal *Architectural Design*. There the wife-and-husband architects Alison and Peter Smithson wrote that an unexecuted house of theirs would have had "no finishes at all internally, the building being a combination of shelter and environment. Bare brick, concrete, and wood.... Had this been built, it would have been the first exponent of the New Brutalism in England."

In addition to its echoes of *art brut*—Jean Dubuffet's name for outsider art—New Brutalism was also an oblique riposte to New Humanism, a set of beliefs inspired by Geoffrey Scott's influential book *The Architecture of Humanism* (1914). But Scott's call for a return to Arts and Crafts design principles in the year that the Great War broke out was scorned as escapist nostalgia by many young midcentury Modernists. Among them was the postwar period's foremost British architecture critic, Reyner Banham, who with his love of modern technology and scant empathy for the Arts and Crafts Movement's focus on social-reform issues belittlingly described New Humanism as "brickwork, segmental arches, pitched roofs, small windows (or small panes at any rate)—picturesque detailing without picturesque planning. It was, in fact, the so-called 'William Morris Revival,' now happily defunct...."

Yet it was not a utopian nineteenth-century dreamland that Brutalism countered as much as the thin, commercialized version of the International Style that after World War II gained ascendance through economic expediency. Brutalism's striking departure from the steel-skeleton-and-glass-skin conformity of routine, profit-oriented Modernism was defined by its contrary emphasis on raw concrete (*béton brut* in French) in massive forms of imposing scale, idiosyncratic shape, rough finish, and uncompromising forcefulness, with a building's inner workings and services—structure, plumbing, electricity, heating, and ventilation—unabashedly exposed and indeed emphasized. Brutalism soon became a worldwide craze, as this comparatively economical means of fabrication offered a cost-effective alternative to hand-riveted metal construction and allowed a broader array of sculptural effects than those obtainable with rectilinear frameworks.

Apart from Brutalism's most influential exemplar—Le Corbusier's Unité d'Habitation in Marseilles (1947–1952), a marvel of multiunit high-rise housing that attracted hordes of young architects even before it was completed—other conspicuous manifestations of the style include Louis Kahn's Richards Medical Research Laboratories at the University of

Pennsylvania in Philadelphia (1957–1960), which was inspired by the distinctively slender medieval defensive towers
of the Tuscan hill town of San Gimignano; Marcel Breuer
and Hamilton Smith's Whitney Museum of American Art in
New York City (1963–1966), a squared-off inverted ziggurat
in concrete and granite complete with a nonfunctioning
moat and drawbridge; and Denys Lasdun's Royal National
Theatre in London (1967–1976), which the retrogressive
Prince Charles once described as "a clever way of building a
nuclear power station in the middle of London without anyone objecting." And although the boldly modeled concrete
architecture of Japan's postwar Metabolist group is often
considered an independent episode, designs such as Kenzo
Tange's Olympic Stadium in Tokyo (1961–1964), with its
swoopingly dynamic tentlike roof, can be placed under the
Brutalist rubric.

The extent to which New Brutalism took hold internationally can be gathered from a geographical range that en-
compasses Paul Rudolph's intricately multilevel Yale Art and
Architecture Building in New Haven (1958–1963; see Illustration 11a) and the cubic heap of Moshe Safdie's Habitat 67
housing at the 1967 World's Fair in Montreal, as well as less
familiar oddities like the rotund Beehive—the New Zealand
Parliament's Executive Wing in Wellington (1964–1977) by
Basil Spence—and Rinaldo Olivieri's La Pyramide (1968–
1973), a mixed-used ziggurat in Abidjan, Ivory Coast. That
global diffusion is further confirmed in byways such as
Skopje, the Macedonian city so extensively (and firmly) re-

built in dramatic concrete forms after a devastating 1963 earthquake that some have suggested that this out-of-the-way destination be promoted to architectural tourists as the "Brutalist Capital of the World."

However, not every big, tough-looking building, even if made of concrete, is necessarily Brutalist. The new popularity of the subject has prompted overeager enthusiasts to take the broadest conceivable definition of the style, regardless of Banham's dictum that "in order to be Brutalist, a building has to meet three criteria, namely the clear exhibition of structure, the valuation of materials 'as found' and memorability as image." Banham, fixated on materials and engineering, asserted that New Brutalism at last fulfilled a central philosophical aim of the Modern Movement. Praising the first celebrated British example of Brutalism, the Smithsons' Hunstanton Secondary Modern School in Norfolk (1950–1954), he wrote in his seminal 1955 *Architectural Review* essay "The New Brutalism":

Whatever has been said about honest use of materials, most modern buildings appear to be made of whitewash or patent glazing, even when they are made of concrete or steel. Hunstanton appears to be made of glass, brick, steel and concrete, and in fact is made of glass, brick, steel and concrete. Water and electricity do not come out of unexplained holes in the wall, but are delivered to the point of use by visible pipes and manifest conduits. One can see what Hunstanton is made of, and how it works, and there is not another thing to see except the play of spaces.

Yet this restrictive attitude about "truth to materials"—a principal Modernist shibboleth that began among moralizing Victorian theorists and has persisted ever since—was in essence little different from the judgmental admonitions of Arts and Crafts adherents about the inherent soullessness of the machine. Banham went on to expand his argument at book length in *The New Brutalism: Ethic or Aesthetic?* (1966), which inexplicably has been out of print for years and deserves republication as a revealing document of architectural historiography by a first-rate polemicist.

There are several reasons for the postmillennial change in perceptions about Brutalism, which remained in fashion for only about twenty years during the 1960s and 1970s. As the landmarks preservation movement has repeatedly demonstrated, what was once underappreciated or even despised in architecture often attains new value when its existence is threatened, whether one personally likes a currently démodé style or not. The most immediate concern about Brutalism now is its conservation, as many of these seemingly invulnerable, fortresslike edifices are beginning to fall apart. Like other experimental architects of the modern age, the Brutalists were more intent on getting their innovative designs built than worrying about how well they would last for the ages, and their command of new materials and construction techniques often lagged behind their visions. But the debate over

whether these purposefully unlovely creations should be restored to their original state or left to decay remains largely
unresolved.

Another major factor in the reexamination of Brutalism is
the part that postgraduate academicians play in methodically advancing topics that have yet to be fully investigated.
While there will always be doctoral dissertations on unex-
amined facets of the great architectural masters, Ph.D. advisers often guide their students toward neglected or
discounted subjects, with the hope that fresh analysis will
yield worthwhile results. Thus we have seen the scholarly
literature steadily progress far into the twentieth century,
and it was only a matter of time until we reached Brutalism.

That there is a definite element of fandom in the Brutalist
revival there can be no doubt. In the introduction to his
paean *Raw Concrete: The Beauty of Brutalism* (2016) the
British architectural historian Barnabas Calder passionately
declares his infatuation:

> I am a lover of concrete. The great outburst of large con-
> crete buildings in the 1960s and '70s, the style known
> as Brutalism, thrills me. I love the unapologetic strength
> of these buildings, and the dazzling confidence of their
> designers in making their substantial mark. I love the
> optimism they seem to embody, their architecture prom-
> ising bullishly that new technologies can improve al-
> most every corner of human life. Most of all, I love the
> way the buildings look: rough, raw concrete, streaked

by rain and dirt, forming punchy, abstract shapes; soaring cliffs of tower block or entire cities within cities.

But it might also be argued that this aggressively Neoprimitive ethos represented an outright rejection of High Modernism's belief in the perfectibility of mankind through advanced technology, a rejection expressed in intentionally crude finishes that hardly improve with age. Brutalism, which reflected the bleak worldview of existentialism so pervasive in the 1950s, reveled in its flagrant uncouthness and lack of finesse in much the same way that the Angry Young Men of postwar British literature, drama, and filmmaking flaunted their contempt for anything that hinted at poshness, polish, or privilege. Where Barnabas Calder sees Brutalism's confidence and optimism, others perceive a palpable angst and inward-turning defensiveness that make many of these designs seem more like penal institutions or military emplacements than housing estates, arts centers, or schools sponsored by an egalitarian and beneficent welfare state.

In yet another familiar progression, subsequent building modes often foster dissatisfactions that make earlier, diametrically different approaches look appealing by comparison, which helps account for major reversals of taste. The wholly uningratiating nature of Brutalism perversely appeals to dystopian undercurrents in modern society, and pessimists both envious of and sickened by today's all-pervasive consumer culture might find this grim aesthetic better suited to the ongoing decline of the postindustrial West—and especially Europe—than a prettified approach to public architecture. Even taking a more positive point of view, after the flimsy cartoon-Classical pastiches of Postmodernism in the 1980s, the nervously fragmented angularity of Deconstructivism in the 1990s, and the postmillennial proliferation of computer-generated Blobitecture, the undeniable material heft and protective aura of Brutalism can seem reassuring to those threatened by an increasingly multivalent and menacing world.

The most substantial study of New Brutalism since Banham's can be found in *Space, Hope, and Brutalism: English Architecture, 1945–1975* (2015) by the British architectural historian Elain Harwood. Although Brutalism became a worldwide trend, its greatest concentration was in Britain, where public building authorities gave overwhelming support to this new direction. A detailed account of that remarkable architectural program is given by John Grindrod in his *Concretopia: A Journey Around the Rebuilding of Postwar Britain* (2013), which lucidly evokes the political and social climate that enabled this style to flourish in a country that before World War II had not embraced Modernism—except for its industrial manifestations—as fully as Germany, France, the Netherlands, the Soviet Union, Czechoslovakia, and Scandinavia.

Like so many other aspects of twentieth-century architecture, the origins of Brutalism can be traced directly back to Le Corbusier, whose pronouncement that *"l'architecture, c'est avec des matières brutes établir des rapports émouvants"* (architecture is the establishing of moving relationships with raw materials) became the veritable gospel of the Brutalists. After he and Pierre Jeanneret completed their stunning series of machinelike Purist villas of the 1920s and early 1930s, the Swiss-French architect became deeply disillusioned with the creative limitations of rationalism and began a decisive turn toward rougher materials and biomorphic forms. These were first seen in his expressive use of concrete at the Pavillon Suisse student housing at the Cité Internationale Universitaire in Paris (1930–1931), and then even more evidently in his Villa Le Sextant (1935) in Les Mathes, France, with its rough stone rubble walls that point directly to the self-consciously primitive aesthetic of Brutalism.

Le Corbusier's long-standing fascination with vernacular culture, amply displayed in his 1911 diary of travels through Southern, Central, and Eastern Europe (posthumously published as Le Voyage d'Orient), was further strengthened by his friendship with Fernand Léger, who likewise idealized folk traditions and sought a similar vitality in his own art as he, too, moved away from an earlier technological aesthetic and toward a vigorous, less refined late style. Although Le Corbusier's theories had a profound influence on the thinking of several generations of British architects, their built works seldom rose to the master's level, unlike their contemporary counterparts in South America, especially the Brazilians Lúcio Costa, Oscar Niemeyer, and Lina Bo Bardi, who used raw concrete with a joyous bravado and sensual abandon rarely seen in British Brutalism.

At times, Brutalism could bring out the best in lesser architects whose work before and after that phase does not seem as interesting, perhaps most notably I. M. Pei. His firm's early jobs for the real estate developer William Zeckendorf Sr. were rather dull sub-Miesian efforts, while his late-career dependence on cautiously segmented and genteely manipulated geometries exhibited considerable technical suavity but little conceptual inventiveness. However, during the 1960s the Pei office produced three of his strongest designs, all in a Brutalist mode: the multitowered National Center for Atmospheric Research in Boulder, Colorado (1961–1967), which owes a clear debt to Kahn's highly publicized Richards labs; the monolithic Everson Museum of Art in Syracuse, New York (1965–1968), influenced by then-prevalent trends in American Minimalist sculpture; and the shadowbox-like Sculpture Wing of the Des Moines Art Center in Iowa (1966–1968), late-Corbusian in its heavily outlined and deeply recessed framing. With this trio of relatively small but monumentally scaled structures, Pei achieved a rare and surprising balance between powerful expression and humane feeling largely unseen elsewhere in his extensive oeuvre.

Contrary to the grungy, pockmarked, damp-stained concrete surfaces typical of most Brutalist buildings, the exteriors of these three Pei structures are all smoothly rendered, the difference owing to the careful craftsmanship of wooden casting molds much more finely finished than usual and often approaching the quality of furniture. Furthermore, the concrete for the Boulder laboratory was mixed with finely ground local red sandstone to harmonize with the surrounding mountainous terrain, whereas that for the Syracuse gallery was similarly augmented with particles of the region's native gray granite. This exacting construction would remain a hallmark of the Pei office and is epitomized by its Grand Louvre expansion of 1983–1993 in Paris, where the perfectionist concrete is indistinguishable from tightly grained limestone. Such grace notes strengthen compositional clarity without seeming overly precious, not unlike the work of Tadao Ando, today's foremost adept of elegant concrete construction, who is often, though incorrectly, regarded as a neo-Brutalist.

The reasons why particular building styles are so prevalent in certain cities—such as Byzantine in Ravenna, Gothic in Bruges, or Modernisme (the Catalan variant of Art Nouveau) in Barcelona—are always rooted in economics and politics. When stability and prosperity attract growing populations and necessitate much new construction within short periods, uncommon architectural coherence emerges. In post–World War II America, the dynamic was rather the opposite, as rapid suburbanization pushed several big cities, financially hard hit since the Great Depression, further into decline. To stem the erosion of their tax base, municipalities such as Philadelphia, St. Louis, and Boston embarked on comprehensive plans to transform their run-down central districts.

The new Boston initiative of the 1960s—led by John F. Collins, the city's mayor for most of that decade, and imple-

mented by Edward J. Logue, prime mover of the Boston Redevelopment Authority—coincided with the apogee of
Brutalism and explains why that city became this country's
foremost repository of this short-lived style. The roster of
designers enlisted to recast the creaking Hub of the Universe
as an up-to-date metropolis included several of the biggest
names in twentieth-century architecture: Le Corbusier, Walter Gropius (then chief partner in the Cambridge, Massachusetts, firm the Architects Collaborative), Josep Lluís Sert,
Breuer, Pei, and Rudolph. By and large, though, the results
were less than wonderful. The nexus of this undertaking was
Government Center, a fifty-six-acre site just to the west of
the Colonial-era Faneuil Hall and the nineteenth-century
Quincy Market. This tripartite modern forum comprised
the John F. Kennedy Federal Building by the Architects Collaborative (1961–1966); Boston City Hall by Kallmann,
McKinnell & Knowles (1962–1969); and the concrete super-
block of Rudolph's Government Service Center (1962–1971).

The semi-enclosed street-level spaces beneath Rudolph's
ponderous and overbearing ensemble—its public concourse
recalls Piranesi's imaginary prisons without his sense of fantasy—provide an object lesson in how seemingly infinite volumes can nonetheless feel alarmingly claustrophobic. As
much as a new generation of Rudolph zealots may hope for
a wider reappreciation of his designs, his posthumous up-
grading seems unlikely to be helped by the Government Service Center's depressing hulk, with its jumbled undercarriage
of sequoia-like columns, bulging balconies, and undulating

stairways, all rendered in vertically corrugated textures of the bush-hammered concrete that became his trademark. (The center's proposed twenty-three-story office tower and a series of surrounding terraces were never executed because of funding cutbacks as the Great Society gave way to the Vietnam War.)

The high-rise Kennedy Federal Building was a wan performance by the Gropius firm, which had just inflicted the dreadful Pan Am Building (1960–1963) on New York City. None of the new Boston projects won as much critical praise as Boston City Hall, which was widely hailed upon its completion as the finest American public building of the postwar period. But this top-heavy citadel, on the former site of the raffish Scollay Square nightlife quarter, came to be seen by the public as forbidding and indeed hostile, and there have been repeated calls for its demolition and replacement with a more welcoming and transparent symbol of civic engagement.

The best of the new Boston designs was a little gem commissioned by a private institution: Le Corbusier's Carpenter Center for the Visual Arts on the Harvard campus in Cambridge (1958–1963). One of only two works he executed in the Western Hemisphere (the other was a house in postwar Argentina), the Carpenter Center shows just how rich and attractive the Brutalist vocabulary could be in the right hands. This five-story structure, squeezed into a narrow site, juxtaposes grid-like masses (which contain art studios) against sinuous *ondulatures* (walkways that slice through the exterior) and a dramatically cranked ramp that rises

1a. Frederick Law Olmsted and Calvert Vaux,
Central Park, New York City, 1857–1873.
They won the contest for this vast urban oasis with a design
that connects the surrounding city through an ingenious
separation of vehicular and pedestrian traffic.

1b. Frederick Law Olmsted and Calvert Vaux,
North Woods, Central Park, New York City, 1857–1873.
Inspired by English Romantic landscape design, the collaborators
devised many natural-looking but wholly man-made tableaux,
such as this cascade in a forest glen.

2a. Antoni Gaudí, Temple Expiatori de la Sagrada Família, Barcelona, 1882– .
The obsessive focus of Gaudí's life, his still-incomplete votary
shrine to the Holy Family is an exuberant hymn to faith.
Despite its improvisational appearance, he carefully engineered
the structure through extensive models and stress tests.

2b. Antoni Gaudí, Casa Milà, Barcelona, 1905–1910.
Nicknamed *La Pedrera* (the quarry) because of its rough-hewn
geological character, this nine-story limestone-clad apartment
building is uncommonly fluid in the way it wraps around a corner site,
and relates to Belgian and French Art Nouveau.

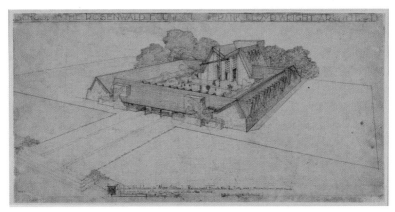

3a. Frank Lloyd Wright, Rosenwald Foundation School (unbuilt project),
Normal and Agricultural Institute, Hampton, Virginia, 1928.
Wright's proposed vocational school for poor blacks is
punctuated by a tall, double-A-frame structure antithetical to
his ground-hugging Prairie Houses of the early 1900s.

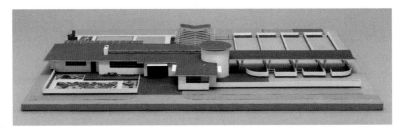

3b. Frank Lloyd Wright, Little Farms Unit project (unbuilt project), 1932–1933.
This prototype for a Depression Era back-to-the-land
resettlement scheme based on regional subsistence agriculture
anticipates the sleek, streamlined forms of the architect's
Johnson Wax building later in that troubled decade.

4a. Josef Hoffmann, Sanatorium Purkersdorf,
Purkersdorf, Austria, 1903–1905.
Modern notions that easy-to-clean interiors free of extraneous ornament are
essential to good health altered hospital and health care design. The severe
exterior of this hydrotherapy spa reflects the belief that simplicity is sanitary.

4b. Josef Hoffmann, Palais Stoclet, Brussels, 1913–1915.
The most opulent of the architect's commissions was this
marble-clad mansion, for which he designed everything from
tableware to gardens. Its dining room glitters with a mosaic mural
by his fellow Viennese Gustav Klimt.

5a. Edwin Lutyens, Munstead Wood, Godalming, Surrey, 1893–1897.
Although this country house is based on rural vernacular traditions,
Lutyens arranged it as an efficient home office for a modern
working woman—the landscape designer Gertrude Jekyll—
and included a photographic darkroom, rare at that time.

5b. Edwin Lutyens, Memorial to the Missing of the Somme,
Theipval, France, 1927–1932.
The antithesis of a triumphal arch, this disturbing
composition seems to cry out like a monstrous mouth and lists
names of British soldiers lost in World War I's worst battle.

6a. Jan Duiker and Bernard Bijvoet, Sanatorium Zonnestraal, Hilversum, the Netherlands, 1926–1931.
Dedicated to healing diamond cutters who contracted tuberculosis through their work, these lightweight pavilions stressed the curative powers of sunlight and air.

6b. Jan Duiker and Bernard Bijvoet, Openlucht School, Amsterdam, the Nertherlands, 1929–1930.
The health craze for outdoor education found urban expression in a structure with walls that could disappear in a daring display of modern engineering.

7a. Albert Speer, Volkshalle, Germania (unbuilt project),
Berlin, 1938.
Cynosure of the chief Nazi architect's plan to remake Berlin into the
world's capital was a 72-story-high dome meant to hold 180,000. Speer
used slave labor to cut stone for this, his most megalomaniacal design.

7b. Gerdy Troost, Great Hall, Berghof, Berchtesgaden, Bavaria, 1935–1937.
Hitler's favorite decorator, Troost took over her husband's architecture
practice after his death and wielded huge influence. The living room of this
alpine retreat featured a panoramic window that rolled down fully.

8a. Alfred Levitt, Levittown Cape Cod house,
Hempstead, New York, 1947.
The most famous of America's mass-production residential builders, the
Levitts capitalized on generous government subsidies for veterans and
pent-up demand for affordable family housing as postwar suburbs boomed.

9a. Ernö Goldfinger, Trellick Tower, London, 1968–1972.
A paragon of New Brutalism in Britain, where that tough-looking style
emerged under the postwar Labour welfare state, this concrete apartment
house was inspired by Le Corbusier's Unité d'habitation in Marseille.

10a. Louis Kahn, Salk Institute for Biological Studies,
La Jolla, California, 1959–1965.
Kahn's Beaux Arts training is clear in this symmetrical
laboratory complex facing the Pacific. The Mexican Minimalist
architect Luis Barragán suggested a bare plaza.

10b. Louis Kahn, Phillips Exeter Academy Library,
Exeter, New Hampshire, 1965–1971.
The soaring atrium of this prep school study center is given
monumental scale by four thirty-foot-wide concrete oculi,
warmed by wood-faced balconies.

11a. Paul Rudolph, Art and Architecture Building,
Yale University, New Haven, Connecticut, 1958–1963.
Boldly claiming a prominent street corner, Rudolph's
intricate Brutalist structure juggles thirty-seven levels within
its seven-story textured concrete carapace.

12a. Minoru Yamasaki, Robertson Hall,
Woodrow Wilson School of Public and International Affairs,
Princeton University, Princeton, New Jersey, 1961–1965.
A prime example of Yamasaki's penchant for
stylized Classical or Gothic motifs.

13a. Lina Bo Bardi, Museum of Art of São Paulo, Brazil, 1957–1969. Had Bo Bardi been a male architect working in the US or Europe rather than a woman in South America, her inventive schemes—like this structurally audacious gallery— would have garnered more acclaim during her lifetime.

13b. Lina Bo Bardi, SESC Pompeia leisure center, São Paulo, Brazil, 1977–1986. Recycled from a 1930s factory, this community services facility for a working-class neighborhood recaptures the dynamism admired in early industrial design.

14a. Frei Otto and Rolf Gutbrod, German Pavilion, Expo 67, Montreal, Quebec, Canada, 1965–1967. Among the most influential concepts in modern architecture, Otto's lightweight tensile and membrane structures elevated the mundane task of roofing large areas.

15a. Frank Gehry, New York by Gehry at Eight Spruce Street,
New York City, 2003–2011.
To cut costs, one elevation of this otherwise undulating
apartment tower was left as flat as a routine office building.

15b. Frank Gehry, Fondation Louis Vuitton, Paris, 2005–2014.
The luxury goods conglomerate LVMH hired Gehry, by then
the world's most celebrated architect, to create a dramatic
kunsthalle for its owner's art collection in the Bois de Boulogne,
and an implicit advertisement for the company.

16a. Renzo Piano Building Workshop, Renzo Piano Pavilion,
Kimbell Art Museum, Fort Worth, 2007–2013.
In his addition to Kahn's landmark, Piano reiterated the colonnaded pavilion
format he more successfully initiated at Houston's Menil Collection.

16b. Renzo Piano Building Workshop,
Fondation Jérôme Seydoux-Pathé, Paris, 2006–2014.
Atop this gemlike cinematheque and film archive, a vaulted ceiling
opens to expansive views of the surrounding city.

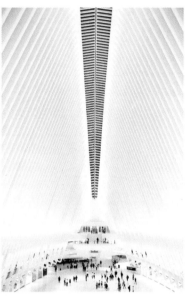

17a and 17b. David Childs/SOM,
One World Trade Center, New York City, 2005–2013 (left);
Santiago Calatrava, World Trade Center Transportation Hub interior,
New York City, 2004–2016 (right). The Twin Towers' replacement
overlooks this shopping mall–cum–train station.

17c. Santiago Calatrava, World Trade Center Transportation Hub,
New York City, 2004–2016.
Although its architect likened his design to a dove of peace,
the finished structure more closely resembled an aggressive stegosaurus
and cost $4 billion, nearly twice the initial estimate.

18a and 18b. Christian de Portzamparc, One57 condominium,
New York City, 2009–2014 (left); Rafael Viñoly, 432 Park Avenue
condominium, New York City, 2011–2015 (right).
Two exemplars of super-tall, super-thin postmillennial Manhattan towers
that altered the Midtown skyline and were dubbed Billionaires' Row.

18c. Alexander Gorlin, Boston Road Supportive Housing,
Bronx, New York, 2013–2016.
Conceived to give the homeless not only shelter but
rehabilitation services, Gorlin's apartment house is as socially
uplifting as it is architecturally superb.

19a. Maya Lin, Vietnam Veterans Memorial, Washington, D.C., 1981–1982. Lin's Minimalist earthwork, inspired by avant-garde trends in 1970s sculpture, has profoundly reshaped contemporary attitudes toward memorial architecture.

19b. Maya Lin, Riggio-Lynch Chapel, Clinton, Tennessee, 2004. The worship-and-meeting space for the Children's Defense Fund leadership training campus evokes Christian symbolism of the church as ship of salvation. Its humble materials echo the ethos of this social advocacy group.

from the sidewalk to the entrance on the building's second level. Both in its piquant ground plan and in its lively elevations, this marvelously collaged composition's play of linear and curving elements brings to mind Picasso's guitar sculptures of 1912–1914, while the brisk *marche* Le Corbusier leads through these powerful concrete volumes is akin to the kinetic internal circulation patterns of Alvar Aalto, unsurpassed in his intuitive understanding of how to convey delight by movement through space.

The postmillennial comeback of Brutalism is not surprising, given a worldwide vogue for strenuously exhibitionistic architecture enabled by computer design, which has resulted in grotesque behemoths far stranger than anything achievable through the relatively low-tech means of concrete construction. Some older observers will see this fascination with grandiosity and ugliness as the return of the repressed, a reminder of why Brutalism fell into disfavor and disrepute in the first place. This was never a style that attempted to convey warmth, comfort, intimacy, or other qualities we tend to associate with an enjoyable way of life, and thus it never won much love except from architectural specialists. Brutalism posited an unsentimental, not to say harsh, view of the modern world, and however heroic its unflinching embodiment of hard realities may have been, most people do not enjoy a daily diet of architectural anxiety and alienation, especially in northern climates under cloudy skies.

One of the first signs of rejection came in J. G. Ballard's dystopian novel *High-Rise* (1975), which is set in a thinly

MAKERS OF MODERN ARCHITECTURE, VOLUME III

fictionalized version of Ernő Goldfinger's Trellick Tower of 1968–1972, in London's North Kensington (not far from an earlier Brutalist residential high-rise, Clifford Wearden and Associates' twenty-four-story Grenfell Tower of 1967, which caught fire in 2017, resulting in the death of seventy-one residents).

Goldfinger's thirty-one-story concrete-framed apartment block, commissioned by the Greater London Council, was based on Le Corbusier's original Unité in Marseilles, although Goldfinger's scheme is nearly twice as high as its prototype (see Illustration 9a). Trellick Tower was well received by its first inhabitants, but as was also true of contemporaneous public housing projects in the United States—especially Minoru Yamasaki's unfairly demonized Pruitt-Igoe housing of 1950–1955 in St. Louis—it quickly descended into crime and squalor as funds for its upkeep and security were slashed.

Neoconservative critics blamed the newfangled architecture rather than larger forces of discriminatory economics, but as sociological studies have since proven, the claim that tall residential complexes breed social malaise is groundless. After Trellick Tower was privatized in the 1980s, when Margaret Thatcher took the British government out of the public housing business, the building's owner-residents increased protection from intruders and paid for long-delayed repairs; it is now a highly desirable property rightly appreciated for its design quality. Ironically enough, it stands as Thatcher's unwitting contribution to preserving the built legacy of the munificent welfare state she worked so hard to destroy through her own distinctive brand of brutalism. And its near contemporary, Grenfell Tower, will long remain a symbol of what can happen when government abdicates its regulatory—and moral—responsibilities in the realm of public welfare, whichever political party is involved.

10

LOUIS KAHN

HOW ODD THAT the towering genius of architecture during the third quarter of the twentieth century—when his most conventionally successful colleagues prized innovation over tradition, analysis over intuition, and logic over emotion—was a mystically inclined savant who sought to reconnect his medium with its spiritual roots. Indeed, he ran wholly counter to prevailing images of the modern architect. Rather than casting himself as a technocratic superman along the lines of the young Le Corbusier or a conduit between man and nature like the twinkling Frank Lloyd Wright, he made his name with an architectural *gran rifiuto,* rejecting the commercial blandishments of an increasingly corporate culture in favor of a quixotic quest to recapture the archaic power of shelter at its most elemental.

This charismatic anachronism was Louis Kahn, who by the time he died in 1974 at the age of seventy-three was widely and correctly considered America's foremost master builder, even though his mature career spanned little more than two decades and he executed only about a dozen important buildings. Posthumous revelations of Kahn's messy personal history have threatened to overshadow his immense professional accomplishments, yet his aura has grown steadily, not just for what he achieved but also because of what has taken place in the built environment since his death. After he almost single-handedly restored architecture's age-old status as an art form, his legacy was quickly squandered by younger coprofessionals. From the mid-1970s onward they have careened from one extreme, short-lived stylistic fad to the next—Postmodernism, Deconstructivism, Blobitecture—and lost sight of the profound values Kahn wanted to convey: timelessness, solidity, nobility, and repose.

Although a great number of books on Kahn's architecture were published in the years immediately following his death, it took more than three decades for a full-length biography to appear—Carter Wiseman's *Louis I. Kahn: Beyond Time and Style: A Life in Architecture* (2007). Another decade would pass until a far more intimate account of his personal and professional activities was presented by Wendy Lesser in *You Say to Brick: The Life of Louis Kahn* (2017). Whereas Wiseman examines eight of the architect's principal buildings in depth, Lesser focuses on five of the same works, what might be termed the Kahn Quintet: his Salk Institute for Biological Studies of 1959–1965 in La Jolla, California; the Kimbell Art Museum of 1966–1972 in Fort Worth, Texas; the Phillips Exeter Academy Library of 1965–1971 in Exeter, New Hampshire; the Indian Institute of Management of

1962–1974 in Ahmedabad, India; and the Sher-e-Bangla Nagar, or National Assembly Building, of 1962–1983 in Dhaka, Bangladesh (see front endpapers).

Each of those designs is a masterpiece, but all are also in some ways imperfect, even the universally beloved Kimbell, with its mastery of the use of light to show works of art against stone walls. Its big failure is the parking lot that fronts the main entrance and brings to mind a suburban strip mall, even though Kahn intended visitors to enter via the recessed courtyard on the opposite side of the building, beautifully landscaped by Harriet Pattison. Happily, what by default became the Kimbell's rear façade was given new life after the opening of the freestanding Renzo Piano Pavilion of 2008–2013 directly across from it.

Problems with some of Kahn's other buildings have been more numerous. The crushing monumentality he sometimes imposed on functions more suited to intimacy is epitomized by the cubic Central Hall of the Exeter library, which is dominated on each of its four sides by circular concrete-framed openings thirty feet in diameter (see Illustration 10b). Exonians call the nearby dining hall, also designed by Kahn, "the crematorium" because of the four tall, ominous chimneys that loom over the single-story structure. Yet that nickname could also apply to the yawning round maws of the library atrium. No amount of nitpicking, however, can diminish his overall contribution, which was nothing less than a complete realignment of architecture's deepest priorities.

That would not seem to be the expected agenda of an

architect who (apart from his fine government-sponsored housing projects in southeastern Pennsylvania with Oscar Stonorov during the 1930s and 1940s) didn't identify strongly with reformist social causes later on, even when they became an urgent matter for many of his colleagues amid the upheavals of the 1960s. However, once Kahn began to attain critical prominence, he stuck to his determination to work solely for high-minded clients. Beyond the patrons of the Kahn Quintet these included universities (Bryn Mawr College, where he built his Erdman Hall Dormitories of 1960–1965); museums (the Yale University Art Gallery of 1951–1953 and the Yale Center for British Art of 1966–1977); scientific institutions (the Richards Medical Research Laboratories of 1957–1960 at the University of Pennsylvania); and religious groups (the First Unitarian Church and School of 1959–1969 in Rochester, New York, and Temple Beth-El Synagogue of 1966–1972 in Chappaqua, New York). How often does any architect get so many prestigious opportunities, and, even more rarely, respond to them with the high sense of purpose Kahn commanded?

His mature designs share a remarkable formal consistency, but without the formulaic repetitiveness one sees, for example, in late-career Ludwig Mies van der Rohe. After much trial and error, Kahn at last learned how to make the grand gesture with simplicity and power. He drew on the gutsy ethos of the Greco-Roman tradition with volumetric heft but no hint of slavish imitation. His urge to create contemporary architecture that would endure through the ages was clearly announced in his essay "Monumentality" (1944), which began with the assertion: "Monumentality in architecture may be defined as a quality, a spiritual quality inherent in a structure which conveys the feeling of its eternity, that it cannot be added to or changed." Kahn's design philosophy was based on a Platonic notion similar to Michelangelo's conviction that all forms are embedded within materials and merely await the artist's touch to be freed. The sculptor believed that he needed only to chip away any parts of a marble block that were not the *David* or the *Pietà* in order to discover those works within. In turn, Kahn pared down his schemes to their most irreducible essentials—monumental mass, pure geometry, numinous natural light—and jettisoned the extraneous trimmings of Classicism without any loss of intensity.

Through his training at Penn under the French-born Beaux Arts–trained architect Paul Philippe Cret, Kahn learned all the compositional elements of the Classical vocabulary, which are evident in the grand, colonnaded, temporary buildings he worked on during his first big job as principal draftsman for the Sesqui-Centennial International Exposition of 1926 in Philadelphia, for which Cret was the master planner. Cret's particular emphasis on Beaux Arts principles such as bilateral symmetry and the *marche* (the central processional route through a building) recurred with particular force in Kahn's late work. These are most evident at the Salk Institute, with its mirror-image, serrated concrete wings flanking a central plaza that sweeps toward the Pacific (see Illustration 10a), and at the National Assembly Building in Dhaka, with its pairs of gigantic cubes and cylinders perforated with colossal circular or triangular openings, all ringed around a central rotunda.

Yet Kahn avoided what the architectural historian Sigfried Giedion criticized as the besetting sin of American Beaux Arts design: "Simply and mechanically transferring emotional luxury-forms from earlier periods to our own." However heavily the past weighed on Kahn's thinking, he was no historical revivalist, and his abstraction and transposition of ancient forms to modern circumstances was on a par with that of such earlier giants as John Soane and Edwin Lutyens, though he went much further than either in dispensing with applied ornament. Less apparent was his enormous debt to Le Corbusier, especially the Swiss-French master's consecration of concrete as worthy of high-style architecture and mysterious modulation of light, above all in the Ronchamp chapel, which he revered. Kahn was early to identify Ronchamp as a hugely significant work, even while some of his coprofessionals did not initially know what to make of this strange biomorphic departure from its designer's earlier machine aesthetic.

When he was about to begin construction on the Salk Institute, his first major project in concrete, Kahn asked a new employee in his office, Fred Langford, how much he knew about that material. When the young man admitted, "Nothing," his boss replied, "That makes two of us," whereupon Langford embarked on a crash course of self-education on the subject. With amazing alacrity he mastered the fine points of a craft that until then had not been executed at a very high level in the United States, and thereby became one of the master's most crucial technical collaborators.

The infelicitous title of Lesser's biography refers to a typically gnomic Kahnism about the inherent nature of materials: "You say to brick, 'What do you want brick?' Brick says to you, 'I like an arch.'" This imaginary dialogue highlights Kahn's surprisingly old-fashioned attitude toward materials and their supposed imperatives—a utilitarian notion so at odds with his insistent spirituality—derived from nineteenth-century British sources, primarily John Ruskin. He indirectly absorbed Ruskin's ideas from an art teacher at Philadelphia's excellent Central High School, a trained architect who inspired the boy to pursue his future profession. As Kahn recalled this adolescent revelation, "Architecture combined my love and desire for artistic creation, painting, and being able to express and stand out," a neat summation of both his soaring artistic aspirations and irrepressible egotism.

That latter quality was perversely reflected in his lifelong attitude toward money. Although Kahn is always portrayed as a hopelessly inept businessman, his disdain for filthy lucre was purposeful, and he remained openly contemptuous of financial go-getters. As he told his longtime engineer, August Komendant, who devised ingenious structural solutions that were beyond Kahn's ken, including the famous vaulted skylight ceilings at the Kimbell:

If you are in the profession of architecture, it is likely that you are not an architect. If you are an architect without thinking of the profession, you might be one. The profession kills your incentive....

You get yourself a good business character, you can really play golf all day and your buildings will be built anyway. But what the devil is that?

From the outset, Kahn was wary of accepting work that he feared would cheapen his image as a great artist-architect. He boasted that "I have refused thousands of dollars that were tainted," and he died nearly half a million dollars in debt. Two years after his death, the state of Pennsylvania rescued his wife, Esther Israeli Kahn, from penury by buying his papers for $450,000. (They are on deposit at Penn.) The architect depended on her income as a medical researcher during most of their forty-three-year marriage, and averred that his undying gratitude prevented him from leaving her for either of the younger women he impregnated. He gave little more than token amounts toward the upkeep of those satellite families, and his widow angrily (if understandably) rejected pleas that she help out his illegitimate children. "They're bastards," she declared. "They're not entitled to anything of Lou's."

During the 1940s and 1950s he took teaching positions at Yale, MIT, and Princeton (to which he commuted while maintaining his architectural practice in Philadelphia), and then ultimately at Penn, for the same reason most other avant-garde architects do: to guarantee a steady income until client fees were able to cover the costs of running an office. A large part of Kahn's legend rests on his fame as a pedagogue, and even though his parallel teaching career was driven by financial necessity, he became renowned for his ability to inspire students with a more elevated vision of professional practice than the technically advanced but psychically stunted approach characteristic of postwar American architectural education.

Although there are several published collections of the architect's lectures, *Kahn at Penn: Transformative Teacher of Architecture* (2015) provided the first in-depth account of his activities as an educator. Its author, James Williamson, was among the students from forty-three countries who received degrees in the architect's fabled master classes at Penn between 1956 to 1974, testimony to Kahn's global pull during his final decades. That there were only sixteen women—including Denise Scott Brown—among the course's 427 graduates is an index of the gender disparity that still persisted in architecture schools. (In recent years, upward of 40 percent of architecture graduates have been women.) Many of Kahn's master class students reckoned the course to have been among the most extraordinary experiences in their lives, but several of them harbored reservations. As Williamson writes:

> He seemed to discourage personal relationships with his students, and my main impression of his personality was its combination of strength and remoteness.

Although he was usually kind enough, I recall few overt expressions of concern for his students. Kahn's idealism, although inspiring, often seemed unrealistic, and in my later professional practice I have continued to struggle to reconcile his lofty ideals with the realities of the marketplace.

Another master class student, John Tyler Sidener Jr., known to the professor as "you from California," felt excluded by the studio's abstruse discourse and worshipful atmosphere:

> [Kahn] talked about the house as a sanctuary, a chapel, with a central space ringed with columns like a small Pantheon. I wasn't ready for that. I'd spent too long on publicly funded school buildings, low-cost housing, and other straight-forward projects. More difficult was this abstract conversation; the hard-core students seemed like they were clustered around a guru under a banyan tree, with conversations only among Kahn... and a few chosen students.

But as others discerned, the most valuable lesson to be learned there was less direct. John Raymond Griffin understood that Kahn's intention was to make his students

> critically examine our underlying thoughts about design...to begin developing our own individual ap-

proaches—and not so much just about architectural design—but also about the larger humanistic principles and purposes which design could or should seek to reveal.

As the historical record amply indicates, Kahn was wildly conflicted within himself: intellectually ambitious yet insufficiently educated save in his specialty; seemingly warm and generous but often aloof and monstrously selfish; endlessly loquacious yet maddeningly obscurantist; at once a wise man and a spoiled child. Although an avid world traveler, he never learned to drive a car. A keyboard virtuoso who helped pay for his education with jobs as a movie-house organist, he could not read musical notation. Physically he presented a similar bundle of contradictions. Though he was short, often rumpled, and facially disfigured, with a high-pitched voice and glasses so thick that he mockingly called himself Mr. Magoo after the purblind cartoon character, he was catnip to the ladies. Kahn's numerous erotic intrigues confirm Henry Kissinger's oft-quoted observation that power is the ultimate aphrodisiac (though here it was a matter of cultural cachet rather than political clout).

The deficiencies of Kahn's appearance notwithstanding, many women found him irresistibly attractive, including his longtime collaborator and lover, Anne Griswold Tyng. Nearly twenty years his junior, she recalled how "on swelteringly hot summer weekend charettes when Lou occasionally worked shirtless, it was hard not to notice how unusually broad his lightly freckled shoulders were in proportion to his slim hips." Vincent Scully, the Yale architectural historian who did more than anyone else to establish and burnish Kahn's critical reputation, lauded his looks in almost mythic terms:

> The impression was of deep warmth and force, compact physical strength, a printless, cat-like walk, glistening Tartar's eyes—only bright blue—a disordered aureole of whitening hair, once red: black suit, loose tie, pencil-sized cigar. It was at this time that he began to unfold into the rather unearthly beauty and command of a Phoenix risen from the fire.

Scully here alludes to the accident that left the future architect with horrific scars on his face and hands. In his native Estonia, the three-year-old Leiser-Itze Schmulowsky (as Kahn was known until he arrived in Philadelphia in 1906) was so mesmerized by the hypnotic glow of lighted coals that he tried to gather them up and suffered burns so severe that they nearly killed him. Though it might be facile to interpret Kahn's strenuous womanizing as overcompensation for his irrevocably damaged countenance, many people seemed not to notice it at all, such was the distracting force of his magnetic personality.

Kahn was unusually promiscuous by the standards of his time and place, fathering three children by three women. The long-concealed chaos of his private life was first revealed in 1997 with the publication of *Louis Kahn to Anne Tyng: The Rome Letters, 1953–1954,* edited by their recipient. Tyng, a glacially beautiful blond WASP who had been one of the first female graduates at Harvard's architecture school, was the golden shiksa goddess of a Jewish architect's dreams. When she became pregnant by Kahn and decided to keep their child, she went to Italy, where her older brother lived, which allowed her to give birth to Alexandra Tyng (who became a realist painter and the spitting image of her father) far from the prying eyes of proper Philadelphians.

Lesser identified yet another Kahn mistress previously unmentioned in the literature. Marie Kuo was a Chinese-born architect who worked in Kahn's firm and began a sexual relationship with him while Tyng was away in Italy. By the end of the 1950s he was involved in overlapping affairs with Kuo, Tyng, and Harriet Pattison, his landscape architect. In a scene worthy of *Les Liaisons dangereuses,* Lesser tells how Tyng overheard an office telephone call in which Kuo assured her mother that she was using birth control and didn't need to worry about an unwanted pregnancy. (Kahn, we learn, would not use condoms, and didn't like his women to take precautions, either.) Although Kuo spoke Mandarin for privacy, she did not realize that Tyng, who was born to Episcopal missionaries in China and raised there, understood her every word.

The architect hardly limited himself to three mistresses, however. One colleague recalled how at parties Kahn "would glom onto some younger woman or other and just press them to the wall—very attractive women, too. And some of them fell for it," though this would be considered sexual harassment or even assault today. Lesser also disclosed Esther Kahn's long-running affair with an acquaintance of her husband's, an unnamed married research scientist who taught at Penn and was blond and Gentile like Tyng. According to the Kahns' daughter, Sue Ann, the architect was "so engrossed in his own world that he probably never even thought about it."

But nothing exposed Kahn's unorthodox family relations more than Nathaniel Kahn's documentary *My Architect: A Son's Journey* (2003), which was nominated for an Academy Award and became a sleeper box-office hit. In it the director—whose mother is Pattison—joins his two older half sisters (Sue Ann is his senior by twenty-two years, Alexandra by eight) in a touching demonstration of how loving families can be forged under the unlikeliest of circumstances. Alas, what they appeared to have most in common was seeking the attention of an affectionate but ruthlessly self-absorbed father who put his work before everything else. Whatever spiritual transcendence Louis Kahn found in his architecture, much emotional wreckage followed in the heedless egotist's wake.

Whereas Wiseman's biography follows a standard cradle-to-grave chronology, Lesser inverts the narrative and begins with Kahn's death, a device often used when a demise is particularly unusual, dramatic, or notorious. Her impressive research skills are on full display as she gives the most complete account yet of the architect's end in a men's room at Manhattan's Pennsylvania Station on St. Patrick's Day in 1974, after which a perfect storm of procedural foul-ups resulted in his distraught families not being notified until two days later. The author debunks several persistent but erroneous notions about the episode, some held by his closest survivors, and gives plausible explanations for what went wrong and why.

Posthumous medical diagnoses are impossible to verify, yet it does seem likely that Kahn was a victim of excessive long-haul air voyages. To be sure, architectural practice was an international affair well before modern aviation, with masters from Bernini to Wright traveling to far-off lands in search of work. But the advent of regular commercial jet service in the late 1950s put unprecedented pressure on architects to routinely transverse vast distances to secure commissions, supervise construction, participate in conferences, give lectures, fulfill visiting professorships, and accept awards, all deemed desirable components of a major international career.

Cardiologists have since identified frequent and lengthy plane journeys as a major risk factor for those with heart disease, and a cause of deep-vein thrombosis, a clot that can now be prevented with advanced blood thinners. Kahn— who in his final year complained of "indigestion," a common misunderstanding of a classic cardiac symptom—was felled by a fatal coronary attack on the last leg of a grueling trek from Ahmedabad, his eighth international trip in four months, several of them halfway around the world. Such a marathon would have been hard on a younger, fitter man, but the toll it took on this workaholic septuagenarian was catastrophic. Because genetics are thought to have an important effect on longevity, and the architect's parents lived into their upper eighties, it might be said that Louis Kahn flew himself to death, a Jet Age Icarus.

11

PAUL RUDOLPH

A FALL FROM critical grace is not uncommon in the arts, but somehow it seems more surprising in architecture than in literature, music, or painting. Buildings tend to remain in the public realm much longer and more conspicuously than books that go out of print, operas that languish unperformed, or paintings relegated to storage. By and large, architecture is simply too expensive to destroy for mere matters of taste. There is no such thing as "out of sight, out of mind" when it comes to an ugly building, whatever the standards for judging one might be. Indeed, the benign neglect of unfashionable architecture in economically marginal areas has long been an inestimable boon to historic preservation.

Among the most acclaimed mid-twentieth-century American architects, none experienced a more precipitous reversal of fortune than Paul Rudolph. During the late 1940s and early 1950s, Rudolph attracted well-deserved attention for the more than two dozen houses he built on the west coast of Florida. These small, sprightly structures displayed what the architectural historian Robin Middleton aptly termed "a very bright-young-boyish charm." Rudolph's informal, lightweight houses demonstrated his dynamic manipulation of space, inventive use of new materials, and rejection of rote domestic conventions. It was thrilling to imagine what he might do on a larger scale with bigger budgets.

At the peak of his career, in the late 1950s and early 1960s, Rudolph was widely deemed destined for greatness. With the death in 1961 of Eero Saarinen, then the preeminent architect of his generation, Rudolph appeared ready to lead the American architectural avant-garde. (Louis Kahn, who was considerably older than both men, began to be perceived as this country's most important contemporary architect only in the late 1960s.) As Rudolph's renown grew, he became preoccupied with two concerns—self-expression and monumentality—that were fundamentally at odds with the empathetic touch and humane feel of his early works.

The extent to which modern architecture had become formulaic by midcentury led Rudolph to ponder how he could stand out from the crowd. His quest for a distinctive stylistic manner led him to adopt the tough vocabulary of New Brutalism, with its vigorously sculptural compositions that made the modular steel-and-glass grids of the Miesian school look somewhat anemic and routine. Rudolph's distinctively American version of Brutalism diverged from that of his foreign peers in his attraction to scenographic design—architecture that begins with a preconceived idea of how a building should look from a specific vantage point, in contrast to the Modernist belief that the internal functions of a structure should determine its external form. However, despite the arresting profiles scenographic design could engender—perhaps most famously in modern architecture the sail-like rooflines of Jørn Utzon's harborfront Sydney Opera House of 1957–1973—the practice struck some as a throwback to nineteenth-century Romanticism.

Another major difference in Rudolph's approach was that instead of using poured concrete like his counterparts abroad, he chose a less demanding and more economical alternative—the rough-finished precast concrete blocks that became his hallmark. Poured-in-place concrete requires costly wooden forms to contain the material until it hardens, whereas precast blocks eliminate that expense and can be used like bricks. Because he wanted to create more voluptuous volumes and richer surface textures than was possible with standard concrete blocks, Rudolph designed a range of precast components with rounded surfaces that could be combined to make a variety of curving forms. These pieces were fabricated with vertical ribs or flutes that mimicked the look of more labor-intensive bush-hammered concrete, which is mechanically distressed to achieve a corrugated surface (and which he used for his Yale Art and Architecture Building). Whether handcrafted or prefabricated, these components gave the exteriors of Rudolph's buildings a fuzzy striped effect often likened to corduroy, although of course not in any way soft.

Such was his publicity juggernaut that the press reflexively

lauded Rudolph's bombastic institutional schemes, epitomized by his eerily cavernous, crushingly heavy Government
Service Center in Boston of 1962–1971—a fortresslike complex with a swirling, multilevel interior that brings to mind
the inner ear of some Brobdingnagian creature. The lack of
critical analysis such overbearing works received at the time
is doubtless attributable to the friendships Rudolph assiduously cultivated with editors and critics in both the professional and general-interest press. Furthermore, his striking
black-and-white renderings—meticulous networks of tiny
lines that convey three-dimensional depth and look terrific
in print—made him a favorite of art directors eager to
achieve layouts with powerful impact.

Perhaps prompted by the historian Sigfried Giedion's influential 1944 essay "The Need for a New Monumentality"
—which argued that modern architecture lacked the imposing presence of earlier building styles—Rudolph sought to
make his designs more monumental. Like many other architects, he equated size with significance and attempted to
turn even lesser public commissions into major statements. A
case in point is his Orange County Government Center of
1963–1971 in Goshen, New York, a grandiose pileup of
boxy concrete forms that seems pompously overreaching for
a small-town office building.

When Rudolph stepped down as the dean of the Yale
School of Architecture in 1965, he grandly announced that
he was moving to New York to become a skyscraper architect, a macho ambition that few true artist-architects would

harbor, let alone openly express. As it turned out, he got to execute tall buildings only late in his career, but that did not stop him from fantasizing about mammoth high-rise projects until he had the chance to build them. Responding to the visionary megastructures proposed in the 1950s by the international collaborative Team 10 and in the 1960s by the Metabolist group in Japan and the Archigram group in Britain, Rudolph in the late 1960s and early 1970s devised hypothetical Manhattan schemes for gigantic agglomerations of mixed-use "plug-in" units that were to be inserted into elongated and towering frameworks reminiscent of children's building kits like Lego bricks, Erector Sets, and Tinkertoys. (Imagining such visionary projects was hardly confined to architects, as demonstrated by Norman Mailer's model for his "Mile High City," some seven feet tall and comprising more than 20,000 Lego pieces, which was used to illustrate the dust jacket of his 1966 book *Cannibals and Christians*.)

Though fortunately none of Rudolph's New York City megastructures was ever built, he applied a low-rise version of the same concept to one of the more imaginative American multiunit housing schemes of the period, Oriental Masonic Gardens of 1968–1971 in New Haven (the exotic name of which referred not to some fanciful real estate marketing concept but to the fraternal organization that sponsored it). Here 148 prefabricated shoebox-shaped units akin to mobile homes—which Rudolph dubbed "the twentieth-century brick"—were grouped in right-angled clusters around courtyards and stacked no higher than two stories.

The barrel-vaulted roof of each "brick" gave a lovely rippling rhythm to the slightly inclined twelve-and-a-half-acre site. Yet as Rudolph later admitted, residents hated the place: their dwellings leaked, some felt the development was as déclassé as a trailer park, and only a decade after its completion this noble experiment was demolished.

In his 2014 monograph on this complex and sometimes confounding figure, the architectural historian Timothy M. Rohan emerged as the foremost posthumous advocate of Rudolph's works. Even though Rohan is wholly sympathetic to his subject, he is far from uncritical about the factors that contributed to Rudolph's career decline. Rohan offers credible insights into how Rudolph's homosexuality was reflected in his work and suggests that his characteristic juxtaposition of defensive, often concrete exteriors and sensuous interiors parallels the dichotomy between his carefully maintained straight public image and his concealed gay private life. However, like several vanguard American artists of the 1960s—including Robert Rauschenberg, Jasper Johns, and Andy Warhol—Rudolph (as well as his architectural contemporaries Philip Johnson and Charles Moore) did not deny his homosexuality, although none of them openly proclaimed it, either.

Paul Marvin Rudolph was born in 1918 in southwestern Kentucky. His father was an itinerant Methodist minister, and as Rudolph observed when he was eighteen, "moving around and being a preacher's son has been hard," although doubtless not nearly as difficult as his emerging awareness of his sexuality given his family, geographic, and generational circumstances. Yet the Rudolphs' fourteen changes of address during his peripatetic childhood also helped him develop an encyclopedic eye for indigenous southern architectural forms. Sensitive and introverted, he took refuge in art and music, and became such an accomplished pianist that he contemplated a concert career until he placed second in a national competition. His need to be number one suddenly emerged as such a strong personal imperative that he there and then shifted his career ambition to the building art.

Rudolph studied architecture at the Alabama Polytechnic Institute (now Auburn University), where at the precocious age of twenty-one he executed his first building, for a professor at the school—the redbrick ranch-style Atkinson house of 1940. His next project was his initial collaboration with Ralph Twitchell, in whose Sarasota architectural office he worked during a gap year before starting a graduate degree. The Twitchell house of 1941 in Siesta Key, Florida, shows the clear influence of Frank Lloyd Wright, a prime example of whose residential work—the Rosenbaum house of 1939 in Florence, Alabama—Rudolph had visited and admired. The Twitchell house closely follows the economical formula Wright called Usonian—usually featuring low roofs and open living areas. The Twitchell house had low-slung massing, an overhanging roof, and concrete-block construction, along with horizontal stained-wood siding and a compact kitchen.

Three months after Rudolph entered the Harvard Graduate School of Design in 1941, the US entered World War II and he enlisted in the navy. After taking maritime architecture courses at MIT, he was stationed at the Brooklyn Navy Yard and put in charge of ship repair. The hands-on knowledge he gained there had a direct effect on his later work, and Rudolph's mastery of low-cost techniques for lightweight framing for houses and new materials such as Cocoon (a spray-on plastic used to mothball disused ship components) resurfaced in his ingenious postwar designs. This was yet another example of how countless young architects transformed their improvisatory wartime experiments into practices that later entered the professional mainstream.

When peace came, Rudolph returned to the Twitchell office and then completed his degree at Harvard, where he won a traveling fellowship that allowed him to witness firsthand the building boom in Europe. He was particularly taken by Le Corbusier's Unité d'Habitation of 1947–1952 in Marseille, with its monumental scale and expressive use of *béton brut*. Although Twitchell made him a partner in 1950, Rudolph later insisted that the designs credited to both men were entirely his own work. Never the most collegial of collaborators, he broke with his early mentor in 1952 and set up his own practice.

Eager to make a name for himself, avoid being typecast as a regional residential specialist, and establish useful contacts nationwide, the hugely ambitious Rudolph accepted teaching positions at architecture schools all across the country, including Cornell, Harvard, MIT, Penn, Tulane, UCLA, and Yale, sometimes overlapping in impractical ways. With considerable effort he juggled his dual design and educational career, and during the academic year ran his small Sarasota practice via telephone and mail. In short order he was awarded such high-profile jobs as the installation for the Museum of Modern Art's wildly popular 1955 photography exhibition "The Family of Man"; the Jewett Arts Center of 1955–1958 at Wellesley College in Massachusetts, a redbrick complex with modernized Gothic overtones reminiscent of Basil Spence's concurrent work in Britain; and several building projects in New Haven, where he became dean of the Yale School of Architecture in 1958. It was a heady ascent for the shy but striving preacher's boy.

Ironically enough, the project that halted Rudolph's rapid career advancement was the Yale Art and Architecture Building of 1958–1963, the plum commission he received soon after arriving in New Haven (see Illustration 11a). This was the latest in university president A. Whitney Griswold's admirable program to bring the best of contemporary architecture to the campus, which included works by Kahn, Saarinen, Johnson, and Gordon Bunshaft. As a series of Rudolph's preparatory renderings show, he gradually but relentlessly inflated the A&A Building (as it was known) from a relatively modest colonnaded structure in his initial version into the Brutalist behemoth that was erected—a nearly cubic core surrounded by a phalanx of windowless towers as forbidding as those of a medieval castle.

The building's many functional flaws soon became unavoidable—thirty-seven different levels were crammed into its seven stories, a preposterous overelaboration of space—and as the social upheavals of the 1960s unfolded, the heroic ethos Rudolph tried to evoke came across to rebellious students as authoritarian posturing. His successor as dean, the scholarly postmodernist Charles Moore, held a view of architecture diametrically opposed to Rudolph's, and had far greater knowledge of and respect for both historical and vernacular traditions. As Moore slyly proclaimed, "I disapprove of the Art and Architecture Building whole-heartedly because it is such a personal manifestation for non-personal use. However, I enjoy very much being in it."

To improve the structure's ill-resolved spatial organization, Moore encouraged students to take matters into their own hands and reconfigure studio spaces as they saw fit. He turned Rudolph's stately penthouse, which had been used for entertaining and as guest quarters for eminent visitors, into a student coffeehouse. Haphazardly altered and poorly maintained, the A&A Building under Moore's deanship became a countercultural mess. Then, in June 1969, a mysterious fire gutted the structure. Although the cause was never determined, Rudolph went to his grave convinced that Moore had somehow incited the destruction of his misunderstood masterpiece. (The building was salvaged, unsympathetically rehabbed, and then finally restored by Gwathmey Siegel & Associates in 2007–2008.)

With his reputation in decline as architectural tastes shifted to more user-friendly schemes, Rudolph pinned his hopes for a comeback on his largest-ever residential scheme, the Bass house of 1970–1972 in Fort Worth, commissioned by the Texas oil heir Sid R. Bass and his first wife, Anne. The A&A Building went up while Bass was a Yale undergraduate and he deeply admired its architect. The admiration between Bass and Rudolph was mutual, and the architect referred to his patron as "my Renaissance prince." Rudolph saw the Bass residence as his equivalent of Fallingwater, Frank Lloyd Wright's most famous house, which helped revive the master's career after a long dry spell. Rudolph's scheme took many cues from that legendary prototype, most notably its tiered arrangement of balconies thrusting outward from a central mast like huge domino tiles set at right angles to one another.

However, the Basses' site lacked the inherent drama of the Appalachian ravine where Wright found a waterfall from which all blessings flowed. Even the addition of an artificial pond by the landscape architect Robert Zion didn't do the trick in Fort Worth. However, thanks to the clients' ample funding, Rudolph was able to use costlier materials and attain a much higher level of execution than ever before. The white-painted steel framework of the Bass house is as precisely crafted as that of its model, Ludwig Mies van der Rohe's Farnsworth house of 1946–1951 in Plano, Illinois. And instead of the painted wood siding of Rudolph's early houses, here he used white porcelain-coated aluminum panels, a deluxe cladding component favored by the then-rising star Richard Meier.

While the expansive (and expensive) Bass house is a far more pleasing composition than Rudolph's Brutalist public works, it offers another example of his deep-seated urge to overcomplicate things, not least in his dragging out the entry sequence to a tedious extreme. He calculated that a visitor would make eight turns and ascend fifteen feet in traveling from the front door to the living room. In contrast, at Alvar Aalto's incomparable Villa Mairea of 1935–1938 in Noormarkku, Finland, visitors move directly from the entry to the heart of this extensive layout in a matter of seconds. Sadly for Rudolph, the Basses did not want images of their house to be published because of security concerns. Without being splashed over the pages of glossy shelter magazines it did not have the restorative effect on his reputation that its architect had so fervently wished for, and his critical rehabilitation never materialized.

Although the critic Michael Sorkin praised Rudolph's own Manhattan penthouse of 1977–1997 as "one of the most amazing pieces of modern urban domestic architecture produced in this country," I had quite a different experience when Rudolph invited me and my wife to a buffet dinner there in 1986, after an opening of his drawings at the Max Protetch Gallery. Throughout that multistory apartment (built atop an existing Beekman Place town house, the lower portions of which the owner rented out for extra income), surface finishes and details were astonishingly shoddy. For example, railings that in photographs seemed to be made of polished chrome were actually covered in peeling Mylar. Floor levels shifted up or down every few feet for no apparent reason, and narrow Plexiglas catwalks spanned chasms open to the stories below. There was so little continuous floor space amid the cavernous volumes that guests that evening huddled on the small carpeted platforms like Little Eva on the ice floes.

Odd sources of dim illumination—underneath stair treads and behind floating wall panels—made navigation treacherous, especially for such older luminaries as the designer Ray Eames and the architectural historian Vincent Scully. There was much stumbling and tripping as we tried to negotiate the labyrinthine circulation paths to and from the food and drinks, and even when we were seated mishaps continued. A large modular coffee table appeared to be composed of alternating cubes of reflective and matte black Lucite. But when someone set a drink down on one of the matte squares, it turned out to be a void and the glass crashed to the story below.

The architect and his longtime, much younger Swiss companion, Ernst Wagner, proudly conducted a house tour, which included such unanticipated sights as a clear Plexiglas bathtub that was fully visible from the level below. This voyeuristic detail seemed a latter-day equivalent of the architect Stanford White's notorious red velvet swing, beneath which he would stand and look up the skirts of young girls he fancied. Whatever erotic allure Rudolph's exhibitionist showpiece might have possessed was subverted by deposits of unidentifiable green matter in the tub's corners.

Understandably, the Rudolph penthouse has become a source of comment among queer theorists. The owner's jaw-dropping bedroom featured floor-to-ceiling mirrors that reflected a white marble Roman male torso and, mounted on the wall behind the white-fur-covered bed, a superscale advertising billboard image of a shirtless, hirsute young man being pawed by a passel of adoring young women. When a story on this startling interior was published in *The New York Times Magazine* in 1967, some saw it as the architect's inadvertent coming out. By the time of our visit the white-fur bedspread had been replaced by one of white leather perforated with metal grommets, which prompted another guest, the longtime MoMA trustee Barbara Jakobson, to ask our host, "What do you call this, Paul, the Stud Room?," which caused him to blush deeply.

But as Rohan notes, "Though highly self-aware and self-critical, Rudolph had several psychological or cognitive blind spots, such as believing that his homosexuality was not apparent to others." He was of course entitled to create for himself whatever fantasy environment he liked, but the penthouse was dangerous for some visitors. As we bid good night to our host, Scully spoke for several of us when he said, "Thanks, Paul, it's been a terrifying evening."

It is one thing to be uncomfortable in someone else's house but quite another to feel not at home in your own. Alexander Hirsch, who commissioned a town house on Manhattan's Upper East Side from Rudolph in 1966–1967, never fully acclimated to that twenty-five-foot-wide structure, which he shared with his companion, Lewis Turner. To be sure, it is a handsome design, fronted by a brown glass façade framed in a monochromatic, Mondrian-like pattern of brown-painted steel I-beams. Visitors enter through a low-ceilinged vestibule and thence into a dramatic double-height living room with a balcony that surrounds its upper periphery. This raised level is reachable only by a flight of floating stair treads that jut out from the side wall without risers or a bannister. The two original inhabitants, then in their sixties, felt this was an accident waiting to happen and tended to stay away from that part of the interior.

Soon after the couple moved in, Rudolph took it upon himself to add a large mural to their living room while they were away on vacation. His campy composition was based on an Italian quattrocento painting that, as Rohan writes, "depicted stylized men in tight-fitting Renaissance costumes with leggings and codpieces." The owner bridled at this unauthorized imposition and refused to pay Rudolph's $1,500 fee, the two stopped speaking, and a few years later Hirsch sold the house. Stories such as this, as well as press reports of several lawsuits lodged against Rudolph, made potential clients think twice before hiring him, and his career went into free fall.

As Rudolph's American commissions dried up, this already solitary figure retreated even further into himself. Though his prospects in this country never recovered, he found an eager new constituency in Southeast Asia. The glitzy highrises he erected there during the 1980s and 1990s—typified by his Bond Centre of 1984–1988, a mixed-use office and hotel complex in Hong Kong, conjoined twin towers bulging with "saddlebags" and clad in mirror glass—gave him the semblance of renewed success, but he never stopped believing he'd been robbed of his rightful place atop the hierarchy of modern architects. In his seventies Rudolph was diagnosed with mesothelioma, a cancer caused by prolonged exposure to asbestos—an occupational hazard in the building trades—and he died in 1997.

Rudolph's diminished posthumous stature is reflected in the unusual number of his buildings that have been destroyed. The most regrettable loss has been his Riverview High School of 1957–1958 in Sarasota, which was torn down in 2009. This early essay in what we now call green architecture—building design that takes regional environmental factors into account, especially for climate control—was a sprawling low-rise complex with an excellent natural ventilation system. However, because the school could not easily be retrofitted for mechanical air-conditioning, now considered essential in Florida, it was needlessly trashed, instead of being converted to another use that could have borne the cost of the renovation and upkeep. And although a plan was floated to save the endangered Orange County Government Center by converting that dilapidated structure into a community arts center, the central portion of the building was razed in 2015.

Rudolph's finest work by far was the Tuskegee University Chapel of 1960–1969 at the historically black college in Tuskegee, Alabama. This nondenominational chapel's angular redbrick exterior, unusually minimalist for Rudolph, conceals one of the most impressive twentieth-century religious spaces in America. The wedge-shaped, brick-walled nave tapers slightly as one nears the chancel, which is configured like an African-American gospel church with risers for a choir, instead of a conventional Christian altar. Most prominent is the pulpit, raised high above the congregation and surmounted by a sleek projecting canopy that signifies the importance of preaching in the black religious experience. Most affecting of all is the supernal illumination that pours down from lateral skylights and imparts a spiritual aura like that achieved by Aalto in his magnificent postwar churches.

Above all, the Tuskegee chapel exudes an embracing quality conspicuously missing in so much of Rudolph's other late work, and hints at what he might have accomplished had he stepped out of his defensive shell more often. The fact that Brutalism went out of fashion was less a factor in his professional decline than his innate inwardness. Louis Kahn, who many consider a Brutalist as well, was far more adept at imbuing his monumental concrete forms with a nobility and humanity that eluded Rudolph. That crucial difference largely accounts for the vast but not unjust disparity in their historical standing today.

12

MINORU YAMASAKI

NOW THAT I'M about to turn seventy I finally feel able to reveal a shameful secret: I was a teenage Yamasaki addict. I have no good excuse for why I got hooked, but Minoru Yamasaki was the first contemporary architect who entranced me. I had already begun my architectural self-education with the early writings of Ada Louise Huxtable in *The New York Times*, where in 1962 she praised the plans for Yamasaki's Robertson Hall of 1961–1965 (home of Princeton University's Woodrow Wilson School of Public and International Affairs) for the way in which "Greco-Roman and Far Eastern influences blend in a series of slender classic columns of Oriental lightness, in a top floor suggesting the cornice of a temple, and in a reflecting pool" and for how "the undertones of the past emerge subtly in a quite advanced and experimental construction" (see Illustration 12a). I thought it was wonderful, too. So much so that as the editor in chief of my high school yearbook, I dragged the baffled members of the National Honor Society fifty miles northeast from our unphotogenic hometown of Camden, New Jersey, to have a group picture taken with us lined up along the white quartzite colonnade of this newly completed Princeton Parthenon. My youthful infatuation with Yamasaki accelerated in January 1963, when he appeared on the cover of *Time*, an honor earlier bestowed on such master builders as Frank Lloyd Wright, Le Corbusier, Richard Neutra, and Eero Saarinen. This accolade seemed likely to propel the fifty-year-old Seattle-born Nisei to the very top of his profession. But he never quite made it, and more than three decades after Yamasaki's death he is unenviably remembered for two large projects that imploded in the most notorious building collapses of modern times. Although neither of these sensationally publicized endings was in any way his fault—and indeed his understanding of advanced engineering prevented the second from being an even worse catstrophe—his critical standing has never risen from the ashes, and he is now regarded, if at all, as a period curiosity.

My disillusionment with Yamasaki began with an eye-opening undergraduate survey course on modern architecture given at Columbia in the late 1960s by Eugene Santomasso, a charismatic young instructor who had studied at Yale with the legendary architectural historian Vincent Scully. Santomasso echoed his mentor's conviction that the period's foremost architect was Louis Kahn and likewise disparaged Yamasaki, whose Wayne State University conference center of 1955–1958 in Detroit, with its diamond-patterned glass-roofed atrium, Scully dismissed as a "twittering aviary."

By 1972 even Huxtable was having second thoughts, and in a dramatic volte-face, ten years after she lauded Roberston Hall she found it characteristic of the "acrobatic novelties and vacuous vulgarities" of postwar American campus design. She sealed the deal when she pinpointed the stylistic contradiction in Yamasaki's design for New York City's World Trade Center of 1962–1976: "Here we have the world's daintiest architecture for the world's biggest buildings." Although it is often assumed that taste is innate, it most certainly can be taught, particularly to the young and impressionable.

But time marches on, and so does the forty-year rule in architectural history, whereby once-admired but subsequently underestimated designers capture the interest of young scholars in search of figures who still await full evaluation. Buildings long deemed passé and unsuccessful can suddenly seem fresh and intriguing to a new generation, just as yesterday's tacky decorative designs can become tomorrow's next cool thing. This has been evident in the steady postmillennial flow of monographs on mid-twentieth-century architects who have undergone a downward critical reversal akin to that of Yamasaki—especially Saarinen, Edward Durell Stone, and Paul Rudolph, none of whom now commands the high artistic respect they all enjoyed around 1960.

Minoru Yamasaki was born in Seattle in 1912, the son of Japanese immigrants who had recently come to America for better economic opportunity but found little. After Congress passed the Chinese Exclusion Act of 1882, employers encouraged immigration from Japan to fill low-wage jobs Americans did not want. A similar reaction against the Japanese later resulted in the Immigration Act of 1924, which banned all Asians from immigrating and doubtless fed the bigotry that confronted the young Yamasaki. Late in life he still harbored bitter feelings about the racial prejudice he faced while growing up, which persisted for decades even as he found the financial success that had eluded his shoe-salesman father.

However, it was a case not only of race but of class, and there was a world of difference between his experience and that of the Chinese-born I. M. Pei, only five years his junior. The MIT-educated Pei came from an aristocratic family, had a faultless instinct for social relations, married an equally patrician Chinese Wellesley graduate—a prime minister, an ambassador, a bank president, and assorted literati are in the couple's genealogies—and they were smoothly accepted into the highest echelons of the American establishment.

Unlike many future architects, Yamasaki did not have artistic leanings as a boy; he excelled instead at math and science, which presaged his keen interest in engineering. But when his Tokyo-based architect uncle, Koken Ito (no relation to the Pritzker Prize winner Toyo Ito), visited Seattle en route to a job in Chicago, the teenager was so entranced by architectural drawings he showed him that he instantly decided to follow his relative's career path. He began the University of Washington's five-year Beaux Arts–oriented architecture program weeks before the 1929 market crash, and during the Great Depression paid for his education with dangerous and exhausting summer stints in the Alaska salmon-canning industry.

Upon graduation Yamasaki headed straight for New York City, where he felt he could escape the discrimination he suffered in Seattle. But like many of his coprofessionals, during the slump he could not find full-time work, and survived on odd jobs until he was hired in 1938 by Shreve, Lamb & Harmon, the architects of the Empire State Building, conceived seven years earlier. He was assigned to the design team for Parkchester, a vast middle-income housing estate in the Bronx sponsored by the Metropolitan Life Insurance Company, the first such development in the US to apply the "towers in the park" concept espoused by Le Corbusier in his unexecuted Ville Radieuse (Radiant City) of 1924, which proposed highrise apartment buildings widely spaced among parklike grounds to supplant densely settled mid-rise neighborhoods.

During World War II, Yamasaki oversaw construction of the firm's huge naval training station on Lake Seneca in upstate New York, which gave him the organizational skills needed to manage large-scale schemes. While occupied with this patriotic work, he had to rescue his parents from being put into an internment camp on the West Coast and brought them to New York, where they were crammed together with the architect, his new wife, and his medical-student brother in a one-bedroom apartment.

When civilian construction resumed after the war, he was recruited by Detroit's foremost architecture office, Smith,

Hinchman & Grylls, to become its chief designer and take the firm in a more Modernist direction. Despite his increase in status and income, Yamasaki still had not escaped racism. Although now well able to afford a house in the upscale Detroit suburbs of Birmingham, Bloomfield Hills, and Grosse Pointe, he found it impossible for an Asian-American to breach those all-white enclaves and eventually bought a nineteenth-century farmhouse in an unincorporated township twenty miles from his office.

Although Yamasaki was already well aware of the priorities of commercial architectural practice—at Shreve, Lamb & Harmon, one partner's mantra was "Finance dictates fenestration, rent rolls rule the parti [the organizational concept of a building]"—he quickly became disillusioned in his new position. As he later observed, "The makeup of a large (several hundred men) office is such that its primary concern has to be to make as much money as possible, forcing it to take almost any kind of work." In such firms, "the turnover...works against the creation of sensitive, responsive architecture." Furthermore, he recalled, "I was never permitted to meet with the client" if design changes were called for, and although this might be attributed to corporate bureaucracy, it is hard not to wonder if there was a racial component to his exclusion.

In 1949 Yamasaki and two office colleagues, Joseph Leinweber and George Hellmuth, set up their own partnership in Detroit, and because of important contacts that the St. Louis–born Hellmuth had in his hometown, they opened a second branch there. (Hellmuth went on to found Hellmuth,

Obata + Kassabaum, now known as HOK, the largest architecture firm in the US.) The combination of Hellmuth's local connections and Yamasaki's Parkchester credentials quickly won them big commissions for public housing in St. Louis, which at the time was in the throes of a thoroughgoing slum clearance and urban renewal campaign.

But if Yamasaki had already been frustrated by the economic incentives of large commercial architecture firms, such constraints were nothing compared to those imposed by the Federal Public Housing Authority, the New Deal agency that regulated the planning, design, and construction of what became known as "the projects." It has been correctly noted that architects of speculative skyscrapers are so limited by economic factors that they can do little more than decorate the exterior of a bulk predetermined by cost accountants. Yamasaki found himself in much the same position when he planned his most controversial work, the Pruitt-Igoe Apartments of 1950–1956 in St. Louis.

Although he kept abreast of recent trends in social housing in Europe, he was stymied in applying those new ideas in this commission because every design decision was subject to a plethora of bureaucratic regulations. The countless mandated requirements—from the minimum size of rooms to the disposition of windows, closets, and appliances—make one wonder how any architect could juggle so many competing demands, stick to the prohibitively low budget prescribed for each unit (under $1,750 per apartment, or around $18,000 today), and still come up with a coherent, let alone beautiful, design.

Whatever small grace notes Yamasaki was able to eke out under these restrictive circumstances were further undermined by budget cuts during the Korean War, which began in 1950 just as his plans were being completed. Nonetheless, the final results, however compromised, were met with grateful enthusiasm by the first inhabitants of Pruitt-Igoe—African-Americans who found the racially segregated development to be a vast improvement over the degrading living conditions they had been inured to. This was confirmed by original residents of the complex who were interviewed by the filmmaker Chad Freidrichs for his corrective 2011 documentary, *The Pruitt-Igoe Myth*. Their appreciative testimony refuted the persistent canard that the alleged debacle of postwar public housing in America—to say nothing of modern architecture as a whole—could be summed up by this noble St. Louis experiment, which ended when the dilapidated, crime-ridden project was demolished, a victim of not so benign neglect, only eighteen years after it opened.

The misconception that high-rise public housing was responsible for social malaise because of its design attributes has been promoted by many opponents of Modernist architecture, most notably the critic Charles Jencks, who began his 1977 polemic *The Language of Post-Modern Architecture* by writing:

Modern architecture died in St. Louis, Missouri on July 15, 1972 at 3.32 pm (or thereabouts) when the infamous Pruitt-Igoe scheme, or rather several of its slab blocks, were given the final *coup de grâce* by dynamite. Previously it had been vandalised, mutilated and defaced by its black inhabitants, and although millions of dollars were pumped back, trying to keep it alive (fixing the broken elevators, repairing smashed windows, repainting), it was finally put out of its misery.

However, as has been amply confirmed by well-informed sociologists, including the housing specialist Herbert Gans, the problems that were allowed to get so unmanageably out of control at Pruitt-Igoe were not architectural in origin. Rather, they had mainly to do with reductions in basic maintenance and social services as government funding for Great Society programs was shifted to the Vietnam War.

Nonetheless, Jencks's assertion has remained indelibly fixed in the public imagination, as indicated by the Victoria and Albert Museum's 2011 design exhibition "Postmodernism: Style and Subversion, 1970–1990," which opened with an enormous photomural of the Pruitt-Igoe towers collapsing amid clouds of dust, like some lurid Victorian tableau of Samson pulling down the pillars of the temple. No architect likes to see his work destroyed, but Yamasaki felt deeply humiliated by the ignominious end of Pruitt-Igoe, and a few years afterward he wrote that "of the buildings we have been involved with over the years I hate this one the most."

None of this could have been foretold at the time of Pruitt-Igoe's completion, and during the 1950s Yamasaki racked up one enviable commission after another. His Lambert–St.

Louis Airport Terminal of 1951–1956, with its sequence of four triple-vaulted concrete canopies, although not quite as audacious as Saarinen's TWA Terminal of 1956–1962 in New York City, nonetheless conveys a similarly evocative image of Jet Age dynamism. Yamasaki was esteemed enough to be chosen for the State Department's embassy architecture program—an initiative meant to advertise the Modernist supremacy of the US—and designed the US Consulate of 1954–1956 in Kobe, Japan.

There he came up with a low-rise grouping of three flat-roofed rectangular structures set around a traditional Japanese landscape garden. In a nod to the local vernacular, he suspended a contemporary metal adaptation of bamboo *sudare* blinds—which although immobile work well to filter daylight—from the projecting upper perimeter of each story. During this commission the architect's exploration of his ancestral homeland intensified a growing desire to bring a more spiritual element—"serenity, surprise, and delight," as he put it—to his work.

In purely formalist terms, however, it is often hard to distinguish Yamasaki's designs from those of his even more celebrated rival Edward Durell Stone, who likewise espoused an approach meant to be more visually enticing than the glass-walled boxes of the debased commercial version of the late International Style. The main difference between the two architects, it now seems, is that Stone wrapped his travertine-clad shoeboxes in pierced screens of vaguely Mughal derivation, whereas Yamasaki preferred outer scrims of

faux-Gothic appliqués and, later on, stylized classical colonnades more familiar to Beverly Hills than to the seven hills
of Rome. In due course a confusing repetitiveness set in to
Yamasaki's work, and it was hard to tell from their exagger-
ated but superficial surface effects whether the building underneath was a synagogue on Chicago's North Shore or an
airport in Dhahran, given how closely the Islamo-Gothic
façades of those two buildings resembled each other.

In 1962 Yamasaki completed his most prestigious commission yet: the United States Science Pavilion at the Century 21 Exposition, more commonly known as the Seattle
World's Fair. This interconnected cluster of six rectangular
white pavilions (now called the Pacific Science Center) is surfaced with stylized Gothic tracery and hovers above a series
of fountain-studded reflecting pools interspersed with plazas.
Over the ensemble soars a freestanding group of five sche-
matic Gothic arches meant to reinforce the quasi-religious
symbolism of what one commentator has called this "virtual
cathedral of science." Yet the architectural hit of the exposition was the Space Needle, Edward E. Carlson and John
Graham Jr.'s *Jetsons*-like observation tower, then the tallest
structure west of the Mississippi. With its hipster-futuristic
styling—like a flying saucer perched atop a hyperelongated
tripod—the Space Needle remains a perennial tourist attraction, while Yamasaki's time-warp design evokes a stage set
on a 1960s *Ed Sullivan Show* excerpt from *Camelot*.

The acclaim that greeted his Seattle World's Fair designs,
however, led to two major high-rise commissions in that

city—the IBM Building of 1962–1964 (which proved that even the simplest architectural box can be awkwardly proportioned) and the Rainier Bank Tower of 1972–1977, both of which, with white exteriors of narrowly spaced vertical ribbing, look much like the skyscrapers Stone was producing at the same time, including his General Motors Building of 1963–1968 in New York City. Leaving aside such oddities as Yamasaki's US Pavilion of 1958–1959 at the World Agricultural Fair in New Delhi—with a sea of gilded onion domes worthy of Las Vegas's Aladdin Hotel—the most bizarre thing he ever created was the Rainier Bank Tower. This twenty-nine-story office block is hoisted atop an upwardly flaring, windowless eleven-story concrete pedestal that at its base is only half the width of the superstructure it supports. Although a tour de force of engineering, the precarious-looking building remains deeply unsettling, especially in the earthquake-prone Pacific Northwest.

Thanks to his burgeoning reputation as a skyscraper architect with an artistic aura, Yamasaki was an obvious candidate for the most ambitious American urban design initiative of the 1960s—the World Trade Center in New York City. This was the pet project of David Rockefeller, the president of Chase Manhattan Bank, who wanted to shore up the faltering value of his family's Lower Manhattan real estate holdings as financial services firms moved from the Wall Street area to midtown or the suburbs. He pursued this grandiose scheme, which never had a sound economic rationale, with the backing of his older brother, New York governor Nelson Rockefeller, whose long tenure in Albany overlapped with most of this fourteen-year undertaking (see frontispiece). The state's chief executive used every power at his disposal to push the quixotic endeavor to completion, including the involvement of the Port Authority of New York and New Jersey, the bistate agency under his political control. The Port Authority had not previously been involved in such an enormous real estate speculation, which comprised ten million square feet of office space that landed on the market with a thud during the worst recession in decades.

The terrible truth is that Yamasaki's posthumous reputation would still be languishing in obscurity were it not for the disaster of September 11, 2001, which propelled him back into the public consciousness for the worst possible reason. Whatever one might think about the aesthetics of his poorly received World Trade Center project, there is no question that the loss of life in the terrorist attack was greatly reduced because of the innovative engineering he employed for the Twin Towers. Notwithstanding widespread shock that the skyscrapers collapsed with such swiftness—the South Tower, the second to be hit, fell after fifty-six minutes, while it took 102 minutes for the North Tower to go down— the real miracle was that these severely damaged hulks remained standing for as long as they did. This allowed an estimated 14,000 to 17,000 people to escape, although many were trapped above the stories hit by the planes, where death was inevitable because emergency stairways were severed.

An unavoidable problem of skyscraper design is that the

higher a structure, the more elevators are needed, thus reducing rentable floor space. And in the case of standard steel- or concrete-frame construction, the number of extra inner columns needed to strengthen super-tall towers adds to the problem. In order to increase the World Trade Center's cost-effectiveness by keeping each story of the towers as free as possible from internal barriers—a necessity in commercial real estate by the 1960s, when the open-office concept began to take hold—Yamasaki decided on a structural system (devised by the Seattle-based engineer John Skilling) whereby the buildings' external walls, made of colossal, hollow steel tubes, became the principal load-bearing support, allowing for unusually open interiors.

Had Yamasaki conformed to conventional internal steel-frame techniques, experts concur, the buildings would have snapped upon the planes' collision and collapsed much sooner and farther afield than they did, with a significantly higher death toll. Indeed, as James Glanz and Eric Lipton write in their authoritative *City in the Sky: The Rise and Fall of the World Trade Center* (2003), an aviation impact study conducted in 1964 to gauge how the structures would withstand being crashed into by a Boeing 707 had concluded:

> The Skilling firm's "total concept" would not just give the twin towers a huge margin of reserve strength to help them survive the initial impact; the peculiarities of their design would let them act almost like a living be-

ing to resist overall failure and collapse even when grievously damaged by the plane.

In the end, what destroyed the buildings was the conflagration fed by tens of thousands of gallons of jet fuel, as was fiendishly projected by the plot's mastermind, Osama bin Laden, who had a degree in civil engineering.

Although the World Trade Center fully conformed to fire-safety standards at the time of its completion, there were misgivings during the planning phase about whether the super-wide Vierendeel trusses that enabled the open-floor spaces, a new concept at the time, were sufficiently fireproofed to withstand such an eventuality. It was the weakening of those elegantly elongated supports, which sagged as fire rapidly spread across the uncompartmentalized interiors, that caused the Twin Towers' concrete floors to collapse onto one another, after which the outer perimeter gave way. By that time Yamasaki had been dead for nearly fifteen years and was spared a loss that surely would have been infinitely more painful to him than even his unjustly maligned Pruitt-Igoe.

13

LINA BO BARDI

THE ONE HUNDREDTH birthday of an overlooked creative innovator sometimes coincides with the revival of a reputation
that is already well already underway. That was the case
with the overdue posthumous lionization of the Italian-
Brazilian architect Lina Bo Bardi, who was born in Rome in
1914 and died in 1992 in her adopted South American homeland at the age of seventy-seven. Bo Bardi's two most important realized schemes are in São Paulo—the Museum of Art
(1957–1969) and the SESC Pompeia, a leisure and cultural
center (1977–1986). They are of such exceptional quality
that one can readily understand why their designer was at
last accorded a high place in the male-dominated canon,
though not why these works did not propel her immediately
to the front rank of the profession during her lifetime. These
incontestable masterpieces, omitted from general histories of
Modern architecture for decades, would not have been so
long overlooked were they made by a man.

Intriguingly contradictory but intelligently resolved, Bo

Bardi's designs are structurally audacious yet uncommonly comfortable, unapologetically untidy yet conceptually rigorous, and confidently dynamic yet suggestively hybrid. Although her architecture stands squarely in the Modernist tradition, she rejected the aggressively machinelike aesthetic favored by many of her male contemporaries, preferring a more relaxed and nuanced vernacular approach. However, as her ingenious recycling of a disused factory into the Pompeia complex demonstrates, she could also embrace industrialism's authentic manifestations and make them invitingly human. This is high-tech that responds to everyday needs and uses modern technical advances to serve them, rather than the more typical postindustrial tendency to put structural showmanship ahead of all other concerns.

Some commentators have interpreted Bo Bardi's belated popularity as a reaction against the all-pervasive commercialism, rampant celebrity-mongering, and dispiriting lack of social awareness in postmillennial architecture. Small wonder that the architect Kazuyo Sejima of the Japanese firm SANAA, the director of the 2010 Venice Architecture Biennale, organized a concise Bo Bardi retrospective as the centerpiece of that prestigious international exhibition. Many viewers felt that Bo Bardi's decades-old designs easily outclassed the sprawling show's surfeit of eye-catching but shallow contemporary offerings.

Typical of the esteem Bo Bardi now commands is her prominent inclusion in Jean-Louis Cohen's authoritative but revisionist survey *The Future of Architecture Since 1889*

(2012), which features a full-page color illustration of Pompeia. She also figures conspicuously in the introduction to Kathleen James-Chakraborty's *Architecture Since 1400* (2014), which includes two photos of the architect's residence, the Glass House of 1950–1951 in São Paulo. And in *Why We Build: Power and Desire in Architecture* (2013), the British architecture critic Rowan Moore devotes an entire chapter to Bo Bardi, whom he calls "the most underrated architect of the twentieth century." But the most important factor in this newfound recognition has been *Lina Bo Bardi* (2013), the first full-length life-and-works, by Zeuler R. M. de A. Lima, an architect and professor at Washington University in St. Louis. Lima's detailed but well-paced monograph is a feat of primary-source scholarship and thoughtful analysis in which he does a masterful job of candidly assessing his brilliant, somewhat erratic, and not always truthful subject. This important contribution to the literature will long remain the essential Bo Bardi publication.

Complementing it is Cathrine Veikos's *Lina Bo Bardi: The Theory of Architectural Practice* (2014), the first English translation of the architect's *Propaedeutic Contribution to the Teaching of Architecture Theory* (1957), the fullest exposition of her design philosophy. (The title's obscure first word means a preliminary introduction to further study.) Bo Bardi's heavily illustrated and footnoted text—similar in format to Robert Venturi's later but far more famous *Complexity and Contradiction in Architecture* (1966)—reveals her deep grounding in the Classical tradition, a product of her interwar

Roman architectural education. Also like Venturi, she extracts applicable contemporary lessons from historical prototypes rather than mining them for directly replicable motifs. Her analogies are most forcefully advanced through provocative juxtapositions of images. She finds Ludwig Mies van der Rohe's Seagram Building in New York a modern counterpart of the Platonically perfect proportions Raphael devised for his Church of Sant'Eligio degli Orefici in Rome. And in pairing a high-rise fantasy project by the Renaissance architect Filarete with a photo of Cass Gilbert's Woolworth Building in New York, she wonders, "Was [Filarete] anticipating the skyscraper?," then answers her own question by asserting that "in the history of men of genius can be found the germs of all anticipations."

Stones Against Diamonds, a collection of Bo Bardi's writings, was issued by London's Architectural Association in 2012. In addition to twenty-two articles she wrote in Italy and Brazil, it includes the transcript of her last lecture, in which she acknowledges her considerable debt to the British scholar Geoffrey Scott's seminal book *The Architecture of Humanism: A Study in the History of Taste* (1914). Her invocation of this now somewhat unfashionable text is typical of her contrarian but principled nature.

Throughout her writings, Bo Bardi's sardonic wit and argumentative personality repeatedly surface, imparting a worldly-wise tone that makes *Stones Against Diamonds* anything but a dry educational treatise. In a profession where personal appearance and public presentation matter a great deal, Bo Bardi (as her photographs show) might be seen as the Anna Magnani of architecture—an earthy, passionate, careworn, chain-smoking, impulsively outspoken character fed up with the hypocrisy of polite society. One perceptive friend, the publisher and playwright Valentino Bompiani, tellingly dubbed her *la dea stanca* (the tired goddess). A defiant outsider sensibility emerges from the architect's prickly but heartfelt pronouncements on the place of architecture in modern society, suffused with a certain resignation quite unlike the utopian optimism of the first-generation Modernists. Yet even Bo Bardi at her most cynical could not have imagined the postmillennial worldwide epidemic of freakishly exhibitionistic construction, marketed as advanced artistic vision but often devoid of the most basic concern for communal life and environmental impact.

Also clear is her belief that design pedagogy ought to discourage what she called "the complex of the individualistic architect"—not as a means of stifling personal creativity but "to create a collective consciousness of architecture in schools, the opposite of an arrogant individualism." This might well be taken as an instinctively feminist stance, given women's known ability to work more cooperatively in professional groups than their male counterparts.

On the other hand, she stubbornly refused to recant her Communist affiliations, even after the horrors of the Gulag had been revealed, and like many pioneering women in her profession she believed more in personal advancement than in solidarity in sisterhood. Thus, in a 1989 lecture, she could deliver the pugnacious and off-putting pronouncement that "I am Stalinist and anti-feminist." In fact, her vision of architecture and her actual work were anything but Stalinist. Why Bo Bardi had been denied her rightful prominence for so long is not difficult to explain. Ingrained prejudice against women in the building art prevailed throughout most of the twentieth century and still has not been fully eradicated. Even the best-remembered female Modernist architects who came of professional age during the decade after World War I and just before Bo Bardi—Margarete Schütte-Lihotzky, Lilly Reich, and Charlotte Perriand—were customarily assigned interior-design tasks by architectural offices headed and largely staffed by men.

This enforced male/female division of labor remained the norm until the end of World War II, when women finally became principals in architectural firms, though they were not always acknowledged as such. (Natalie de Blois, a former Skidmore, Owings & Merrill partner who died in 2013 at ninety-two, was responsible for designs sometimes attributed to the firm's senior designer, Gordon Bunshaft, such as her jewel-like Pepsi-Cola Building of 1958–1960 in New York City). The few postwar women architects who did receive rightful recognition worked in partnership with their husbands, including the British team of Alison and Peter Smithson and the American couple Denise Scott Brown and Robert Venturi.

Achillina di Enrico Bo was born four months after the outbreak of World War I to a family who lived in a Roman working-class neighborhood near the Vatican. From an early age Lina, as she was known, harbored extraordinary, not to say grandiose, ambitions. "I never wanted to be young," she later recalled. "What I really wanted was to have a history. At the age of twenty-five, I wanted to write my memoirs, but I didn't have the material." Like many other women who went on to achieve success in male-dominated professions, she identified with her father, a small-time building contractor with artistic yearnings. (An amateur painter, he befriended Giorgio de Chirico, who did a portrait of the young Lina.) She displayed unusual skill at drawing, and in 1930 entered the Liceo Artistico di Roma. Upon receiving her degree four years later, she enrolled at the Rome School of Architecture, where two professors had a decisive impact on her architectural thinking.

The historian and urban planner Gustavo Giovannoni was a strong advocate of *ambientismo* (contextualism)—designing buildings to fit in with their immediate surroundings in scale and material—as well as a staunch preservationist. Her other early mentor, Marcello Piacentini, the president of the National Fascist Union of Architects, undertook huge Stripped Classical commissions for the Mussolini regime that included a new campus for the University of Rome and the city's EUR district (planned for the subsequently aborted 1942 World's Fair). Especially strong was Piacentini's emphasis on being an *architetto totale*—a complete architect, equally conversant with new construction, restoration of old buildings, and city planning (a range Bo Bardi extended even further to include the design of interiors, furniture, and jewelry).

She received her degree in 1939 and then moved to Milan, where the progressive design scene was much more drawn to the rationalist ideas of the Bauhaus and Le Corbusier than to Mussolini Modernism. Two months after her arrival, Italy entered World War II, a time "when nothing was built, only destroyed," as she put it. Bo supported herself during the conflict with graphic design and illustration jobs, especially for *Lo Stile*, a design magazine spun off by the architect and industrial designer Gio Ponti from his influential journal *Domus*. In 1946 she married Pietro Maria Bardi, a journalist and art dealer fourteen years her senior, who had cultivated strong ties to Mussolini. As Zeuler Lima points out, there is no evidence to support her claim that she had worked with the anti-Fascist resistance, and although she aligned herself with the Communist Party after 1943, her close association with Ponti—whose early support for Mussolini has been rationalized by apologists as more patriotic than ideological—impelled the newly married couple to quit Italy when the Communists gained ascendance in the first postwar elections.

Pietro Bardi already had connections in Brazil, where he traveled in 1934 to sell art to prosperous Italian expatriates. With his dismal postwar prospects in Italy, friends in Rome's Brazilian embassy set up a series of commercial exhibitions for him in Rio de Janeiro. There he attracted the attention of the culturally ambitious press magnate Assis Chateaubriand (known as Chatô), who wanted to foster a Brazilian arts scene commensurate with the country's increasing international identity as a major center of modern architecture, an emergence signaled by "Brazil Builds: Architecture New and Old, 1652–1942," a popular exhibition held at New York's Museum of Modern Art in 1943.

Bo Bardi, who had yet to build anything, received a chilly reception from the leading figures of the country's architectural avant-garde. Lúcio Costa told her, "You're so dull, so many drawings," while his colleague Oscar Niemeyer averred that "Europeans make things seem too complicated." Yet she contradicted both those competitive putdowns with her first completed work, the Casa de Vidro (Glass House), the sublimely simple yet uncommonly elegant residence she created for herself and her husband in São Paulo. Not the least interesting aspect of this rectangular Minimalist structure with transparent peripheral walls is its close relation to two more renowned contemporaneous domestic designs: Mies van der Rohe's Farnsworth house of 1945–1951 in Plano, Illinois, and Philip Johnson's Glass House of 1949–1950 in New Canaan, Connecticut. Yet the considerable differences among this trio of glass houses tell us a great deal about why Bo Bardi has gained such an ardent postmillennial following.

The much-vaunted intention of Mies's and Johnson's inhabitable glass vitrines was to make interiors at one with nature. Johnson referred to the sylvan views from his Glass

House as "the world's most expensive wallpaper," but as often happened with this self-critical nihilist, his wisecrack contained a kernel of harsh truth. Both his and Mies's shoebox-shaped structures present themselves as industrially made objects, but they were in fact exquisitely custom-crafted villas for the rich. The Casa de Vidro is much like the Mies and Johnson houses (all are more or less flat-topped, though the roof of the Brazilian version inclines slightly downward from a center ridge for rain run-off). However, Bo Bardi's house differs from the others in being sited on a steep hillside, to say nothing of being considerably more economical than its expensively detailed American analogs. And the underlying concrete slab of the São Paulo residence is elevated on a series of tall, thin aluminum poles, with the structure fully touching the earth only at the uppermost, rear portion of the slope.

This was the first building to be erected in a newly developed residential neighborhood, and completion photos depict a rather barren setting reminiscent of the Hollywood Hills. Indeed, Bo Bardi's lightweight, open-to-the-outdoors design, framed in thin members of white-painted metal, brings to mind the experimental Case Study Houses of the late 1940s and early 1950s in Southern California. Yet just a few years after its construction, the Casa de Vidro was engulfed in a lush tangle of greenery, and it now feels like a subtropical tree house.

Bo Bardi's populist outlook was antithetical to the grandiose vision realized in the Brazilian heartland by Costa and

Niemeyer—the former's urban plan and the latter's principal structures for Brasília, the start-from-scratch capital city decreed by President Juscelino Kubitschek de Oliveira in 1956 and essentially completed within his five-year term of office. Whereas Bo Bardi was immediately taken by her new country's multicultural folkloric traditions and multiracial vernacular culture, her best-known Brazilian coprofessionals were much more concerned with how to recast an essentially European Baroque monumentality in High Modernist terms.

Furthermore, the creators of Brasília paid scant attention to the housing and transportation needs of the sizable labor force needed to serve the capital city's bureaucracy. These omissions resulted in a host of messy ad hoc stopgaps by local residents to correct Costa and Niemeyer's enormous functional lapses. Bo Bardi was one of the few contemporary critics of these architectural stars, and certainly the most insightful. In 1958, just as construction of Brasília was getting underway, she wrote "architecture or Architecture"—a short, urgent warning about the disturbing direction Niemeyer's schemes were taking, away from his smaller early works (today his most admired designs) and toward the megalomaniacal scale typified by the new city's flying saucer–like parliament building:

> More than the buildings of Brasília—which, according to Niemeyer himself, are irreproachable in their conception and purity—we like the church in Pampulha and the house in Vassouras, which have attracted

international attention on account of their simplicity, their human proportions, the modest and poetic expression of a life that rejects that very despondency, that struggle between social needs and architecture— the struggle that Niemeyer claims to have overcome by setting out, as the aim of his architecture, a formal position that denies all human values....

In contrast, Bo Bardi found ways to combine the large dimensions appropriate to the public sphere with an intimate scale that gives the users of her buildings a sense of both individual presence and group connection that Niemeyer was generally unable to achieve in his works from Brasília onward, when colossal geometric formalism became his overriding principle. An unlikely, but in her hands fully integrated balance between the monumental and the personal was achieved with striking imagination in the Museum of Art of São Paulo (MASP), an institution founded in 1947 by Chatô, directed by Pietro Bardi, and during its first decade housed in temporary display spaces designed by his wife within existing structures.

Among the Bardis' beliefs was that pictures ought not to be hung on a wall like bourgeois decorative elements but instead displayed on freestanding easels that give a closer idea of their means of production. Thanks to Chatô's strong-arm acquisition tactics—the unscrupulous publisher, who has been called the Brazilian Citizen Kane, blackmailed prominent figures with threats of newspaper exposés in re-

turn for "donations" of cash and art to his new museum—
Pietro Bardi was able to quickly assemble what at that time
was the most important public art collection in South America with works, for example, by Manet, Cézanne, and Van Gogh.

MASP offered a revolutionary rethinking of the art museum and was the embodiment of the Bardis' belief in architecture as a prime agent for social cohesion rather than aesthetic self-indulgence or a benefactor's status. Their innovative ideas about the museum as an educational institution responsive to the public and not just a repository of precious objects were reflected in Bo Bardi's equally inventive design solutions for welcoming entry areas, flexible exhibition spaces, and a casual atmosphere that emphasized art as a pleasure for everyone, not just an informed elite. To be sure, Edward Durell Stone and Philip L. Goodwin's Museum of Modern Art of 1936–1939 in New York had already made a notable departure from the formality and monumentality of traditional Beaux Arts gallery design and toward a relaxed domestic scale that reminded twentieth-century New Yorkers more of their apartments than of princely palaces. But MASP took such democratic notions even further, though its architectonic presence is anything but recessive.

In an unexecuted 1952 scheme for a museum at the seashore (illustrated on the cover of *Habitat*, the influential art-and-design magazine the Bardis founded), Bo Bardi devised an elongated shoebox form that would have been hoisted one story above the ground by four inverted, squared-off

U-shaped trusses of red-painted steel clamped across the gallery enclosure's narrower dimension. In a further refinement of that unusual format, MASP is an even bolder feat of engineering, with just two gigantic red-painted steel trusses that span and support the two-story glass-walled gallery container longitudinally rather than laterally (see Illustration 13a). The configuration provides two urbanistic benefits: it elevates the museum above the busy vehicular traffic streets that flank it to the north and south, and the underside of the building creates a roof for the open-sided gathering place at ground level. This large outdoor space, protected from sudden tropical downpours, is used for public events of all sorts, and remains one of São Paulo's most memorable modern civic venues.

The open-plan exhibition areas suspended above this plaza were conceived to be optimally adaptable for various kinds of art, with interchangeable partitions and freestanding display elements. Curators were thereby encouraged to rethink visitors' progression through exhibitions, which in conventional institutions with fixed walls allows little or no deviation from a strictly imposed route. The wide-ranging possibilities here give an entirely different character to the art-viewing experience, and the MASP approach is now standard practice at contemporary art institutions, especially because the unpredictable display requirements for today's large installation pieces, video art, and other nontraditional mediums—so different from even the most advanced painting and sculpture of the Bardis' heyday—have made easily transformable interiors mandatory.

Although the ground-level public space of MASP functions wonderfully as a social condenser, it is surpassed in that respect by Bo Bardi's final major work, the SESC Pompeia leisure center. Many early Modernists, most conspicuously Le Corbusier and Walter Gropius, admired the no-nonsense functionalist aesthetic of late-nineteenth- and early-twentieth-century industrial structures. In homage, they designed schools, cultural institutions, and residences that closely resembled utilitarian construction (signified by Le Corbusier's famous definition of the house as "a machine for living in"). By the 1970s this practice had become so accepted that forward-thinking architects and their patrons decided to convert actual factories and warehouses into museums, theaters, and other arts facilities rather than trying to replicate the industrial look from scratch.

In 1971, Brazil's Serviço Social de Comércio (SESC, the public outreach arm of the country's trade organizations, established to quell unrest among laborers) acquired an obsolete 1938 steel-barrel factory in a working-class São Paulo quarter for a community center (see Illustration 13b). SESC originally planned to tear down the prefabricated, reinforced-concrete structure to make way for a new building. But the recent and much-publicized success of San Francisco's Ghirardelli Square of 1962–1965—an abandoned chocolate factory that the architect William Wurster and the landscape architect Lawrence Halprin reconceived as a retail-and-restaurant complex and became a major tourist attraction—prompted the decision to retain the existing São Paulo structure.

Because it had already been temporarily retrofitted and clearly worked well as a neighborhood gathering place, Bo Bardi advised that this fine example of industrial architecture (based on the pioneering structural concepts of the French engineer François Hennebique) merely be tidied up and preserved. Into that imposing shell—dominated by soaring concrete volumes that bring to mind the monumental Brutalism of Louis Kahn—she inserted her comprehensive series of domestically scaled innovations, each fulfilling a specific function.

These included everything from her colorful and tactile interior and furniture designs to her programming for exhibitions and performances. In her egalitarian view of art, both high art and popular culture were presented without hierarchical distinctions in the center's flexible display galleries. A wide range of educational and vocational activities are still offered in classrooms and a library, but there is also a full array of sports facilities (including a swimming pool), areas where people can play games, meet friends, and socialize in a variety of ways, as well as a theater and a community lunch restaurant that at night becomes a beer garden. As Zeuler Lima writes:

> SESC Pompeia offered a concrete example of one of Bo Bardi's main pursuits: to show that "culture is a fact of everyday reality," not a special event or even the domain of the educated elite.... [She] imagined it, as many in the center's staff still do, as an antidote to con-

sumer society and a space for human imagination and shared participation.

With the Pompeia commission, Bo Bardi cut out the middleman, as it were, by adapting an old factory while preserving its gritty character. This remarkable advance in architectural thinking anticipated the widespread vogue for recycling former industrial facilities into exhibition galleries, epitomized by Richard Gluckman's transformation of a warehouse into the Dia Center for the Arts in New York (1987) and Jacques Herzog and Pierre de Meuron's conversion of London's Bankside Power Station into the Tate Modern (1995–2000). Furthermore, Bo Bardi's celebration of her design's workaday origins and its overwhelmingly warm reception make it a direct antecedent of New York City's postmillennial public-works wonder, the High Line (2003–2014), which likewise turned derelict infrastructure into an instantly beloved community treasure.

On the cover of Zeuler Lima's splendid study is an image that perfectly sums up what might be called the Bo Bardi Touch. This black-and-white photographic detail shows an irregular opening cut into a concrete wall of the architect's Teatro Gregório de Matos of 1986–1987 in the Brazilian city of Salvador (one of nine theaters she designed). Instead of the geometric precision associated with the Bauhaus, this amoeboid aperture—which she called a *fustella* (perforation punch, in Italian)—brings to mind a rougher version of the free-form outlines of Alvar Aalto's biomorphic Savoy Vase

(1936). Executed with the nonchalant facture typical of Bo Bardi, this unruly form reminds us that she much preferred to focus on how architecture feels rather than the way it looks. Robert Venturi famously wrote, "I am for messy vitality over obvious unity," and in that same spirit the designs of Lina Bo Bardi exert a vivifying and unifying effect that architecture can impart only when the need for a better social life is genuinely important to the architect's imagination.

14

FREI OTTO

FEW ARTISTS CAN be said to have fundamentally reshaped the basic nature of their medium, as did James Joyce by supplanting the linear narrative of the conventional novel with a swirling stream of consciousness, or Wassily Kandinsky by expanding painting from the depiction of realistic scenes to an abstract evocation of inward emotions, or Alexander Calder by transforming sculpture from a static earthbound mass into a kinetic object floating through space. Thus although twentieth-century architecture was replete with countless innovations in structure and materials, none of its practitioners rethought the very basics of construction and presented an alternative to millennia of received design concepts more successfully than the German architect and engineer Frei Otto.

During his heyday in the 1960s and 1970s, Otto had an enormous influence on younger architects who followed his example and thought beyond the repetitive shoebox forms that dominated postwar commercial design. Otto's great contribution was the modern tensile tent, its exterior made from synthetic materials reinforced with metal mesh, unlike its cloth antecedents. Perfected in the 1950s and brought to worldwide attention during the next two decades, Otto's ideas have since become so pervasive that the advances he pioneered are now perceived as a generic development rather than attributable to a single person, which has contributed to amnesia about his central place in twentieth-century architectural history.

Otto's hallmark inventions—lightweight tensile and membrane canopies that can shelter large areas both economically and beautifully—were no pie-in-the-sky visionary proposals like those of so many of his avant-garde contemporaries. Instead, these eminently practical schemes offered imaginative solutions to real problems, but also pointed the way to freer attitudes that would flourish, though with very mixed results, toward the end of the millennium. In his 1996 essay "Architektur Natur," Otto provocatively asserted that all architects can be assigned to one of three categories: "*Arrangeur, Diebe und Erfinder*" (arrangers, thieves, and inventors). By arrangers he clearly meant those who merely manipulate known forms into other configurations, while of course the thieves even more expeditiously steal the ideas of others. And given the countless uncredited knockoffs of his designs he surely must have considered the second group as the most numerous.

Yet to the end of his life Otto remained remarkably modest about his own achievements, and when he was informed that he was about to be given the Pritzker Architecture Prize at the age of eighty-nine, he averred that "I have never done anything to gain this prize." Others demurred, and if he would not explicitly describe himself as an inventor, his most knowledgeable and accomplished colleagues certainly would. He was known to be exceptionally generous in stressing the broadly collaborative nature of the architectural process in a profession where many design principals arrogate a disproportionate amount of credit for themselves. The brilliant Irish structural engineer Peter Rice (1935–1992)—who worked closely with Otto but is now perhaps best remembered for his louvered ceiling light-filtering system at Renzo Piano's Menil Collection of 1982–1986 in Houston—placed Otto firmly among the *Erfinder* when in his book *An Engineer Imagines* (1994) he likened him to the British Victorian mechanical and civil engineer Isambard Kingdom Brunel, the innovative builder of bridges, tunnels, railways, and ships at the apogee of the Industrial Revolution:

> Think of the way Brunel worked and the kind of things he did, the broad range of activities he covered. He must have worked similarly to Frei. Frei uses intuition backed up by physics rather than mathematics. He has a strong physical sense. . . . We should call him an inventor.

Unlike Brunel, however, Otto's commissions were not always prompted by social movements of the highest import, which may have something to do with why his reputation is not stronger today. For example, in 1977 he devised a system of upwardly flaring, umbrellalike stage canopies of white fabric for the British rock band Pink Floyd's *In the Flesh* international concert tour. Easily dismantled and moved from one performance venue to the next, Otto's sheltering design gave the impression of a field of Art Nouveau flowers and represented a degree of visual artistic seriousness rarely equaled in the world of rock and roll, but still, it was only rock and roll.

By the time Otto died, in 2017, less than three months shy of his ninetieth birthday, he had become a virtually forgotten figure among the general public, and even architectural devotees could be forgiven for thinking that he had expired years earlier. This was largely owed to his having executed very few projects during his last decades, and his path-breaking schemes had long been eclipsed by far more dramatic structures made possible by computer-aided design, which was in its infancy during his creative prime.

Otto's most conspicuous late-career effort was his collaboration with the much-younger Shigeru Ban (a major exponent of variations on the German's lightweight structures, though often made of more low-tech materials) for the Japanese pavilion of 1997–1999 at Expo 2000 in Hannover, Germany. This approximately oblong, clear-span exhibition hall was overarched by an undulating latticed roof composed of reinforced cardboard tubes (a Ban signature). It swelled upward in three equal segments and evoked the buoyant biomorphic spirit of Otto's work of a half-century before, while reconfirming his strong effect on successive generations of followers.

Frei Paul Otto was born in 1925 near Chemnitz in Saxony but grew up in Berlin. His uncommon first name—which means "free" in German and was his mother's personal motto—reflected the liberal values of his idealistic parents, members of the Deutscher Werkbund (German Work Federation), a social reform group that promoted, among other causes, decent modern housing for all, educating the public in principles of good design, and closer collaboration between craftsmen and industry. Otto's father and grandfather were both sculptors engaged primarily in carving gravestones, and it was expected that young Frei would follow them in the family business. A teacher at his vocational school introduced the teenaged Otto to sail gliding—then a popular sport in the flat, lake-studded terrain around Berlin—which shaped his fascination for lightweight structures. He also showed an unusual aptitude for making models, and it was decided that he was talented enough to merit training as a master builder.

He commenced his architectural studies at the Technische Hochschule Berlin in 1943, but soon afterward he was conscripted into the Luftwaffe because of his expertise in amateur aviation, a fortunate assignment at a time when German ground forces were being decimated on the Eastern Front. Captured by the Allies, he was incarcerated for two years in France near Chartres, during which he served as a prison-camp architect, a position that forced him to address the most basic function of architecture—cover from the elements—

which under wartime circumstances had to be provided quickly, economically, and improvisationally, requirements that would establish Otto's principal priorities and define them thereafter. He later explained that the daily sight of the spires of Chartres Cathedral inspired him to devise the tented structures that offered the most immediate solution to the need for shelter in the camp.

After his release, he resumed his education at his old school (which had been renamed the Technische Universität Berlin) and confronted the central challenge of his emergent generation of German architects: how to create large-scale buildings that avoided any taint of Nazi design, which was typified by a ponderous, ornamentally stripped Classicism rendered in heavy materials, particularly stone. Otto's familiarity with aeronautical engineering led him to devise a diametric alternative to that forbidden monumentality. He began to experiment with ultralightweight forms that derived from thin-membrane airplane parts made from reinforced fabric, the antithesis of the crushing mass favored by Hitler and his chief architectural henchman, Albert Speer.

In 1950 Otto won a travel stipend that allowed him to visit the United States for six months, where with remarkable self-confidence for a twenty-five-year-old he gained introductions to several of the loftiest pioneers of modern architecture, then in the final phases of their careers, including Frank Lloyd Wright, Erich Mendelsohn, Richard Neutra, and Ludwig Mies van der Rohe. In due course he became particularly close to Mies, to the extent that when the aged master was building his Neue Nationalgalerie of 1965–1968 in Berlin, he turned to Otto for advice on the museum's unusually large free-span roof, whereupon the younger architecture suggested an elegant correction to calculations that allowed for fewer and less-conspicuous interior supports. This successful recommendation reflected Otto's equal authority as both an engineer and an architect, a rare combination in that many master builders must collaborate with structural consultants to determine if what they have designed will actually stand up, as did Louis Kahn with his indispensible engineering adviser, August Komendant.

One of Otto's earliest public successes was the gossamer-light dance pavilion he designed in 1957 for the Federal Garden Exhibition in Cologne, a five-peaked, mast-supported, white-fabric canopy in the highly stylized shape of an exotic bloom, which nicely evoked the botanical theme of the event. This scheme was in effect a sketch for his much larger essays in this same mode over the years to come, for although not all architectural ideas first essayed in small dimensions can be successfully enlarged, Otto's could, almost without exception. Furthermore, in contrast to many of his contemporaries, he rejected the Neoprimitive Brutalist aesthetic favored by Le Corbusier after World War II, as well as the widespread New Brutalism that followed it. Otto's organic approach was much more like that of Antoni Gaudí, whose extensive research into naturally occurring structures was likewise the basis for startlingly new architectural forms that appear deceptively delicate yet possess the power of industrial elements. Otto took his cues from phenomena such as the way soap film spans a gap with maximum efficiency or the extraordinary tensile strength displayed by fragile-looking but in fact quite resilient spiderwebs.

In order to advance his theories and apply them to a wider variety of uses, in 1964 Otto founded his think tank-cum-studio, the Institut für leichte Flächentragwerke (Institute for Lightweight Structures), at the University of Stuttgart. It, and his professional office, Atelier Frei Otto, located in the small town of Warmbronn west of Stuttgart—became the central vehicles for developing his ideas and the training grounds for several generations of followers who disseminated his concepts internationally. Among the latter is Otto's frequent collaborator Mahmoud Bodo Rasch, who developed a thriving practice in the Middle East, where his tented coverings and large retractable umbrellas have been widely used for shading outdoor public spaces, especially at religious pilgrimage sites.

Otto felt a special kinship with his three-decade-older American counterpart R. Buckminster Fuller, a fellow enthusiast of lightweight structures and the father of the geodesic dome, his greatest structural innovation. The self-aggrandizing fabulist Fuller and the self-effacing moralist Otto could not have been more different personally, but their ingenious designs shared similar limitations. Though both were widely promoted as panaceas for a host of architectural tasks, Fuller's domes and Otto's tents were essentially roofing systems. Despite those structures' ability to economically shelter an interior, it was much trickier to subdivide their internal volumes for specific functional purposes, a drawback that inhibited their wider acceptance.

The curvature of a geodesic structure renders space around its inner periphery almost useless for at least several feet as it meets the ground, while the center of a dome of substantial size is often higher than required except for purely structural reasons. Similarly, a large tensile tent must be suspended from vertical supports that can disrupt an internal expanse, and the problem of how the roof turns into a wall was often inadequately resolved.

During the 1960s, after a decade of designing increasingly large, more complex tents for trade shows and outdoor stages in several German and Swiss cities, Otto received two high-profile, career-defining commissions. Perhaps aware that no German architect of the postwar period had yet achieved the international renown achieved by such celebrated figures as Mies, Mendelsohn, and Walter Gropius, the West German government asked him to design both its display at Expo 67, the Montreal world's fair (see Illustration 14a), and a vast multistructure complex for the 1972 Olympics in Munich. Together, Otto's eye-catching experiments made his international reputation, as well as that of his engineering associate Jörg Schlaich. What appears even more impressive in hindsight is that until the early 1970s, Otto created his structures without the benefit of today's sophisticated software, and instead worked out the complicated dynamics of each effort with costly, labor-intensive study models.

His German Pavilion at the Montreal exposition caused a sensation, not least because its swooping profile had a decidedly Romantic air to it, quite different from the undisputed architectural hit of the fair, Habitat 67, by the Israeli-born Canadian Moshe Safdie. This 146-unit housing complex, which resembles a pileup of Lego blocks, was rightly praised for its refreshing combination of sculptural power (the result of the architect's skillful composition of 348 identical prefabricated concrete modules), his commitment to humane scale, and his welcome departure from the predominance of the monolithic high-rise postwar apartment block as defined by Le Corbusier's Unité d'Habitation. In contrast to this pragmatic paradigm of multiunit housing, Otto's ethereal, high-masted, peak-roofed German Pavilion was the stuff of fairy-tale visions. One can thus understand his disclaimer, delivered when he was honored with an exhibition in Munich on the occasion of his eightieth birthday, that "*Ich habe wenig gebaut. Ich habe viele Luftschlösser ersonnen.*" (I have built little. I have dreamed up many castles in the air.)

That same feeling permeated his Olympic scheme five years later. I was in Munich during the 1972 games and still recall the thrilling effect of dappled sunlight that filtered through the translucent fabric overhead as one walked through the curving sequence of exhibition and refreshment tents that snaked around the Olympic Stadium. (For this commission, Schlaich invented a new set of computer analysis tools to execute Otto's design, a historic first in the profession.) Otto's next major commission—which along with Montreal and

Munich comprise his three most significant projects—was the Manheim Multihalle of 1970–1975, an exhibition center most notable for its sinuous wood-lath latticed roof. The American structural engineer Guy Nordenson, peerless in his ability to clearly explain the work of his coprofessionals to a lay audience, described Otto's great trio in almost poetic terms in this excerpt from his obituary of the German master for *Artforum*:

> Despite their rational origin in the minimal surfaces of mathematics (famously explored through soap-film models) the Montreal, Munich, and Mannheim roofs are exquisite forms that hover somewhere between landscape and cloud, their airy, immaterial structures belying their size....
>
> The composition of these structures—the tilt of the masts, the varied sizes and extent of the webs of cable or wood lath—have the inevitable quality of the most carefully contrived landscapes. While the authorship of each of the three projects is spread between [*sic*] the many collaborators, the language is clearly one invented by Otto.

Where we should correctly place Otto in the history of modern architecture remains an open question. The work of Frank Gehry has shown how digital programming tools that were unavailable to Otto—who was nonetheless the very first to use computer-generated data to plan his Munich stadium scheme, three decades before Gehry's epochal Guggenheim Museum Bilbao—could advance an audacious recasting of architecture from rectilinear convention to free-form exuberance.

Many earlier precursors to these developments have been suggested, from the German Expressionist Hermann Finsterlin to the Danish modernist Jørn Utzon, for whose Sydney Opera House of 1957–1973 Otto served as a structural consultant after the building's completion had ground to a halt until the means to execute this unconventional design were finally worked out.

Yet Otto—whose extremely early use of aeronautic prototypes was paralleled decades later by Gehry's brilliant adaptation of CATIA software (devised for the design of irregularly shaped airplane components) to architectural applications—now seems the most convincing forerunner of today's boundless biomorphism. However directly these connections are reckoned, there can be no doubt that Otto helped lift his homeland out of the darkest period in its political and cultural history through his marvelously wrought designs, which conveyed not only stunning technical finesse but, more importantly, a spiritual lightness of being.

On March 9, 2015—two months after being informed confidentially that he'd been named the fortieth recipient of the Pritzker Architecture Prize—Otto died, and just under the wire, as the award's rather nebulous and occasionally malleable bylaws stipulate that it cannot be given posthumously. By again reaching into what might be termed the back catalog of twentieth-century architecture, the jury's decision to honor Otto recalled the joint bestowal of the 1988 prize on Oscar Niemeyer and Gordon Bunshaft, who were then eighty and seventy-nine respectively. Though long past their creative prime, they personified a meridian moment of High Modernism, and the same might be inferred about the selection of Otto at a time of irresolute architectural values.

In his late-life mediation "Architektur Natur," Otto had harked back to one of the most familiar (if also most frequently misunderstood) dictums of Modernism, *"weniger ist mehr"* (less is more), which is now most closely associated with Mies (who apparently first invoked it only as late as 1947) but was used in various similar forms by several artists and writers during the eighteenth and nineteenth centuries. Yet Otto obviously was intrigued by this formulation in quite another way from the stylistic reductivism it represented to the Minimalist Mies:

> "Less is more," this phrase fascinates me: fewer houses, less material, less concrete, less energy but for use with that which is available for humanistic uses. . . . To build in concert with nature and to make much out of little. Better to build nothing at all than to build too much! Those were old and new goals.

If Otto were some medieval master intent on putting his indelible mark on *Baukunst*—the building art—one can fully imagine him making a personal motto from four German words in that declaration of principles: *"Aus wenig viel machen*" (To make much out of little). This is a rare sentiment to be embraced by an architect, since most of them are driven to make even more out of much, and thus Otto's selfless embrace of the exact opposite remains all the more extraordinary and moving.

15

FRANK GEHRY

STRANGE AS IT would have seemed when he burst upon the avant-garde architectural scene four decades ago, Frank Gehry, the volcanic improviser of free-form structures unlike anything seen since the irrational fantasies of German Expressionists in the early twentieth century, eventually attained the stature of those visionaries' antithetical contemporary Ludwig Mies van der Rohe, the hyperrational codifier of modern architectural reason. Though Gehry's design precepts have been nowhere nearly as regularized as Mies's, Gehry Technologies—the computer-programming offshoot of his Los Angeles–based office, Gehry Partners—pioneered and later disseminated the digital means for architects to realize irregular structural shapes (colloquially known as Blobitecture) of a kind once attainable only through laborious craftsmanship, like those of Antoni Gaudí. The world today perceives the building art in an entirely different light thanks to Gehry, not least because of his firm's software, which has given countless others the ability to design just as unconventionally as he has.

The Gehry office's breakthrough application to architecture of the aeronautical computer-design program CATIA enabled the construction of his masterpiece, the Guggenheim Museum Bilbao of 1991–1997 in Spain. The rapturous reception of that building led to the so-called Bilbao Effect, a salubrious influence on the city's economy that in turn has spurred countless other municipalities to fund grandiose architectural schemes to attract cultural tourism. Gehry's software has since made the creation of eccentric buildings economically feasible for clients who once would have rejected deviations from the cost-efficient regularity of Mies's rectilinear modular formula. As a result, Gehry's transformative contribution has become an intrinsic part of present-day practice, which makes it easy to take his revolutionary advances for granted, in the same way that Mies's were by the end of his life.

Recognition of Gehry's singular place in contemporary architecture was particularly evident in Paris during the fall of 2014 with the opening of his Fondation Louis Vuitton of 2005–2014 (see Illustration 15b) and a simultaneous Centre Pompidou retrospective of his six-decade career. This large show, which comprised 255 drawings and 67 models covering 60 projects, traced his rise from a scrappy maverick with artistic hankerings to the most important American architect since Louis Kahn. It was at least a thrice-told tale (if one counts the Walker Art Center's reputation-making 1986

FRANK GEHRY

Gehry survey organized by Mildred Friedman, who also curated the Guggenheim Museum overview in 2001) but one
well worth reiterating, considering his immense impact on
the redirection of modern architecture.

Gehry spent the first twenty years of his career as a very
creditable commercial architect for figures as divergent as
Victor Gruen (the Los Angeles–based Viennese émigré often
called the father of the American shopping mall) and the
more socially conscious James Rouse (who promoted racially
integrated communities such as the Rouse Company's new
town of Columbia, Maryland, where Gehry executed several
buildings). As his artistic ambitions came to the fore, Gehry
set up his own office in Los Angeles in 1962 and began to
produce self-consciously avant-garde designs. What stands
out most about those early independent works is an essential
and quite touching humility, a quality present even in such
radical proposals as his unexecuted Familian house of 1977–
1978, a multiangular design for a Santa Monica site that
evokes a veritable avalanche of lumber. But even though that
client got cold feet, the project now looks perfectly plausible
as a home because Gehry during the intervening decades has
so thoroughly reshaped our basic notions of habitability.

However, Gehry's postmillennial work has tended to be
anything but humble. This is especially true of his extravagant Fondation Louis Vuitton, which is the equivalent of
fifteen stories high and from certain angles imparts the overbearing aggressiveness projected by the tilting Cor-Ten steel
sculptures of the architect's competitive friend—or perhaps

249

"frenemy"—Richard Serra. The Vuitton building, which occupies a verdant site in the northern part of the Bois de Boulogne, was an instant popular hit. It continues a long history of Parisian modern wonders at once novel and bizarre, typified by the Montgolfier balloon, Foucault's pendulum, the Eiffel Tower, and the *Spirit of St. Louis*, all of which combined technological novelty with conceptual audacity and drew *tout le monde* to come out and gawk at the latest sensation in the city that for centuries has been the world's epicenter of new fashions of every sort.

The Pompidou's exhibition subliminally suggested that if there has been a climactic year for Gehry it may well have come with the completion of the Walt Disney Concert Hall of 1989–2003 in Los Angeles, which proved that he could maintain his extraordinary level of success after Bilbao. Between Disney and Vuitton he executed some twenty-three commissions, but with several exceptions—such as his superb IAC Building of 2003–2007 on the West Side Highway in Manhattan's Chelsea district, a mid-rise office building clad in curving white-fritted glass—few of those post-Disney efforts are likely to be counted among the highlights of Gehry's oeuvre.

For example, the awkward Peter B. Lewis Science Library of 2002–2008 at Princeton University makes a disappointing memorial to its donor, who was Gehry's most generous client. The architect has termed his unbuilt Lewis house of 1985–1995 for Lyndhurst, Ohio, "my MacArthur grant" because the $5 million in fees it earned him (on a budget that ballooned to an incomprehensible $82 million) subsidized a crucial phase in his creative growth. The seventy-six-story Lower Manhattan apartment tower unfortunately named New York by Gehry at Eight Spruce Street (2003–2011) fulfilled the architect's long-cherished dream of erecting a skyscraper (see Illustration 15a). But rather than an extruded version of his cohesively biomorphic compositions, this stainless-steel-clad high-rise is voluptuously modeled with wavelike surfaces on only three of its four sides. The flat south façade, which seems to have been sliced off from the building's undulating portions like a roasted turkey breast, gives that elevation the cut-rate appearance of a speculative office building.

Later proposals were even more open to question. Gehry's LUMA Foundation/Parc des Ateliers of 2014–2018 for an arts organization in Arles, France, brings to mind a stainless-steel tornado. Also in 2014, images of a design dubbed the Flower Building were released, his part of a joint venture with Norman Foster for the redevelopment of London's Battersea Power Station site. Yet this galumphing oddity summons up not so much a bouquet of blossoms as the dancing hippos in the "Waltz of the Flowers" sequence of Walt Disney's *Fantasia* (a resemblance once cited by the architecture critic Michael Sorkin apropos of the Disney Concert Hall, but which seems even more apt here).

Gehry claimed in one of his annoyingly kvetchy interviews that his museum commissions dried up after Bilbao, but the caesura was only temporary, like actors who can't find roles following an Oscar win. After that watershed commission he carried out a boisterous 2004–2008 renovation of the Beaux Arts–style Art Gallery of Ontario in his native Toronto; built the low-budget Ohr-O'Keeffe Museum of Art of 2000–2010 in Biloxi, Mississippi (which was heavily damaged by Hurricane Katrina in 2005 and had to be virtually rebuilt); and his commission for the Guggenheim Abu Dhabi was announced in 2009. However, that last project has been delayed long beyond its original anticipated completion date and its ultimate fate remains unclear, despite reassurances from the client that the scheme will be executed. Far more promising if uncharacteristically restrained is his 2014 master plan for reconfiguring and expanding the Philadelphia Museum of Art, which is expected to be completed in 2020. Thus hopes were understandably high among Gehry's admirers that his private museum in the French capital would mark a return to the top of his game.

The Fondation Louis Vuitton is Gehry's second work in Paris, two decades after his American Center of 1988–1994 opened in the city's eastern Bercy quarter. That cultural-exchange institution—with a playful limestone, glass, and zinc exterior that resembles a charming Cubist collage of a cityscape—closed nineteen months after its completion because the overoptimistic client spent too much on it. (The building was finally taken over by the Cinémathèque Française in 2005, when its interiors were extensively reworked.)

The Vuitton commission came to Gehry with an apparent element of rivalry behind it. In 2000, the luxury goods conglomerateur François Pinault (whose Kering group's subsidiaries include Gucci, Yves Saint Laurent, and Alexander McQueen) declared his intention to build a $195 million contemporary art museum designed by Tadao Ando on the Île Seguin in the Seine, southwest of central Paris. Pinault canceled the project in 2005 because of civic administrative delays and instead bought the Palazzo Grassi in Venice to display his extensive holdings.

However, in 2017 he won approval from the city of Paris to have Ando transform Nicolas Le Camus de Mézières's Corn Exchange of 1763–1767—a circular, domed structure with a free-span rotunda sixty-four feet in diameter, located not far from the Centre Pompidou—into an art gallery where his collection will be shown.

A year after Pinault's initial proposal was floated, Bernard Arnault (the chairman and CEO of LVMH Moët Hennessy–Louis Vuitton—the holding company for such prestigious labels as Dior, Givenchy, and Guerlain—generally considered Pinault's principal competitor) announced plans to sponsor a cultural center in Paris by Gehry, an even bigger architectural star than Ando, in a move viewed by some as corporate one-upmanship. There was a heated public debate over permitting the Fondation Louis Vuitton to build on a Bois de Boulogne site long owned by LVMH's Dior subsidiary, but France's National Assembly ultimately settled the matter, declaring Gehry's building "a major work of art for the whole world," and the undertaking proceeded.

An admirable example of a contemporary art center built by a luxury goods purveyor is the Fondation Cartier, which was founded in 1984 and a decade later moved into the wonderful building on the Boulevard Raspail designed for it by Jean Nouvel. One of his strongest yet most discreet designs, this rectilinear, multilayered glass-walled structure has aged exceptionally well, thanks not only to the inherent quality of the scheme but also because of excellent maintenance. More importantly, the Fondation Cartier's programming has been consistently superb. To be sure, using art and architecture to increase the cachet of expensive consumer goods is hardly a new idea. More than a century ago, Helena Rubinstein adorned her Paris cosmetics salon with sculptures by her protégé Elie Nadelman. In the 1930s, the couturiere Elsa Schiaparelli collaborated with Jean Cocteau and Salvador Dalí on designs for clothing and accessories, and after World War II the Czech-born entrepreneur Zika Ascher commissioned silk scarves from more than fifty artists, including Matisse and Calder. And since the turn of the millennium, luxury-goods companies have been commissioning high-profile retail stores from prominent architects, including Gehry as well as a host of other Pritzker Prize winners such as Ando, Zaha Hadid, Jacques Herzog and Pierre de Meuron, Toyo Ito, Rem Koolhaas, Renzo Piano, and Kazuyo Sejima and Ryue Nishizawa of SANAA.

Particularly active in this sphere is LVMH, which has solicited handbag designs from such well-known contemporary artists as Yayoi Kusama, Takashi Murakami, Richard Prince, and Cindy Sherman, as well as Gehry, whose Twisted Box handbag was for sale in the new building's gift shop at the time of the opening in 2014 for €3,000 ($3,775). As Jean-Paul Claverie, Arnault's longtime art adviser and later head of the holding company's cultural philanthropy, told *The Art Newspaper* in 1997, "LVMH is just a name. With art, we are building our image." The Fondation Cartier demonstrated that a commercially sponsored art gallery can add a great deal to the life of a city even as well endowed with cultural offerings as Paris.

But where the line is to be drawn between beneficence and promotion remains a big question, especially as the commodification of art unceasingly advances into realms unimagined even by Andy Warhol, who anticipated this development in the 1960s. For example, it may have seemed a lighthearted jest to stack vintage Louis Vuitton steamer trunks on the walls of the Gehry building's restaurant and gift shop in imitation of a Donald Judd shelf sculpture, but the gesture seems no more appealing than the gleaming, nine-foot-high metal LV logo attached to a wall above the building's main entrance. This is, to be sure, a private institution, but its credibility would have been notably enhanced if such self-promotional flourishes were toned down in the interest of focusing on the art within, as is the case at the Cartier Foundation, which eschews its sponsor's double-C logo.

It is axiomatic among architecture editors and art directors that if a building is not very good, then one should use images of it at sundown; if it is worse than that, show it reflected in water at twilight; if it is truly awful, shoot it after dark in the snow. This perhaps explains why several publications, including *Architectural Digest, Vanity Fair,* and *The New York Times,* depicted Gehry's Vuitton gallery in a dim crepuscular glow, rising above its shallow pools and dramatic stepped cascade. Recourse to special photographic lighting does address one of this building's basic shortcomings, however, for in a city where it is overcast much of the time, a glass-skinned structure is bound to look rather dull quite often, which is true of the Fondation Louis Vuitton, despite Gehry's best efforts to imbue it with high drama.

The twin peaks of Gehry's career—Bilbao and Disney—are both clad in the silvery titanium that became the hallmark material of his career's second half, superseding the chain-link fencing, corrugated metal, and chicken-wire glass that gave his early experimental work a louche, combative quality that repelled some potential clients but earned him street cred as a tough avant-garde artist. Glass was chosen for the Vuitton gallery's exterior because of restrictions imposed by the city to keep the building from appearing too massive. The structure is enveloped by a dozen gigantic steel-framed, white-fritted-glass "sails" in a series of complementary arcs hoisted on an elaborate armature of 179 steel and wood tripods. These curving, billboard-like surfaces thrust outward from the "icebergs," as Gehry called the concrete-paneled internal gallery structures. The lifting looks very heavy indeed, and at points the concatenation of multiple support elements seems like a chaotic pileup of Mark di Suvero sculptures. It then becomes easy to believe the astonishing statistic that this building contains more than twice the steel used in the Eiffel Tower.

By adopting such a costly and effortful dual structural system—there seem to be two buildings in one here, just as Santiago Calatrava's overly complicated bridges are said to duplicate their task—Gehry was able to combine a sensuously sculptural carapace of glass with workable display spaces within (a format he earlier employed for a very different function at his Hotel Marqués de Riscal of 1999–2006 in Spain). He was stung by criticism that his most famous structure is inimical to art—"Every museum director I know hated Bilbao," he claimed, with much hyperbole and typical self-pity. Thus even though the eccentric interior volumes of his masterpiece are in fact wonderfully hospitable to certain kinds of art, such as Serra's sculptures (it also includes several conventional galleries), he clearly wanted to avoid difficulties in showing the LVMH collection.

In its clear separation between free-form exterior and straightforward interior, the Vuitton building also recalls Gehry's Richard B. Fisher Center for the Performing Arts of 1997–2003 at Bard College in Annandale-on-Hudson, New York. There, a utilitarian shed of the sort that might be used for a suburban big-box store is fronted with billowing titanium sheets, a contrast not unlike Palladio's Venetian churches with their highly articulated stone façades and mundane brick side and rear elevations. Although hardly on a par with Gehry's Experience Music Project of 1995–2000 (now the Museum of Pop Culture) in Seattle, arguably the worst building of his entire career, the Fondation Louis Vuitton is notably lacking in repose, a quality not incompatible with dynamism, as both Bilbao and Disney demonstrate.

The metal skins of the Bilbao museum and the Los Angeles auditorium conceal the necessary workings beneath serenely opaque surfaces. In contrast, the Vuitton building's translucent exterior reveals a plethora of angular underpinnings that would have been best left hidden. This building's obviously high level of execution has caused some observers to question whether it could possibly have cost only $135 million, a widely reported figure that LVMH will neither confirm nor deny. As Claverie told *The New York Times*, "In philanthropy, we never express figures because we want the dream and the emotion to speak for itself [*sic*]."

On its south flank the Fondation Louis Vuitton fronts one of the undulating roadways that snake through the Bois in the English Romantic manner. Passing into the main portal on that elevation, one enters a vast, amorphous central court some thirty feet high. This space is surmounted by a flat ceiling with banal detailing more befitting a suburban outlet mall than a high-style art museum. Tilting outer glass walls offer views of the surrounding park, with a pleasant café on the north side enlivened by a swarming school of Gehry's whimsical plastic-laminate Fish Lamps, first produced in the 1980s, suspended from the ceiling.

Adjacent to this entry area is the upper level of a double-height auditorium. Oddly for an interior that frequently will need to be darkened for performances, it has two large glass window walls with blackout curtains concealed above them. Here is displayed one of several site-specific works the foundation commissioned for the building—a vertically striped, rainbow-spectrum stage curtain (which could be easily confused with a gay pride flag) and five monochromatic panels by Ellsworth Kelly, which are positioned around the large room and double as acoustical absorption baffles. Moving outward from the building's core one quickly becomes disoriented. For a structure with such a plethora of circulation —corridors, stairways, catwalks, escalators, and elevators seem to spring up at every turn—it is difficult to make your way methodically from gallery to gallery and from level to level.

The most enjoyable parts of the structure are its outdoor terraces, which encircle the "icebergs" at different levels. Some of them offer panoramic views of Paris beyond the treetops of the Bois. The upper reaches of Gehry's vitreous spinnakers provide an intriguing frame for some of the vistas, though they occlude others and create landscape slivers that Manhattan real estate brokers would term partial park views. It was once said of the Eiffel Tower that it was the most agreeable spot in Paris because it was the one place where one could not see the Eiffel Tower. That is not at all the case with the Fondation Louis Vuitton, but it may take some time before it fulfills its ambitious mission to become an equal among the City of Light's formidable array of cultural landmarks.

16

RENZO PIANO

THE SINGULAR POSITION held by Renzo Piano—among the most respected master builders at the end of the twentieth and the beginning of the twenty-first century, when he seemed to have a veritable monopoly on the most prestigious cultural commissions—owed much to a pervasive (if seldom articulated) fear among benefactors of cultural institutions that the building art in some essential sense had moved beyond their comprehension. The unexpected emergence of Frank Gehry as his generation's most celebrated architect, confirmed by his ecstatically praised Guggenheim Museum Bilbao, created a slipstream of rapid acceptance for such younger practitioners as Zaha Hadid, Daniel Libeskind, and Santiago Calatrava, all exponents of what has been called the architecture of spectacle, which emphasizes extreme novelty and high drama rather than qualities of timelessness, beauty, and repose that were more prized in earlier epochs.

Following the Bilbao sensation, uncertainty about how

well this kind of exhibitionistic design would pass the test of time brought many museum building committees to Piano, whose Menil Collection of 1982–1986 in Houston has certainly done just that. If anything, the Menil is now even more esteemed than when it first opened. Piano's next museum jobs in Texas—his Cy Twombly Gallery of 1992–1995 next to the Menil in Houston and Nasher Sculpture Center of 1999–2003 in Dallas—reiterated his unparalleled understanding of how to harness the harsh daylight of the Sun Belt to maximum effect in naturally illuminated interiors. This particular skill, along with his reputation for a dependably understated elegance and an exceptionally agreeable personal demeanor not always found among avant-garde architects, made him the obvious candidate for yet another Texas commission, one of the utmost sensitivity: an addition to Louis Kahn's revered Kimbell Art Museum of 1966–1972 in Fort Worth, by general consensus the greatest gallery building of the modern era.

The announcement that Piano had been chosen for this delicate task was greeted with widespread relief among architectural aficionados, for clearly the job was in safe hands. It also prevented some from raising the indelicate question of why this project was being undertaken in the first place. For if the Kimbell's undeniable magic derives from its being about as perfect as any art museum could possibly be, why mess with success? Yet even this most gemlike and personal of institutions—an oasis of intimacy in a period when both the physical size and attendance figures of museums are aggressively aggrandized to the detriment of viewing art—could not escape the plutocratic peer-group pressure that demands that museums expand in every respect.

Happily, the addition to the Kimbell—chivalrously named the Renzo Piano Pavilion to honor its designer and emphasize it as a separate architectural entity instead of an appendage of Kahn's original structure—turned out to be far from the desecration some feared (see Illustration 16a). About the worst one could say about it is that the $135 million building is not very distinguished, especially in light of the Nasher only thirty-two miles away in Dallas. When I revisited the Nasher at the time of the Piano addition's opening, the older building struck me as its designer's equivalent of Kahn's Kimbell, a warm and embracing fusion of art and architecture that seems increasingly remarkable each time one returns. It defies precise definition of exactly why it is so wonderful, that elusive quality of all truly great architecture.

To be sure, matters would be much improved had the freestanding Renzo Piano Pavilion been placed elsewhere on the Kimbell's ample property—specifically a vacant lot just across Van Cliburn Way to the east of the Kahn galleries, used as an auxiliary parking lot for Tadao Ando's Modern Art Museum of Fort Worth (1997–2002). Piano devised a promising initial plan for that unobtrusive location, but the Modern Art Museum wanted to keep the parking lot (even though the land is actually owned by the Kimbell) and a different scheme was prepared for the site to the west of the Kahn building, where the 101,000-square-foot addition now stands. Those closest to the project privately reported that the museum's longtime president and chairman, Kay Kimbell Forston—a niece and namesake of Kay Kimbell, the Fort Worth entrepreneur who upon his death in 1964 left his entire fortune of $100 million, big money in those days, to create the museum—hoped to avoid conflict with Anne Windfohr Marion, a Modern Art Museum trustee and local social powerhouse, and thus did not press her property rights. On matters such as this the history of architecture sometimes hinges.

The new pavilion's design reiterates the format Piano has used in several other museum buildings: a low-rise rectangle with a flat overhanging roof supported by a modern version of the Classical colonnade, a single continuous row of columns set out from the structure's outer walls and supporting the extended roof above the configuration, first seen at the Menil Collection. However, here there is an odd disjunction between the somewhat vacant three-hundred-foot-long entry façade—from which you see the Kahn building across a broad grassy lawn—and the busy one-hundred-foot-long side elevations, which overlook streets to the north and south.

The Piano addition is connected to the Kahn building by an underground parking garage and by a walkway across the lawn between them. Most visitors will leave their cars in the garage and ascend by stairs or elevator to the new structure; there is no direct access for the public to the Kahn building from the garage, though those using the original aboveground parking lot will enter the old galleries through the east door as before. A subterranean tunnel between the two can be used upon request by people in wheelchairs.

The pavilion's tripartite front is bland beyond the worst norms of Minimalism, with a pair of blank concrete walls that frame a central segment of ground-to-roof glass panels and portals, the detailing of which is routine at best. As one stands in the west-facing courtyard of the Kahn building—with its famous grove of yaupon hollies designed by Harriet Pattison, the architect's landscape architect and mother of his son, Nathaniel Kahn—the Piano addition nearly fades away. Alas, the same cannot be said of its overwrought north and south ends, which seem ill-proportioned thanks to the massive, hundred-foot-long, gray-stained, laminated Douglas fir roof beams that jut beyond the glass walls beneath them and give the composition a top-heavy quality reminiscent of 1970s Brutalism. Supporting those narrower elevations, a row of eleven squared-off concrete columns (echoing the corner supports of the Kahn gallery's porticoes) are spaced a mere ten feet apart and thus make the building appear to be sinking under its own weight.

The Renzo Piano Pavilion is actually two separate structures conjoined: an entry-and-gallery pavilion, behind which, half-buried beneath a green-roof earth berm, is a subterranean component that contains a double-height, 298-seat auditorium; a handsome library; various education facilities, including classrooms and children's art studios; and a cave-like gallery dedicated to works of Asian art. The main virtue of this crepuscular space is that it allows fragile works with stringent light-control requirements—such as scrolls, screens, and textiles—to be displayed together. Despite deferential gestures to the Kahn building, the addition blocks the once westward-sweeping vista toward another cornerstone of Fort Worth's estimable cultural district, Philip Johnson's Amon Carter Museum of American Art of 1958–1961, from his so-called Ballet School Period of fussy sub-Classicism. Though hardly in the same architectural league as Kahn's Kimbell, the Amon Carter when seen from a distance did possess a certain campy charm akin to a folly at the terminus of a Baroque garden axis. However, that view is now obscured behind an ungainly concrete retaining wall that props up the submerged portions of the Renzo Piano Pavilion.

In an initial miscalculation, the Kimbell decided to temporarily display its permanent collection in the Piano Pavilion while it housed a 2013 inaugural loan exhibition, "The Age of Picasso and Matisse: Modern Masters from the Art Institute of Chicago," made possible by the temporary dislocation of that museum's best twentieth-century paintings. Ironically, this superb show owed something to Piano as well, because the works became available when the problem-plagued third floor of his Modern Wing of 2001–2009 at the Art Institute was closed for seven months of repair work only four years after the addition's completion. The switch invited some unfortunate comparisons. Kahn's interiors, with their celebrated skylit concrete ceiling vaults and use of creamy travertine on the walls, virtually caress pictures shown within them, in an almost uncanny melding of sensitively proportioned volume and mysteriously modulated light. Not surprisingly, the Art Institute's finest modern pictures looked better in the original Kimbell than they ever have at home.

Although the Kimbell's Old Master paintings could be adequately viewed when temporarily installed in Piano's new galleries, they unquestionably seemed less magical there than they customarily do in Kahn's spaces, where they fairly glow. The works that fare best in the Piano Pavilion's three major display areas are the non-European sculptures mounted in the pellucidly lit north gallery (illuminated, as is the south gallery, by a combination of natural and artificial overhead lighting). Among them are the museum's choice pre-Columbian artifacts and superb African tribal objects, the latter exemplified by an Ife terra-cotta head, circa 1100–1300 CE, one of the finest treasures from that continent in this hemisphere. The pavilion's best feature is its exquisitely wrought concrete walls—supervised by the Dottor Group, an Italian architectural restoration firm—which were poured in unusually large and smoothly finished wooden formworks to minimize the seams and circular indentations that can be so distracting when viewing art against conventionally made concrete surfaces. The material exudes a low-key silvery sheen thanks to a 2 percent addition of titanium to the ingredients. It is the most ravishing concrete I have ever seen in the United States.

On a whole, though, the Renzo Piano Pavilion quickly

faded into the middle rank of Piano's oeuvre, neither at the top (the Nasher and Menil) nor the bottom (the Broad Contemporary Art Museum of 2003–2008 in Los Angeles and the Morgan Library and Museum of 2000–2006 in New York). The Fort Worth pavilion is but one of the architect's twenty-five museum buildings, and he cannot be expected to produce a hit every time. One can easily imagine an outcome at the Kimbell better in several respects—a structure lighter, more ethereal, and livelier than this dull affair. Yet we should also be grateful that the designer and his client were so cautious. The most important requirement they faced vis-à-vis Kahn's masterpiece could be summed up in the opening words of the Hippocratic oath—"First, do no harm"—and in that respect they undoubtedly succeeded. The extreme preoccupation over the success or failure of the Renzo Piano Pavilion is indicative of the dominance that architecture has disproportionately assumed in the evaluation of art institutions since Gehry's Guggenheim Bilbao. This is not to say that the buildings in which works of art are housed should be beside the point, but great architecture alone does not guarantee a great museum.

Although the low-rise, colonnaded rectangle has been Piano's most familiar museum format, he has diverged from it several times, as in the undulating steel-framed roof of his Zentrum Paul Klee of 1999–2005 in Bern, Switzerland, and the sail-like glass canopy that overarches his Astrup Fearnley Museum of Modern Art of 2009–2012 in Oslo. Another postmillennial museum design by his Paris office—the Fondation Jérôme Seydoux-Pathé of 2006–2014 in Paris—is similarly biomorphic, and yet the architect also had to take into account the landmark structure behind which his scheme was to be erected. (Although this nineteenth-century vestige is hardly a major treasure on a par with the Kimbell, the city of Paris carefully guards the overall texture of is architectural fabric, and buildings that are not of the highest significance are protected all the same.)

In the fall of 2014, while *le tout* Paris and architecture enthusiasts were agog over the debut of Gehry's assertively spectacular and lavishly publicized Fondation Louis Vuitton in the Bois de Boulogne (see Illustration 15b), Piano's little gem opened with no fanfare five miles to the southeast in the 13th arrondissement (not far from Dominique Perrault's quadruple-glass-towered Bibliothèque Nationale de France of 1989–1995). The Fondation Jérôme Seydoux-Pathé is a museum, archive, and cinematheque for Pathé, the pioneering French film company (see Illustration 16b). With its ingenious demonstration of how to insert a work of avant-garde architecture into a historic setting, this voluptuously swelling aluminum-and-glass-clad form—instantly likened to an armadillo—ranks among Piano's best works.

At just 23,000 square feet, Piano's five-story jewel displays his particular strengths to perfection: the sleek engineering of its bold forms, the exquisite craftsmanship of its interior finishes, the way its arching translucent roof skillfully modulates daylight, and the aura of elevated calm throughout. These same qualities likewise typify what I have called the Piano Quartet, the four intimately scaled art galleries (Menil, Twombly, Nasher, and Beyeler Foundation Museum) at the core of his achievement. The discreetly restrained Pathé Foundation, on the broad Avenue des Gobelins, occupies a keyhole-shaped footprint connected to the back of a freestanding Beaux Arts façade with an entry arch featuring Neoclassical bas-reliefs of Drama and Comedy by the young Auguste Rodin. This site once housed the Théâtre des Gobelins, an early cinema owned by the Pathé company, which was founded at the dawn of cinematography in 1896.

The ground floor of the new building is raked upward about six feet from front to back, toward a small garden landscaped with birch trees visible through a glass wall at the rear of the site. Stairs lead down to a subterranean seventy-seat screening room for silent films, adjoining an exhibition gallery where early-twentieth-century Pathé movie posters are displayed. On the second story is another gallery, devoted to an array of period movie cameras and projectors set out on a long, narrow platform without protective glass, which gives the antique cinematic hardware the air of a contemporary sculpture installation.

The two levels above this are devoted to climate-controlled archival storage and offices, and then, at the very top of the building, Piano's pièce de résistance: the research center. This soaring open-plan space, which encloses a conference area as well as desks for researchers, is defined by a sequence of thirty-eight laminated larchwood arches that increase in size toward the center of the dazzling glass-roofed aerie. The canopy's outer surface is clad with approximately seven thousand perforated aluminum louvers that filter daylight but afford soft-focus views of the surrounding cityscape. The graceful ebb and flow of the double-curved roof and the immaculate facture of the wooden parabolas that support it impart an organic, Aalto-like warmth to what otherwise might have seemed a chilly high-tech exercise in precision engineering. Attention to detail throughout is impressive but unobtrusive, perhaps most tellingly in the internal stairways, a necessity on which some firms would not expend much effort. These vertical circulation spaces have unpainted concrete walls almost as smoothly finished as those in the Renzo Piano Pavilion, and here are ideally complemented by yellow-and-orange linoleum flooring on the steps and landings, as well as by stylish squared-off stainless-steel handrails.

Choosing Piano for this project was somewhat of a family affair. The building was commissioned by Pathé's CEO, the billionaire Jérôme Seydoux, whose relatives have had a notable association with the architect dating back to his early career. Seydoux's mother was a member of the hugely rich Schlumberger clan, whose oil equipment firm is headquartered near Paris in a Piano building of 1981–1984. She was also a first cousin of Dominique de Menil, née Schlumberger, the legendary Franco-American art collector and aesthete who with her husband, John, commissioned the Menil Collection.

In certain respects the Fondation Jérôme Seydoux-Pathé brings to mind the DZ Bank Building of 1995–2001 in Berlin by Gehry, who similarly juxtaposed a decorous classicizing façade (of his own design, rather than a vestige as in the Paris project) with biomorphic volumes concealed behind it. In Gehry's scheme, a horsehead-like stainless-steel-wrapped conference room is set within a fish-form glass-roofed atrium. The Pathé foundation's billowing metal-and-glass-clad roof is barely visible from the Avenue des Gobelins, and is best viewed from the small garden tucked behind the structure. In both instances, the conservative character of the buildings' immediate neighborhood has been respected, while visitors experience an unexpected spatial revelation as they move inside.

However, the Pathé building is wholly different from Gehry's hulking Fondation Louis Vuitton, not only in its structural suavity and organizational clarity but also in the former's notable reticence, antithetical to the Vuitton showplace's insistent self-advertisement. To be sure, there is also a great disparity in size between the two structures: Gehry's rises fifty-six feet higher and is a hundred thousand square feet larger. But the real dichotomy is not just architectural but spiritual. The splendid Fondation Jérôme Seydoux-Pathé quietly amplifies the cultural contributions of its sponsor's historic enterprise, rather than exploiting artistic cachet as a mere promotional and marketing tool. The scant attention the Pathé facility received upon its completion, especially in contrast to the media feeding frenzy that surrounded the opening of the Vuitton gallery, is all the more a pity since it far surpasses other, much higher-profile museum projects by the Renzo Piano Building Workshop (RPBW). The firm's compact but corporate-looking additions to the Morgan Library and Museum and Boston's Isabella Stewart Gardner Museum of 2005–2012 have disappointed many admirers of those venerable institutions.

The fall of 2014 also saw the opening of the Piano firm's renovation and expansion of the Harvard Art Museums—a project that consolidated the university's Fogg Art Museum, Busch-Reisinger Museum, and Arthur M. Sackler Museum. This scheme drew sharp criticism for the way it connects the new ensemble to Le Corbusier's adjacent Carpenter Center for the Visual Arts of 1959–1962. The Princeton architectural historian Beatriz Colomina went so far as to denounce it as "a crime against humanity" for the damage she claims it does to the "mythical" Le Corbusier building. Yet the following May, RPBW's Whitney Museum of American Art of 2009–2015 in New York City's Meatpacking District drew strong praise from most critics and was an instant hit with the public after the museum moved its collections from Marcel Breuer's landmark Brutalist building of 1963–1966 on Manhattan's Upper East Side.

These highly variable outcomes indicate that far from being able to guarantee that his buildings will resist seeming dated decades after their completion—a claim Piano has never made in any case—this undoubted master is no more able than any other architect to escape shifting perceptions of long-term transcendence. One plausible explanation for the uneven reception of his firm's output is its extraordinarily high volume of one-off cultural commissions. These projects are far more time-consuming than commercial structures, which involve repetitive tasks that in most firms are routinely handled by assistants rather than principals. Another factor is almost certainly the individual design team in charge of each highly collaborative scheme, and a formidable task therefore awaits future architectural historians in trying to unravel why and how the Piano office operated at its best.

17

DAVID CHILDS /
SANTIAGO CALATRAVA

NO URBAN DESIGN project in modern American experience
aroused such high expectations and intense scrutiny as the
rebuilding of the World Trade Center site in New York City.
It took fifteen years after the terrorist assault of September
11, 2001, for the principal structures of this sixteen-acre
parcel in Lower Manhattan to be completed. In a field where
time is money in a very direct sense (because of interest pay-
ments on the vast sums borrowed to finance big construction
projects), such a long gestation period usually signifies not
judicious deliberation on the part of planners, developers,
designers, engineers, and contractors but rather economic,
political, or bureaucratic problems that can impede a speedy
and cost-efficient conclusion. Indeed, the revival of the dev-
astated World Trade Center site was repeatedly dogged by
obstacles of every conceivable sort from start to finish.

In contrast to this slow-motion rollout, it took less than a
decade to erect the Associated Architects' twenty-two-acre,

fourteen-building Rockefeller Center of 1930–1939, which was accomplished without benefit of the countless technological advances devised since then or the mammoth government subsidies allocated to the remaking of what became known as Ground Zero. That swiftness was owed in part to the project being underwritten by the richest family in America during the Great Depression, when jobs were scarce and both designers and laborers were grateful for work, but the endeavor was a logistical triumph nonetheless. With Ground Zero, the lengthy delay reflected the project's divided and ambiguous leadership as well as the fractious political tenor of the times.

Who was really in charge of this undertaking remained a persistent and vexing question throughout. However, as several studies have made abundantly clear, the transformation of the World Trade Center site was hampered to a shameful degree by the intransigent self-interest of both individuals and institutions. As a result, an effort ostensibly meant to display our country's unified spirit in response to an unprecedented calamity instead showed that communal altruism of the sort that helped America survive the Great Depression and triumph in World War II had largely become a thing of the past. Although all major construction schemes face tremendous problems, the World Trade Center rebuilding encapsulates everything that is wrong with urban development in a period when, as in so many other aspects of our public life, the communal good of the many is sacrificed to the selfish gain of the few.

The actual and emotional centerpiece of the grouping is the magnificent National September 11 Memorial of 2003–2011, the hypnotic pair of reflecting pools recording the names of victims by the architect Michael Arad, and the surrounding park by the landscape architect Peter Walker, which was dedicated on the tenth anniversary of the disaster. In May 2014 came the opening of the adjacent National September 11 Museum, a much less successful design that resulted from a shotgun marriage between two wholly mismatched firms, the high-style Norwegian-based collaborative Snøhetta (which designed the trendily off-kilter exterior) and the workaday New York office Davis Brody Bond (responsible for the awkward interiors). This doomed division of labor produced a disjointed building that unintentionally mirrors the continuing conflicts over the way the 2001 attacks should be interpreted.

Three of the five reflective, glass-skinned office towers that will ultimately surround Arad's pools were finished fifteen years after the attack: the vapid 7 World Trade Center (2006) by David Childs of Skidmore, Owings & Merrill; the equally disappointing 4 World Trade Center (2013) by Fumihiko Maki; and the Western Hemisphere's tallest skyscraper, Childs's One World Trade Center (2013), a 1,776-foot-tall monolith that supplants Minoru Yamasaki's Twin Towers of 1966–1977 (see Illustration 17a). Not as bad architecturally as it is conceptually, One World Trade Center is faute de mieux the best of the lot.

The chief virtues of this building—which was initially

277

dubbed the Freedom Tower by New York Governor George Pataki but later "rebranded" to tone down jingoistic associations that might scare off potential tenants—are that it effectively addresses the huge open space to its south, including Arad and Walker's memorial, and overpowers its lackluster neighbors. Though hardly an intriguing work of architecture, it nonetheless succeeds in anchoring the unruly scrum of contiguous lower structures through the sheer force of its gigantic scale and simple sculptural presence. The building's symmetrical, upwardly tapering, prismatic contours make it stand out clearly against the Lower Manhattan skyline, especially when slanting sunlight gives its four angled corners a clear contrast against the rest of its mirrorlike glass cladding. If not ideally proportioned in its height-to-mass ratio, Childs's tower comes close enough to being an agreeable composition and is a notable improvement over the architect's other conspicuous Manhattan skyscrapers—the chunky Postmodern campanile of his Worldwide Plaza of 1986–1989 in Midtown West (which occupies the entire city block between 49th and 50th Streets and Eighth and Ninth Avenues) and his glitzy twin-towered Time Warner Center of 2000–2003 on Columbus Circle.

David Magie Childs, who could reasonably claim to be the most successful corporate architect in postmillennial America, was born in 1941 in Princeton, where his father was a professor of classics at the university. After prepping at Deerfield he went to Yale and then its school of architecture, where he received a masters degree in 1967. Four years later

he joined the Washington, D.C., branch of Skidmore, Owings & Merrill (SOM), the large multicity (and later multinational) firm, and in 1984 moved to its New York office, where
he was named chairman in 1991 and served in that post for a
decade. A fixture in the empyrean of American design offi-
cialdom, Childs was a member of the National Capital Planning Commission, chairman of the US Commission of Fine
Arts, and has sat on the boards of numerous cultural institutions, including the Museum of Modern Art. Better connected than this you do not get in the world of architecture.

The way in which Childs secured the Freedom Tower/One
World Trade Center job for SOM but himself in particular
could provide a master class in the politics of major league
architecture and urbanism. The details of Childs's eventual
emergence at the forefront of a huge field of contenders is far
too complex to fully recapitulate here. Briefly, though, just
six weeks before the 2001 disaster, the New York real estate
developer Larry Silverstein bought a ninety-nine-year lease
on the World Trade Center from the Port Authority of New
York and New Jersey and then hired SOM to renovate the
Twin Towers. Three decades after the double colossi first
opened they were in a generally run-down condition and not
at all competitive with more recently built, technologically
advanced skyscrapers in Lower Manhattan. Thus SOM was
already on the scene by September 11, and it was delusional
for anyone to think that the full-service megafirm would re-
linquish such an immensely lucrative reconstruction job,
which was only its to lose, not anyone else's to win.

This was well understood by Childs, who stood aside from the clamor that surrounded what most people imagined to be an open competition to determine the site's future. As a seasoned veteran of New York City real estate wars—the intricacies of which can scarcely be comprehended by even the most experienced outsiders, as was discovered by Yoshio Taniguchi during the construction of his Museum of Modern Art expansion of 1997–2004—Childs knew that property rights in this country supersede all other considerations when it comes to building in the public realm. Furthermore, he understood that government officials would have no recourse other than to go along with decisions made by Ground Zero's lawful leaseholder, unless they were prepared to give in to Silverstein's outrageous financial demands. Longtime observers of the New York construction industry barely raised an eyebrow when they saw the clueless tyro Daniel Libeskind, nominal master planner of the Trade Center site, blown away like tumbleweed.

Anticipating this, Childs and his SOM team produced a fully implementable design in record time. Unparalleled security concerns required that the reinforced concrete-and-steel base of One World Trade Center, approximately nineteen stories high, be as impenetrable as a 1950s atomic bomb shelter. In a dubious attempt to prettify this veritable fortification, Childs originally intended to cover it with two thousand clear prismatic glass panels and welded aluminum-and-glass screens. However, after $10 million had been spent on this decorative flourish, it proved too technically daunting to execute, and more conventional glazing was substituted. In the end, One World Trade Center, which cost $3.9 billion—nearly twice the price of Western Europe's tallest building, Renzo Piano's $1.9 billion Shard of 2000–2013, on London's South Bank—became the world's most expensive skyscraper by a wide margin.

The tower's interior is far stranger than its straightforward exterior, understandably because of urgent protective measures. Visitors to the observatory on the 102nd floor (2.3 million came during its first year) are shepherded through a labyrinthine series of unnervingly lighted and plastic-feeling walkways and holding areas on the ground floor, where security checks are made before they arrive at the Sky Pod Elevators. These lifts propel them to the summit in forty-two seconds, while an animated time-lapse video, brilliantly designed by the California firms Blur Studio and Hettema Group, plays on nine seventy-nine-inch high-definition screens that line the elevator cabs. This simulation imagines how an eastward outlook from the site appeared during the past five centuries, beginning with lightly forested marshes circa 1500 and, a century later, gabled Dutch houses that pop up and vanish. In due course the skyscrapers that made Manhattan world-famous shoot heavenward and are replaced by ever-taller ones. Finally, for a fleeting four seconds, we catch a peripheral glimpse of one of the vertically striped Twin Towers, which swiftly vanishes, happily without any sign of what took place. One exits from this intense ride thankful for the majestic panoramic views that extend peacefully in every direction beyond the glass-walled rooftop gallery.

Without knowledge of Ground Zero's terrible history, Childs's design would seem even less exceptional, just another super-colossal, shiny skyscraper made possible by all sorts of advanced engineering marvels but unmistakably a thing of the past because of its fundamental lack of forward-thinking urban planning ideas. It seems impossible to see this as anything other than a placeholder for half of what once stood in its approximate place, a feeling reinforced by the eloquent voids of Arad's heartrending memorial right in front of it.

The most architecturally ambitious portion of the ensemble, Santiago Calatrava's World Trade Center Transportation Hub (commonly called the Oculus), opened to the public in 2016, though with no fanfare whatever, doubtless to avoid drawing further attention to this stupendous waste of public funds. Born in Valencia in 1951, Calatrava studied architecture in his hometown before taking a doctorate in civil engineering from the Eidgenössische Technische Hochschule (ETH) in Zurich in 1981. His rise was astoundingly rapid, and by the time he was thirty he had completed eight projects—most of them transportation infrastructure—in Switzerland, Germany, and Spain. The Transportation Hub commission was a direct result of Calatrava's determination, as he turned fifty in 2001, to widen his wildly successful Zurich-based practice to the United States. When he got the job in 2003, he opened a New York office with the coy corporate name of Festina Lente LLP (Latin for "make haste slowly") to oversee its execution. As things transpired, the project took twelve years to finish instead of the five originally promised, and part of its exorbitant $4 billion price will be paid over decades to come by commuters in the form of higher transit fares. The fortune spent on this kitschy jeu d'esprit— nearly twice its already unconscionable initial estimate of $2.2 billion—is even more outrageous for a facility that serves only 40,000 commuters on an average weekday, as opposed to the 750,000 who pass through Grand Central Terminal daily. Astoundingly, the Transportation Hub wound up costing $1 billion more than One World Trade Center itself.

Calatrava's budgetary excesses were already well known among professionals by the time he received this commission. But the Lower Manhattan Development Corporation (LMDC)—the joint city-state body established to carry out the reconstruction—had just gone through a bruising public struggle to select a master planner for the entire site, and in its eagerness for an architectural showpiece paid insufficient attention to the Spanish architect's troublesome track record and fell for the maudlin sentimentalism of his design. What was originally likened by its creator to a fluttering *paloma de la paz* (dove of peace) because of its white, winglike, upwardly flaring rooflines seems more like a steroidal stegosaurus that wandered onto the set of a sci-fi flick and died there (see Illustration 17c). And instead of an ennobling civic concourse on the order of Grand Central or Charles Follen McKim's endlessly lamented Pennsylvania Station, what we now have on top of the new transit facilities is an eerily dead-feeling, retro-futuristic, Space Age Gothic shopping mall with acres of highly polished, very slippery white marble flooring like some urban tundra (see Illustration 17b).

Formally known as Westfield World Trade Center, it is filled with the same predictable mix of chain retailers one can find in countless airports worldwide: Banana Republic, Hugo Boss, Breitling, Dior, and on through the global designer-label alphabet. (The Westfield Corporation is an Australian-based British-American shopping center company.) Far from this being the "exhilarating nave of a genuine people's cathedral" that Paul Goldberger claimed it to be in *Vanity Fair*, Calatrava's superfluous shopping shrine is merely what the Germans call a *Konsumtempel* (temple of consumption), and a generic one at that.

Still to come among the ensemble's components are 2 World Trade Center by the Bjarke Ingels Group (BIG) and 3 World Trade Center by the office of Richard Rogers. Plans are doubtful for a putative 5 World Trade Center (to replace the former Deutsche Bank Building, which was irreparably damaged by debris from the collapse of the Twin Towers and laboriously dismantled) and no architect has been selected. And there will be no 6 World Trade Center to replace that eight-story component of Yamasaki's original five-building World Trade Center ensemble, also destroyed on September 11.

The prodigious public interest in the resurrection of Ground Zero quickly prompted three books about the first phases of the effort, all aimed at a general readership and published within four months of one another around the disaster's third anniversary. Goldberger's *Up from Zero: Politics, Architecture, and the Rebuilding of New York* (2004) was one of his typically well-reported but never indiscreet overviews. Philip Nobel's *Sixteen Acres: Architecture and the Outrageous Struggle for the Future of Ground Zero* (2005) offered a juicier, more anecdotal account of the same events. But both books suffered from a lack of adequate illustrations, a shortcoming rectified by Suzanne Stephens's pictorially rich compendium *Imagining Ground Zero: Official and Unofficial Proposals for the World Trade Center Site* (2004).

A decade after that initial flurry of publications, what is likely to remain the definitive account of this tortuous and unedifying saga appeared, Lynne B. Sagalyn's *Power at Ground Zero: Politics, Money, and the Remaking of Lower Manhattan* (2016). Sagalyn, who retired as a professor of real estate at the Columbia University Business School, insists that there are no heroes or villains in her narrative. However, her meticulous and exceptionally clear exposition of the essential facts provides more than enough evidence for readers to come to their own, and often damning, conclusions, especially about Silverstein.

Her exhaustive research exposed some fascinating interrelationships in the upper echelons of the city's power elite, which will be unsurprising to those who know how the financial and cultural capital of the US really works, and insider glimpses are rarely documented as directly as she does here. For example, she tells how the well-connected attorney Edward Hayes, a "New York political infighter" and "go-to guy," urged Governor Pataki, a former Columbia Law School contemporary of his, to pick Daniel Libeskind's scheme in the competition for the site's master plan. Hayes had been introduced to Libeskind and his business-manager wife, Nina, by Victoria Newhouse—an architectural historian and the wife of the publishing magnate S.I. Newhouse Jr.— who was avid to see Libeskind win the commission. Pataki reassured Hayes that he was already in favor of Libeskind's proposal and indeed intervened at the last moment to ensure that he was chosen. It was a pyrrhic victory for the architect, however. Libeskind assumed that winning the contest would also entitle him to design the Freedom Tower, but because of his limited experience with such large-scale projects, he was forced to collaborate with Childs, who edged him out of the commission with Machiavellian dispatch.

Si Newhouse resurfaces later in the story when the question of who would actually occupy the Freedom Tower becomes an urgent matter. His Condé Nast Publications was identified as the ideal "anchor tenant" by Silverstein's long-time leasing broker, Mary Ann Tighe of CBRE, the world's largest commercial real estate services firm, who had known the publisher for decades. Given the perceived danger of another terrorist attack, this would not be an easy sell, but Tighe recalled that Condé Nast had been previously receptive to an undesirable address at the right price: it relocated from its longtime Madison Avenue headquarters to the newly built 4 Times Square in 1999, when that area still had a seedy aura. The developer of 4 Times Square, the Durst Organization, received tax incentives estimated at more than $280 million, which allowed it to give Condé Nast very favorable terms, a classic example of corporate welfare at taxpayer expense. Durst partnered with the cash-strapped Silverstein on One World Trade Center once it became an active, risk-free proposition, and Condé Nast agreed to move to Ground Zero when it was offered yet another sweetheart deal on a property widely deemed to be very difficult to rent.

A more visible display of influence was orchestrated by Herbert Muschamp, the *New York Times* architecture critic from 1992 to 2004. As Frank Gehry told the writer Clay Risen, the architect and the critic dined together in Manhattan the night before the Twin Towers attack, and the ensuing catastrophe so traumatized Muschamp that he felt unable to leave his forty-fourth-floor Tribeca apartment, several blocks north of Ground Zero, for some time afterward. Thus he deprived the Newspaper of Record of his immediate insights on the biggest architectural news story of modern times for nearly three weeks. Perhaps to compensate for this glaring lapse, he organized a special issue of *The New York Times Magazine* that presented his notions of how the site ought to be reconfigured, which was published the Sunday before the first anniversary of September 11.

Muschamp had been dismayed that several months earlier the LMDC and the Port Authority had selected the architectural and planning office Beyer Blinder Belle (BBB) to develop a master plan. Although that partnership had won universal praise for its exemplary restoration of Grand Central Station that began in 1990, the *Times* critic deemed BBB insufficiently adventurous for this assignment. Accordingly he invited many of his favorite practitioners, older figures of the New York avant-garde as well as younger trendsetters, to submit their own ideas and assigned parts of the project to them. The fact that these hypothetical schemes lacked even the most basic information that architects need to draw up design proposals—a budget and a functional program beyond vague designations (school, arts center, and the like)—seemed not to bother either Muschamp or his nominees. As Sagalyn writes in one of her rare overt expressions of disapproval:

> This was not city building. Architecture may be art and city building calls for artlike understanding of the fabric of a place, but a city is not a blank canvas to paint at will as Muschamp was advocating with his study project, most unrealistically....
>
> Irresponsibly, Muschamp had preemptively pronounced his personal opinion of what was likely to result before BBB had even drawn a single line. Did this belong in the news section of the paper? Where does the press cross the line between presenting the news to inform the public and aiming to become a player by advocating a particular vision—other than on the editorial page?

Yet this self-appointed planner was scarcely oblivious to urban design realpolitik (nor were the LMDC and the Port Authority, which swiftly withdrew the commission from BBB and announced an open competition to find a new planning firm). Immediately after Libeskind's master plan was chosen over Rafael Viñoly's proposal—the latter centered by a scaffold-like, smaller reiteration of the Twin Towers that Muschamp championed but that Pataki tactlessly likened to a pair of skeletons—the critic made an astonishing volte-face and wrote that the best scheme had won after all.

This aesthetic influence-peddling, whether in the back corridors of government, the salons of the powerful, or the nation's most prestigious newspaper, was nothing compared to the nonstop machinations of the pivotal figure in this tawdry drama, Silverstein, who before September 11 had been considered a fairly minor player and something of a bottom-fisher among the big-deal *machers* of the New York real estate establishment. Although Sagalyn's portrait of Silverstein accords with the general outlines of previously published reports, here he emerges even more unfavorably as his actions are recounted in greater detail than ever before, thanks to the author's extensive interviews and her informants' willingness to speak candidly about him (an indication of how much rancor he aroused). At the heart of the matter was Silverstein's unshakable determination that all ten million square feet of office space lost in the Twin Towers' collapse be replaced, a position driven by his desire to protect the maximum future profitability of his investment.

However, this did not accord with the changing economic realities of postmillennial Lower Manhattan, and his sheer stubbornness struck the New York City mayor Michael Bloomberg and the technocratic urbanists around him as fundamentally uninformed and misguided (to put it in the most polite terms). Sagalyn quotes Daniel Doctoroff, Bloomberg's deputy mayor for economic development and rebuilding, as pointing out that "Lower Manhattan before 9/11 had a growing residential population, but it had been losing worker population since 1970," even as the construction of the original World Trade Center was still underway. The changing demographic needs of this part of the city, Doctoroff said, "were swept under the rug in the wake of 9/11 by this kind of nostalgia for the World Trade Center and the tremendous emotion that existed."

The Bloomberg administration favored a varied mix of components with less emphasis on offices and more housing units, in line with the growing residential character of the Financial District, where many old commercial buildings that are no longer suitable for today's high-tech businesses had already been converted to apartments, often very costly ones, a trend that continued apace during the second decade of the millennium. But Silverstein's representatives (including Tighe) aggressively pressed his case for a full ten-million-square-foot build-out, and hammered home the questionable assertion that the boom-or-bust nature of New York City building cycles demanded readiness for the next inevitable upswing (this was before the international market meltdown of 2008). Conveniently omitted by the developer's team was the financial history of the World Trade Center. The complex was built during a recessionary period, and it took until the 1980s for it to finally turn a profit; it did so only because of the artificial life support of state government agencies that had been transplanted to the Twin Towers by New York governor Nelson Rockefeller, a brother of that quixotic scheme's mastermind, David Rockefeller, who held top positions at the Chase Manhattan Bank from 1957 to 1981.

Bloomberg and his advisers repeatedly tried to gain control of the beleaguered project and impose the focused leadership and purposeful direction it lacked. Their most ingenious attempt was a Solomonic solution advanced by Roy Bahat, then a twenty-four-year-old aide to Doctoroff, who suggested a swap of the land underneath Kennedy and LaGuardia airports—the city owns that real estate but the Port Authority runs the facilities on it—in return for the Trade Center acreage, owned by the Port Authority. This would have allowed the city to invoke eminent domain, cancel Silverstein's lease, and be done with him. Although the *Times* praised this as "the most creative idea to arise from the Lower Manhattan redevelopment process so far," the trade-off foundered not only because of the tangled economics of how evaluations for the respective assets would be calculated but also because it was stymied by officials who foresaw themselves losing power if the deal went through.

As is typical of such betrayals of the public trust, there was more than enough blame to go around. Sagalyn names

names, and they include Port Authority vice-chairman Charles Gargano, described by the author as "'a loyal Pataki soldier'... said to be riled by the swap proposal, a threat to his influence; he had already been 'a loser in a bid to control the [LMDC]'. In the end it was a political decision—for Governor Pataki." At that time Pataki harbored presidential ambitions and felt that his continuing involvement in rebuilding Ground Zero would elevate his national reputation. As a result of these and other complications, the swap died in June 2003.

Whatever one might think of Bloomberg's often high-handed approach to urbanism and civic governance, which tended to favor corporate interests at the expense of other concerns, there can be little doubt that he did a number of very good things for New York City during his long tenure as mayor and would have been a far better overseer of the World Trade Center redevelopment than any other major figure on the scene at that time. Among the institutions involved in the rebuilding, none is portrayed more critically by Sagalyn than the Port Authority, and rightly so. Its preference for investing in chancy real estate speculations instead of focusing on an overburdened transportation system and crumbling regional infrastructure remains a long-running scandal, and a thorough overhaul of that bistate agency would seem to be the only solution to correcting the abuses detailed so revealingly by Sagalyn.

High among other factors that greatly complicated the rebuilding of the Trade Center site were recent advances in

DNA verification methods. The conjunction of those new capacities with the 2001 catastrophe served as the basis for a thoughtful and solidly informed meditation, *Who Owns the Dead?: The Science and Politics of Death at Ground Zero* (2016) by Jay D. Aronson, a professor at Carnegie Mellon University and director of its Center for Human Rights Science. Because it is now easier than ever to identify human remains found at sites of mass disasters, expectations ran high among many bereaved families that they might reclaim some corporeal vestige of their dead relatives. It was once expected that those lost at sea would lie forever asleep in the deep, much as soldiers killed in foreign wars would be buried near where they fell. However, modern science has encouraged a broad belief that the retrieval of physical matter, no matter how tiny, is essential to attaining "closure"—that vaunted but elusive goal of contemporary grieving.

Fifteen years after the catastrophe, remains of 1,113 of the disaster's victims—or some 40 percent of the death toll—were still unidentified. At several points during the slow, painstaking, dignified, and respectful recovery process, officials announced that the search had been concluded, but family members who had not yet been given definitive physical proof demanded further forensic analysis. As it turned out, though, spot checks confirmed that minute amounts of residue from the victims were still discernible in the surrounding area, a finding that prompted an even more microscopic investigation, which in some areas went inch by inch through newly discovered concentrations of possible physical evidence. This renewed task was pursued with a vigilance that the participating experts vouchsafed was much more thorough than any they had witnessed before, and it verged on the exactitude of an archaeological dig. As a result, additional names were subsequently associated with the powdery particulate.

But to what end was this search increasingly obsessive? As Aronson writes:

> The thought of unidentified remains is unnerving, especially for a society that wants to believe it has the technical capacity to provide some measure of certainty in an uncertain world. . . . It is ironic, then, that the individualization of the victims of the World Trade Center has made it more politically palatable for the US government to engage in a seemingly perpetual war that has created innumerable casualties in Afghanistan, Iraq, Pakistan, Yemen, and elsewhere.

The truth of the matter, though, was that no one—the dead of September 11, their survivors, or the American public at large—would be allowed to rest in peace.

18

CHRISTIAN DE PORTZAMPARC / RAFAEL VIÑOLY / ALEXANDER GORLIN

THE SKYLINE OF New York went through a century and a quarter of increasingly dramatic changes after the completion of Bradford Gilbert's steel-framed, eleven-story Tower Building of 1889, arguably the city's first skyscraper, which was demolished in 1914. But during the second decade of the twenty-first century a strange and sudden transformation altered New York's character radically. Although a rash of so-called sliver towers emerged in Manhattan during the 1980s, often on midblock sites that exploited loopholes in zoning laws, none of them made a notable impact on the city's vertical profile. But that began to change when New York became a magnet for international capital on a scale unprecedented in its history.

Since New York's founding in the early seventeenth century as a Dutch trading outpost, most of its residents have been renters rather than owners. From the pre-Revolutionary period until World War II, tenants were uniformly given three months' notice of annual rent increases on February 1 (known as Rent Day). Many then sought cheaper deals, and when all leases expired on May 1 (called Moving Day), as many as a million residents changed homes. Beginning in 2014, another, more specialized real estate frenzy took hold in the city, signaling a recovery from the collapse of financial markets in 2008, and its most visible manifestations involved some of the world's richest people. In December 2014 a long-anticipated threshold was crossed when a duplex penthouse atop the French architect Christian de Portzamparc's One57 condominium of 2009–2014, built by the Extell Development Company on West 57th Street between Sixth and Seventh Avenues, sold for $100,471,452.77 (see Illustration 18a). In the same year, seven more apartments in that building changed hands for between $32 million and $56 million each, which together accounted for more than a third of New York's two dozen biggest residential transactions of 2014. In January 2015 a duplex there fetched $90 million.

Portzamparc's tower of monetary power stands two blocks south of Central Park, at the epicenter of Manhattan's densest concentration of top-of-the-line apartment construction since Fifth and Park Avenues were built up between the two world wars. The block directly west of One57 awaits the completion of another Extell venture, Nordstrom Tower of 2014–2019, designed by Adrian Smith (architect of the world's tallest structure, the Burj Khalifa of 2003–2010 in Dubai) and Gordon Gill. Comprising a branch of the Nordstrom's fashion retailer at street level, a hotel above the store, and condos on the uppermost stories—unobstructed park views commence at 225 feet, hence this sequence—it rises next to and over Henry Hardenbergh's Art Students League of 1891–1892 and will become the city's tallest residential building at 1,775 feet when it opens.

Nordstrom's effortful piggybacking was made possible not only by creative engineering but also by the developer's purchase of the art school's air rights—that is, the titular transfer of empty vertical space above nearby buildings never used to the full extent permissible by zoning laws. Such stratagems are an essential part of the complex legal and economic equation (what the skyscraper historian Carol Willis has termed "invisible Monopoly," after the board game) that has allowed these super-tall, super-thin towers to multiply in Midtown North, as planners and police call the neighborhood.

Several similar towers are underway around 23rd Street near Madison Square and in Lower Manhattan, but the rarefied calculus of this niche market hinges on location. Thus, even though seasoned New Yorkers have long deemed Central Park South somewhat socially marginal—during the 1980s brokers dubbed it "Mistress Row" for the many kept women with apartments there—or the province of out-of-towners who frequented its fancy hotels (the Plaza, the St. Moritz, Essex House) and touristy restaurants (Trader Vic's, Rumpelmayer's, Mickey Mantle's—which are now gone), foreign buyers still consider it the golden core of the Big Apple.

On the same block as One57, SHoP Architects' 111 West 57th Street will have the dubious distinction of being the world's slenderest building, thanks to the extreme contrast between its tiny 60-foot-wide base and attenuated 1,421-foot height. By way of comparison, the base-to-height ratio of Minoru Yamasaki's World Trade Center was 1:7; 111 West 57th Street's will be 1:23. Like both One57 and Nordstrom, 111 will have a glass curtain wall, and its full-floor apartments will all afford views north to Central Park panoramas. Despite its being a technical feat of engineering—the building is heavily weighted at its top to stabilize it in high winds—111 will be an annoyingly intrusive and yet strangely elusive urban presence, the architectural equivalent of Chauncey Gardner, Peter Sellers's here-but-not-here character in Hal Ashby's film *Being There* (1979).

The two financial prototypes for this new breed of ultra-luxury towers were David Childs and Mustafa Kemal Abadan's Time Warner Center of 2000–2003 on Columbus Circle and Robert A. M. Stern's 15 Central Park West of 2005–2008, both a few blocks north of 57th Street. These condominiums were specifically designed to attract an emergent class of plutocrats who might have difficulty buying into Manhattan's most exclusive cooperative apartment buildings, whose boards of directors, unaccountable to antidiscrimination laws, routinely blackballed Jews, blacks, gays, single women, show-business performers, or anyone whose source of wealth they considered less than respectable.

The 1990s witnessed the high-tech, telecommunications, and dot-com booms, the rise of hedge funds, the privatization of the former Soviet Union's natural resources, and the ascendance of China's state-controlled capitalism. Together, these developments radically altered standards of private wealth worldwide. In the top bracket of Manhattan real estate there were said to be only fifty or so extremely desirable apartment houses, symptomatic of the oddly persistent scarcity of premium housing in America's financial hub. Here was a gaping hole at the high end of the market begging to be filled, and if nature abhors a vacuum, no less do New York real estate developers hate missing out on a sure source of big money.

Although major fortunes have increasingly trumped religious, racial, or social biases, some Manhattan co-ops require purchasers to have liquid assets equal to many multiples of an apartment's price, which has limited sales of them to an even smaller portion of the so-called one percent. If you buy a co-op, you buy shares in the building; if you want to leave, it is up to you to sell the shares to someone who can win approval of the board of directors. Conversely, if a condominium board turns down a sale it must buy back the apartment, an effective deterrent to rejection. Thus the offspring of deposed African dictators are as welcome at condos as Social Register scions, and this ease of access has attracted shady characters who would never get past the boards of the toniest old-guard citadels.

Well after 15 Central Park West was completed, high-priced resales there continued to dominate the Big Deals column in *The New York Times* Sunday real estate section, which celebrated each week's largest residential property closings. Until the $100 million blockbuster at One57 in 2014, the most expensive apartment in town had been 15 Central Park West's penthouse, which the former Citigroup CEO Sanford Weill sold in 2011 to a daughter of a Russian oligarch for $88 million. Weill more than doubled his investment four years after buying the full-floor flat for a then-record $42.4 million. Nothing succeeds commercially like mimicry of success, and Stern's limestone-clad, neotraditional design for that building was closely modeled after the 1920s and 1930s apartment houses of Rosario Candela, the Sicilian-born architect whose uncommonly capacious, generously detailed apartments are widely judged the city's most coveted. (The second-costliest New York residential transfer in 2014 amounted to $71 million at Candela's legendary 740 Park Avenue.) Stern's 15 Central Park West has been termed "the Limestone Jesus" because this $950 million endeavor was seen by many to have miraculously risen from the dead after the 2008 crash killed off several other grandiose development schemes.

The stupendous financial success of 15 Central Park West has brought its architect many more apartment building commissions, including 220 Central Park South, a condominium two blocks due north of Nordstrom—so due that the buildings' respective developers waged a costly legal battle because 220 would have blocked Nordstrom's park views. The lawsuit was settled when each party agreed to shift its tower—Stern's to the west, Smith and Gill's to the east—and Extell received $194 million from the builder at 220 Central

Park South for an adjoining Central Park South parking garage, demolition of which allowed construction to proceed. The two broader elevations of Stern's building face east–west rather than north–south, but at a mere 950 feet it will rank only tenth-highest among Manhattan skyscrapers. This late-Deco pastiche in some ways is preferable to the other new condos crowding the area, which, *faute de mieux*, indicates the generally low architectural state of New York's postmillennial housing for the super-rich.

The Manhattan high-rise that had everyone talking when it seemed to materialize almost overnight during the summer of 2014 is 432 Park Avenue, the skinny eighty-nine-story spire that soars above the northwest corner of East 56th Street and Park on the site of the old Drake Hotel (see Illustration 18b). It was designed by the New York–based architect Rafael Viñoly, and became the highest residential structure in the Western Hemisphere at 1,397 feet, as well as New York City's second-tallest building (after David Childs's One World Trade Center). Actually, it was the loftiest by twenty-eight feet in terms of habitable space, since a broadcasting mast accounts for the uppermost 408 feet of the Childs tower.

Many observers have reported being bemused, not to say unnerved, by the Viñoly building's strange ubiquitousness. Visible throughout all five boroughs and as far away as Long Island and New Jersey, the tower startles both visitors and natives with its looming omnipresence, and seems to follow you around like a bad conscience. One doesn't hear much about 432 Park's design for the good reason that artistic niceties are almost beside the point in the mathematical conjuring that brought it and its peers into being. You could even say this structure resembles a three-dimensional balance sheet more than a fully articulated architectural façade. And while Stern clings to a passé Postmodernism—his Manhattan jobs are drenched in a gooey nostalgia tinged with outer-borough longing akin to Gershwin via Woody Allen—Viñoly hews closely to the reductive aesthetic of High Modernism.

Rafael Viñoly Beceiro was born in 1944 in Montevideo, Uruguay. His father was a movie director with twenty-eight films to his credit, his mother a mathematics teacher. After receiving degrees in architecture from the University of Buenos Aires in 1968 and 1969, he worked for the better part of the next decade in Argentina. His early activities there became a sudden controversy in 2003 when, on the morning the master planner for the rebuilding of the World Trade Center was to be selected, *The Wall Street Journal* published a front-page story recounting that Viñoly had worked for the murderous right-wing military junta that sponsored the FIFA World Cup stadium of 1976–1978 in Mendoza, Argentina. Although Viñoly was indeed a member of the design team for that arena, he immigrated to the United States the year it was completed, and set up his own office in Manhattan in 1983. However, the eleventh-hour *Journal* story may have been damaging enough to tip the scales in favor of the other finalist, Daniel Libeskind, who won the coveted Ground Zero commission.

This was a rare setback for Viñoly, but not his only case

of bad publicity. His 20 Fenchurch Street skyscraper of 2009–2014 in London's financial district—nicknamed "the Walkie-Talkie"—acted as a concave mirror that focused hotspots of up to 243 degrees Fahrenheit on its immediate surroundings. A similar problem also occurred at the architect's Vdara Hotel of 2006–2009 in Las Vegas, where what workers called "the Vdara death ray" was strong enough to melt plastic cups and burn hair. In both instances the buildings' surfaces were given a protective film to reduce this solar effect, which Viñoly blamed on global warming.

Although less laser-like in its environmental impact, the exterior of Viñoly's 432 Park Avenue imparts a graphic feel accentuated by the flatness of the building's four identical sides, as well as the bold contrast between its dark glass windows (six large square panes per story) and white concrete panels that frame the Minimalist fenestration. But what most sets this oddly disturbing composition apart is the way it shoots straight upward to its full, vertiginous height, with none of the horizontal setbacks or vertical indentations that define the classic Art Deco apartment houses Stern cribs for his pastiches.

Together with the Viñoly building's relatively small footprint (ninety-three feet square, about one quarter the length of a football field), this uninterrupted ascent was made possible by city regulations that waive upper-story "wedding cake" setback requirements—instituted in 1916 to prevent overbuilt Lower Manhattan streets from turning into lightless, airless canyons—but only if a building occupies no more than one quarter of its lot. Yet when prices for Manhattan residences in prime locations started going through the roof, it hardly seemed wasteful to leave 75 percent of a plot empty on a $1.25 billion speculation like 432 Park. Among these proportionally attenuated but financially overloaded towers, design elements not directly tied to profit were often downgraded or eliminated as overall costs climbed. For example, Portzamparc poetically predicted that the rippling glass exterior he initially planned for One57 would evoke a cascading waterfall. As executed, however, the flat surface of the building's variously blue, gray, and silver panes fades into a pixelated blur even from a short distance. With these mathematically generated super-spires, it's best to paraphrase Mae West: "Architecture has nothing to do with it."

Architectural prestige, however, had a great deal to do with why Portzamparc was chosen for this assignment in the first place, specifically his being awarded the the Pritzker Architecture Prize in 1994, just before his fiftieth birthday, reportedly thanks to the strenuous electioneering of Ada Louise Huxtable, the longtime *New York Times* architecture critic and Pritzker juror. Portzamparc's selection was surprising given his relative lack of built works, and was based largely on the City of Music of 1984–1995 in Paris, a lesser component of President François Mitterrand's Grands Projets, the series of eight major public works that more famously include I. M. Pei's Louvre Pyramid and Gae Aulenti's Musée d'Orsay.

Portzamparc was born in Casablanca in 1944, the son of a peripatetic French army officer. He began studying architecture at the École des Beaux-Arts in Paris in 1962, amid what his countrymen now nostalgically call *les trente glorieuses*—the thirty glorious years from 1945 to 1975 bracketed by the end of World War II and the OPEC oil embargo, a period of economic growth that saw France recoup much of the international prestige it lost with its humiliating defeat and occupation by Nazi Germany. Despite that general postwar optimism, the young Portzamparc questioned whether he wanted to become an architect at all, and it took him seven years to receive his degree.

Upon graduation he did not work as a design architect but became involved with sociologically oriented research groups that investigated urban housing patterns and practices. He applied ideas that he learned through direct contact with residents to his first major built project, Les Hautes Formes of 1975–1979, a six-building, 209-unit cluster of social housing sponsored by the city of Paris in the 13th arrondissement. The scheme struck a sensible balance between then-fashionable Postmodernist and older Modernist approaches, which has saved it from now seeming as dated as contemporaneous Postmodern housing estates near Paris by Ricardo Bofill, Manuel Nuñez, and others. Portzamparc opened his own architectural office in 1980, but his roster of seventeen completed works over the ensuing three-and-a-half decades hardly seems as impressive as the output of most other Pritzker winners. Yet so potent is the imprimatur of that prize that Portzamparc—still not a household name beyond architecture experts—was deemed desirable enough by One57's developers to serve as a lure for international buyers.

The convergent forces that have shaped Manhattan's super-tall, super-thin towers were examined in "Sky High and the Logic of Luxury," an illuminating exhibition held in 2013 at the Skyscraper Museum in New York just as these remarkable mutants were beginning to drastically alter the cityscape. If anything, this prescient overview curated by Carol Willis came a bit too prematurely to fully benefit from the dawning public awareness that a singular departure was upon us. As she wrote for the exhibition's wall texts:

Beginning around 2012, sales of condos in ultra-luxury buildings reached $8,000–$10,000 per sq.ft. and in some cases even higher. These records have set a new standard that developers use to raise the budget for project expenses. The "logic of luxury" is the idea that high development costs for a project are good business strategy if they can produce extraordinary profits....

Expensive land and air rights, "starchitect" design fees, special engineering and construction, extra-high ceilings, and abundant amenities all factor in a simple math that stratospheric sale prices justify....

Sophisticated engineering and advances in material strengths have made these spindles possible, but it is the excited market for premium Manhattan real estate that is driving both heights and prices skyward. Predicated on Central Park views and other exceptional vistas, these aeries appeal to a distinct clientele to whom developers direct their marketing psychology.

Willis is not the only analyst to draw direct connections between the sudden emergence of this construction binge and the workings of high finance. Now more New York real estate than ever is held by absentee owners, and in at least five large Manhattan condominiums most units are not primary residences. Although many such pieds-à-terre are doubtless used by Americans, they are most attractive to foreign nationals eager to secure a foothold in the US in the event of trouble in their homelands. International capital flight has thus been the decisive impetus in this booming sector of the New York property market, as people from all over the world seek a relatively stable haven for themselves and their assets.

In February 2015, *The New York Times* published "Towers of Secrecy," a five-part investigative series by Louise Story and Stephanie Saul that focused on condominium buyers from four countries (India, Malaysia, Mexico, and Russia). They revealed how clandestine ownership of apartments in the city's most expensive buildings is often abetted through shell companies, to say nothing of a veritable industry of New York City facilitators. For example, the reporters found that a majority of apartments in a half-dozen luxury condos were nominally owned through entities that are often obscure, including One57 (77 percent), Time Warner Center (64 percent), and 15 Central Park West (58 percent). And 58 percent of New York City condominiums are paid for entirely in cash, which makes buyers more untraceable because no mortgage documentation is involved. As Story and Saul write:

> An entire chain of people involved in high-end real estate sales—lawyers, accountants, title brokers, escrow agents, real estate agents, condo boards and building workers—often operate with blinders on. As Rudy Tauscher, a former manager of condos at Time Warner, said: "The building doesn't know where the money is coming from. We're not interested."

A report jointly issued in February 2015 by Wealth-X (a self-described "private wealth consultancy") and Sotheby's International Real Estate confirmed that New York had become the world's favorite refuge for second-home buyers from abroad (London was number two, though that status is now uncertain because of Brexit). The largest proportion of non-American purchasers of residential real estate in the city were British, contradicting conventional wisdom that Russians and Chinese were dominant. Although *The New York Times* reported that in the year ending in March 2014 Chinese buyers accounted for $22 billion in real estate sales in the US—almost a quarter of all purchases by foreigners— they prefer suburban houses to metropolitan apartments.

According to one Sotheby's broker, "New York City is the concrete jungle, much like Beijing or Shanghai. Long Island offers fresh air, no pollution, the waterfront." Whether such strong foreign interest can be sustained given the xenophobic worldview of the Trump administration and its imposition of travel bans remains to be seen.

The stratospheric amounts at stake in these Manhattan towers perhaps can best be understood by comparison with today's contemporary art market, where multimillion-dollar paintings and sculptures have become favored instruments in the global transfer of vast and largely unregulated sums. The more expensive the object, the more money can be shifted internationally in one transaction, with the artworks themselves—mere markers to some degree—making a useful stopover at the Geneva Freeport, the tax-free air entrepôt in Switzerland used by dealers and collectors to reduce or eliminate import duties and value-added taxes. However, much as the new super-tall New York condos may serve that same general purpose, these are no works of art. If, as Goethe posited, architecture is frozen music, then these buildings are vertical money.

Interestingly, there's a clear architectural disparity between the bloated behemoths of Midtown North and the smaller, livelier, but scarcely inexpensive condominiums clustered around the High Line two miles to the southwest in Chelsea. Unlike the rebuilt 57th Street corridor, which quickly became known as Billionaires' Row—where city-planning loopholes have been cunningly exploited to capitalize on the immense profits to be reaped from supersized condominiums—areas adjacent to the High Line have not been "upzoned." Higher buildings are largely confined to nearby north–south avenues.

The enormous popular success of the High Line and the arty cachet of its environs have made this a much sought after neighborhood among affluent young creative sorts. The city's principal contemporary art galleries now crowd the trestle in the West 10s and 20s, and the Whitney Museum of American Art saw its attendance figures triple after it moved into its new home at the southern end of the linear park in 2015. As a result, developers have been willing to sponsor architecturally inventive schemes in West Chelsea to appeal to an audience more aesthetically sophisticated than the cautious foreign investors who gravitate to blue-chip Midtown North.

The art world favorite Annabelle Selldorf has designed both galleries and apartments near the High Line. However, developers favor Pritzker Prize winners for the implicit cultural validation they bring to a project, as Portzamparc did when Extell hired him to design One57. The Pritzker laureates Shigeru Ban and Jean Nouvel have built condominiums near the High Line, and one of the last works designed by the award's 2004 recipient, Zaha Hadid, is her thirty-nine-unit condo of 2013–2018 at 28th Street. This swoopingly streamlined eleven-story composition—in a retro-futuristic style—rivaled prices achieved in Midtown North with a penthouse that had a reported $35 million asking price. And that building's developer, Related Companies, enlisted yet another Pritzker honoree, Rem Koolhaas of the firm OMA, to do a condo next to the High Line at West 18th Street.

In tandem with all this high-priced development, New York City housing since the turn of the millennium has become far less affordable (especially for young people, except for those who work in financial services, information technology, or other highly lucrative fields). In 2016 the median price paid for apartments in the city rose to a new high of $1.2 million, with the median for condos reaching $3.1 million. Gone are the days when aspiring writers, artists, actors, dancers, and other low-earning bohemians could count on finding a solo dwelling in Manhattan. Apart from the new-found fashionableness of Brooklyn—whose hippest sections are now prohibitively expensive—even the remotest reaches of the five boroughs are being gentrified, and longtime tenants sometimes find themselves priced out of their neighborhoods.

To combat this trend, New York State Senator Brad Hoylman of Manhattan in 2014 said he would sponsor a bill to impose a property tax surcharge on nonprimary residences in New York City valued at $5 million and higher, which one study says could generate some $665 million to subsidize low- and middle-income housing. Predictably, the city's powerful real estate industry—largely controlled by a few dozen family-owned firms, some with long-standing ties to politicians of both major parties—vigorously opposed the idea. Nonetheless, this brave initiative was surely more equitable than incentives given to developers of Manhattan's new safe-deposit boxes in the sky. As Charles V. Bagli reported in the *Times* in February 2015, under New York City's Property Tax Exemption Program, known as 421a, the $100 million apartment at One57 qualified for a 95 percent tax cut worth about $360,000. (Such abatements decrease over time and usually expire in twenty-five years or less.)

In return for these breaks, developers were required to create housing for low-income tenants, but fewer than 10 percent of new dwellings in the city have been earmarked as such. Some of those subsidized units are located in the new luxury towers themselves (though in a few instances are accessible only through a separate entrance that activists have scorned as "the poor door"). Developers can also support off-site affordable housing in order to qualify apartments for 421a status, as Extell did with One57 by underwriting sixty-six such units in the Bronx. However, in his 2015 State of the City address, Mayor Bill de Blasio asserted that "the city has for decades let developers write their own rules.... Sometimes projects included affordable housing... but far too often, they did not."

De Blasio identified six neighborhoods outside Manhattan where developers would be compelled to build 80,000 units of affordable housing over the next decade, and twice that number of market-rate properties in general. In postmillennial New York, no one has it as bad as the growing homeless population, which between 2006 and 2014 increased by 93 percent to more than 60,000, a good-sized city in itself.

By the end of 2017 that number had ballooned to 76,000, a 4 percent increase over the preceding year. Appropriately enough considering those appalling figures, the finest apartment building completed in New York City during this marathon of hyper-expensive construction is Alexander Gorlin's Boston Road Supportive Housing of 2013–2016, which was created specifically to help alleviate the homeless crisis (see Illustration 18c). In several respects this twelve-story, 154-unit structure in the gritty Morrisania section of the South Bronx is far from the aeries of Billionaires' Row and the avant-garde condos around the High Line. It fairly jumps out of its drab surroundings thanks to its crisp colorful design, with a strikingly fresh, deceptively simple, but carefully composed façade that mixes and mashes bright metal panels in syncopated rhythms that make you wonder why so many New York City buildings have to be so boring.

Easily visible on the southern horizon from the upper stories of Gorlin's building is the inescapable 432 Park Avenue. Yet although these two residences were erected with vastly disparate budgets and entirely different inhabitants in mind, the notable contrast in quality between Viñoly's magic beanstalk and Gorlin's pragmatic gem proves that America's ever-widening gap between rich and poor is neither inevitable nor unbridgeable when it comes to architecture. Boston Road was conceived not for society's most privileged members but for its least—once-homeless elderly people, survivors of HIV/AIDS, and the growing ranks of the urban poor. Still, beauty is as beauty does, and the strong social underpinnings of Boston Road give it a significance beyond mere good looks.

Gorlin knows both components of this equation better than most of his fellow American professionals. Born to a middle-class family in Queens, New York, in 1955, he studied architecture as an undergraduate at Cooper Union during the mid-1970s. He went on to get a master's degree from Yale, which exposed him to a more patrician view of architecture. After stints working for I. M. Pei and Kohn Pedersen Fox, Gorlin founded his own New York office in 1987. On the one hand, he does a thriving business in clean-lined, exquisitely detailed Modernist houses and interiors for the rich, as well as aesthetically ambitious synagogues for wealthy Jewish congregations. On the other hand, he feels a moral obligation to do less remunerative but more socially beneficial work, and subsidizes the time he spends on such undertakings with the proceeds from his more lucrative commissions, like an architectural Robin Hood. Thus a substantial part of his practice has been devoted to collaborations with Breaking Ground—a private organization founded (as Common Ground) in 1990 to address homelessness with housing that reintegrates residents into the community rather than simply sheltering them. This initiative seems a particularly vital contribution now that new publicly financed dwellings are a thing of the past.

The quality of design Gorlin has achieved with the Boston Road Supportive Housing, for which he had a very limited construction budget of $30 million, or about $325 per square foot, approximately half what luxury Manhattan condos were built for at that time, is extraordinary by any standard. Boston Road's most arresting physical aspect is its handsome exterior. Unlike almost all other mid-block buildings in big cities, which usually have unfinished-looking sides and backs, each elevation of this L-shaped configuration is as fully surfaced and detailed as the lively street façade. The structure is clad in dark gray brick, a perfect foil for the primary and secondary hues Gorlin chose for the metal panels between windows. The interiors are equally successful and show how much can be achieved with very little. The apartments—all 350-foot studios with a private, windowless bath and integral kitchen—are virtually indistinguishable from a new breed of "micro-apartments" that began appearing around the same time in New York in response to skyrocketing real estate values. At one of them, Camel Place on Manhattan's East 27th Street, a 360-square-foot studio rented in 2015 for $2,920 a month, as opposed to $550 here (where fees are gauged on ability to pay).

In addition to Boston Road's shared amenities—which include an exercise room with fitness machines on a par with commercial gyms, a bike room, a computer center, and a laundry room—the facility contains ample common areas for its full array of social services. Among them are a resident nurse, a twelve-step program, nutritional and weight-loss guidance, career counseling, and discussion groups, all aimed at propelling residents into self-sufficient lives among the larger community. As other Breaking Ground facilities have demonstrated, these all-important support and monitoring activities can prevent recidivism to a remarkable extent. Boston Road's model of a mixed population of former vagrants alongside low-income workers is an important step forward in destigmatizing homelessness, and the proximity of employed residents with others just off the streets likewise provides a potentially motivating example of self-help.

None of the demographic shifts reflected in these New York City housing patterns, high and low, is accidental. During his twelve years in office, Mayor Bloomberg repeatedly declared his intention to make New York—long renowned for turning generations of poor immigrants into middle-class taxpayers—into what the political blogger Alex Pareene has characterized as the billionaire businessman's "perfectly engineered technocratic dream city." As Bloomberg said in 2013, "If we could get every billionaire around the world to move here it would be a godsend." In fact, he believes that economic inequality in the city is attributable not to growing poverty among the many but to burgeoning wealth among the few:

> The reason [the income gap] is so big is that at the higher end we've been able to do something that none of these other cities can do, and that is attract a lot of the very wealthy from around the country and around the world. They are the ones that pay a lot of the taxes. They're the ones that spend a lot of money in the stores and restaurants and create a big chunk of our economy.

And we take the tax revenues from those people to help people throughout the entire rest of the spectrum.

Such persistent Reagan-era fantasies of trickle-down economics aside, Bloomberg's brand of wealth redistribution would seem more heavily weighted toward plutocrats than paupers. A dispassionate but ultimately critical analysis of the three-term mayor's grand vision for Darwinian upscale urbanism can be found in *Bloomberg's New York: Class and Governance in the Luxury City* by the anthropologist Julian Brash, which received insufficient attention when it was published in 2011. Brash shows that the mayor imagined the city

as a place of competition, elite sociality, cosmopolitanism, and luxury, populated by ambitious, creative, hardworking, and intelligent innovators. . . . The Bloomberg Way constituted an effort to establish the dominance of the ascendant postindustrial elite vis-à-vis other social groupings in New York City.

This had, according to its critics on both the left and the right, "deleterious effects . . . on small businesses, the middle class, and taxpayers."

This race to erect ever-higher, ever-more-luxurious Manhattan condominiums recalls the early-twentieth-century competition to win New York City bragging rights for the world's tallest building, as one record-breaking tower after another rose in dizzying succession. Yet not one of New York's postmillennial claimants to that lineage possesses an iota of the aesthetic élan that distinguished those early skyscrapers, internationally renowned as America's signal contribution to modern architectural form—for example, the Woolworth, Chrysler, and Empire State buildings. In contrast, the smokestack-like protuberances that now disrupt the skyline of midtown Manhattan signify the steadily widening international gap between the unimaginably rich and the unconscionably poor. Those of us who believe that architecture invariably (and often unintentionally) embodies the values of those who sponsor it will look upon these etiolated oddities less with wonder over their cunning mechanics than with revulsion over the larger, even uglier machinations they more accurately represent.

19

MAYA LIN

OLDER ARTISTS WHO struggle futilely for recognition often envy those who achieve great success at an early age. But never being able to surpass or even equal a youthful triumph can be a cruel fate for those who believe you are only as good as your latest work. This is the potentially daunting reality that Maya Lin has lived with since she skyrocketed to fame at the age of twenty-one, when during her senior year as a Yale undergraduate architecture major she won the open design competition that resulted in the most influential public monument created since World War II: the Vietnam Veterans Memorial of 1981–1982 in Washington, D.C. (see Illustration 19a).

Although Lin's rigorously abstract scheme—devoid of the representational elements and allegorical imagery typical of war monuments since ancient times—provoked great controversy in some quarters when it was chosen from among the 1,421 contest entries, her powerful melding of the period's two main avant-garde sculptural developments, Minimalism and Earth Art, fundamentally recast popular notions of commemorative architecture. This symmetrical composition of two wedge-shaped, vertically paneled, polished black granite walls, set at a 125-degree angle to each other and sunk ten feet below grade at their deepest, is inscribed with the names of 58,307 American military personnel who died as a result of the Vietnam War between 1957 and 1975.

The sloping walkway parallel to this 493-foot-long expanse of stone begins at street level and then reaches its nadir at the monument's midpoint. The transit along the declivity gives one the palpable impression of being swamped by a tide of mortality as the rows of names rise higher and higher above one's head. Then, as the pedestrian path begins to ascend at the structure's midpoint, the opposite occurs, the sensation ebbing and abating as one reaches the flat expanse of the National Mall once again, filled with relief that the flood of names has finally ended. It is not uncommon to see visitors in tears after they have negotiated this symbolic abyss, a journey made all the more unnerving because of the unconsoling directness of the experience. However, the stunning physical immediacy of Lin's design could not be conveyed in preparatory drawings or models, and thus its visceral impact was unanticipated by many until the monument was completed.

The adage that success has many fathers but failure is an orphan certainly pertains to those involved with the Vietnam Veterans Memorial commission, although the person most responsible for its triumphant outcome—the artist herself—has never tried to arrogate sole credit for what became a hugely complicated and highly politicized process. Robert Doubek, who served as the executive director of the Vietnam Veterans Memorial Fund (the nonprofit organization created in 1979 to raise money for the monument's construction), in 2015 published a heartfelt memoir of the struggle to bring this patriotic dream to fruition, and he was not at all reticent in aggrandizing the part he played. As the definite article in his subtitle suggests, *Creating the Vietnam Veterans Memorial: The Inside Story* is not only a first-person but also a one-sided account of this frequently contentious saga.

Nonetheless, for all its flaws and self-serving paybacks, this is a valuable contribution to the memorial's historiography, above all in Doubek's portrayal of the conflicting forces that vied for supremacy. We get a vivid sense of the emotions Lin's design aroused among those who felt her scheme was disrespectful to the memory of the fallen because of its uncompromising abstraction and the way it is dug into the earth—a grave, a pit, a latrine, detractors charged—rather than physically elevated to a position of high honor.

Doubek admits that he was no fan of Lin's design as it emerged from the crowd of other submissions during the selection process. "[Her] sketches and drawings were very amateurish," he writes, "and the black shapes said nothing to me. 'What the hell is that?' I had thought." A very different reaction came from the West Point–trained Jack Wheeler, co-founder (with another former soldier, Jan Scruggs) and chairman of the Vietnam Veterans Memorial Fund, who instantly declared, "It's a work of genius." Doubek still didn't get it.

"I had anticipated a messiah emerging from the mists of competition-land," he recalls of his first meeting with Lin. "But she didn't have a lot to say and didn't seem to know or care much about us. I felt like I had let a genie out of the bottle only to have the genie chill out." Things between them never improved greatly, and in the book's postscript the author sourly notes that it was only in 2007 that "Lin for the first time expressed thanks to me and the others with VVMF," oblivious to why it may have taken her so long. But Doubek's obtuseness was far from the worst adversity Lin faced, as she endured vicious sexist and racist attacks from those outraged that an Asian woman—a "gook," many openly said—should determine how the Vietnam War was memorialized for the ages.

Concerted objections to Lin's design among veterans' groups led to the addition of a naturalistic bronze statue, Frederick Hart's *The Three Soldiers*, which depicts a trio of zombielike combatants who exhibit the so-called thousand-yard stare of battle-hardened warriors. Unveiled a year after the main memorial's completion, this kitschy tableau was at least placed far enough away from the great earthwork to inflict minimum damage. Not surprisingly, Hart's hyper-masculine lineup spurred feminists in turn to demand yet another sculptural supplement to the site, which resulted in the Vietnam Women's Memorial (1993), a bronze figural group by Glenna Goodacre that shows three servicewomen tending to a wounded GI in the attitudes of an overcrowded but still male-centered *Pietà*.

The pervasive influence of Lin's masterwork has been repeatedly demonstrated in a period when traditional forms of architecture and sculpture have come to seem wholly inadequate in memorializing events once deemed unimaginable, most clearly the attack on the World Trade Center in 2001. Michael Arad and Peter Walker's National September 11 Memorial on the site of that catastrophe reinterprets several of Lin's concepts in highly original ways. So as not to become architecture's Lady of Perpetual Mourning, she has turned down all but three subsequent offers to design memorials, including that at Ground Zero. (The other two commemorative commissions she accepted were the Civil Rights Memorial of 1989 in Montgomery, Alabama, and the Women's Table of 1993 at Yale, which was commissioned in 1989 to mark twenty years of coeducation at her alma mater.) She has promised that her final effort in that vein will be What Is Missing?, which is intended to raise awareness of species extinction and protection.

Lin turned instead to environmental sculptures, as well as to a smaller number of modestly scaled buildings that have led some to underestimate her degree of professional ambition. Yet in contrast to architecture as many men in the profession still would define it—the bigger, costlier, and showier the better—her meditative view of the building art provides a means for expressing poetic impulses about humanity's place in the natural, rather than man-made, environment. Indeed,

Lin's steadfast determination to ignore the corruptions of modern publicity—that fatal addiction of postmillennial culture, signified in her profession by the hideous neologism "starchitect"—has been among her most important qualities.

It could be said that such indifference is easy for someone whose place in architectural history is already secure. But the blatant degree to which some of Lin's colleagues in the profession, female as well as male, have fallen in with the contemporary celebrity industry offers a cautionary contrast. When Jerry Seinfeld was once asked how he could ever possibly exceed the phenomenal success of his eponymous TV sitcom, which ended in 1998, he replied in words that echo Lin's attitude: "There's only one way to top it. And that's to remain an artist and not a 'star.'"

Maya Ying Lin was born in 1959 to culturally sophisticated and professionally accomplished Chinese immigrants in Athens, Ohio, where her parents—who met as students at the University of Washington—moved that year to take up posts at Ohio University. Her mother, Julia Ming-hui Chang Lin, was a poet and scholar of Chinese literature. Her father, Henry Huan Lin, a renowned studio potter, founded the school's ceramics program and later became the dean of its College of Fine Arts. His older half sister, Lin Huiyin, China's first female architect, married the architect Liang Sicheng, known as the father of modern architecture in his country. Liang, who studied at the University of Pennsylvania under the Classicist Paul Cret (as did his exact contemporary Louis Kahn), maintained close ties to the West, and after World War II served as China's representative on the architectural advisory committee that oversaw the design of the United Nations headquarters in New York. His posthumously published *Chinese Architecture: A Pictorial History* (1984) remains the basic English-language introduction to that subject.

Maya Lin's more distant antecedents were no less distinguished, as was revealed in a 2016 episode of the PBS series *Finding Your Roots*, with Henry Louis Gates Jr., in which the Harvard historian showed her a copy of a scroll that purportedly traces the Lin family's origins directly back to her ninety-ninth great-grandfather in 1092 BCE. Gates also identified one of her maternal great-grandmothers, Ye Deyi (born 1885), a gynecologist and pediatrician who was among China's first female physicians. Lin's self-assurance in entering a field still dominated by men doubtless owes much to her parents' encouragement, but it is hard not to wonder if genetics also played a significant part.

Her gift for the sympathetic placement of architecture within a landscape is of a piece with her strong sculptural instincts, and most evident in her work at Haley Farm, the 157-acre rural campus of the Children's Defense Fund in northeastern Tennessee. Her two buildings there, though quite different from each other, are nonetheless alike in their thoughtful siting, humane scale, humble materials, and appropriateness to their function, and symbolically evoke the enclave's purpose as a training and conference center for young community activists of color. Her first project on the property—the Langston Hughes Library of 1999—was a remodeling of an 1860s barn of a form particular to the region: a rectangular shed raised one story above the ground, atop a considerably smaller pair of grain-storage cribs composed of horizontally stacked logs. (A similar top-heavy configuration is seen in Scandinavian folk architecture.) Lin treated the existing building as a precious historic artifact, but to support the significant added weight of heavily laden bookshelves she inserted an entirely new steel framework within the wood-frame structure.

She employed an equally timeless form for the nearby Riggio-Lynch Chapel of 2004, a simple but beautifully crafted wooden structure whose subtly curving contours recall those of a boat, a reference that harks back to early Christian iconography of the church as a barque akin to that of Jesus and his apostles as they fished on the Sea of Galilee (see Illustration 19b). Indeed, the architectural term "nave"— the main enclosure of a sanctuary—derives from the Latin *navis* (ship). An extra layer of symbolism attaches to this seemingly beached vessel on the edge of a pond fringed by weeping willows. The finely crafted but economical unpainted particleboard interior of the windowless chapel is illuminated by skylights, and one's focus is directed to the central pulpit in the grand tradition of black preaching churches.

Lin has demonstrated a similar topographic sensitivity in her remarkable series of earthwork sculptures, which began with *The Wave Field* (1995). It was commissioned for the interior courtyard of an aerospace building at the University of Michigan in Ann Arbor, which was named in memory of an alumnus, François-Xavier Bagnoud, a helicopter rescue pilot who died in an air accident at age twenty-four. (He was a great-grandson of Simón Patiño, the Bolivian "Tin King," and *The Wave Field* was underwritten by Bagnoud's philanthropic mother.) Eager to express the freedom and fluidity of youth and aeronautics, Lin found inspiration in the undulating, parallel lines of a water current called a Stokes wave. Using that pattern as a model, she demarcated a one-hundred-foot square, had its surface shaped on the diagonal into rows of swelling grass-covered hillocks three to five feet high, and achieved an effect of rippling propulsion akin to a verdant meadow beneath the rotors of a chopper during liftoff.

At once specific in its commemorative purpose but generalized in its abstract, hypnotic beauty, *The Wave Field*, now a popular campus gathering place, demonstrates Lin's genius for transforming profound personal loss into a force for social cohesion, no less so than in her most famous work. The architect has since produced two variations on this theme: *Flutter* (2005), for a federal courthouse in Miami, Florida; and the eleven-acre *Storm King Wavefield* (2009) at Storm King, the sculpture park in Orange County, New York. The latter installation is more extensive than its predecessors not only in area but also in the size of the waves, which here vary from ten to eighteen feet high, with a separation of some forty feet between each row of mounds, proportions that approximate the sensation of being on a stormy sea where one's view of the horizon is blocked by tall swells. *Storm King*

Wavefield gives those who climb up and down the slopes to reach its centermost folds a palpable sense of being engulfed by the forces of nature, an immersive experience not unlike that of the Vietnam Veterans Memorial, but without the political meaning imputed to that earlier work.

Related to the wave fields but more reminiscent of the land forms built over a five-thousand-year period by Native American cultures collectively known as the Mound Builders are Lin's "Earth Drawings." These include *Eleven Minute Line* (2004) at the Wanås Foundation sculpture park in southern Sweden and *Kentucky Line* (2008) near Louisville, both of which extend like gigantic snakes across their rural settings. These works are less pictographic than their ancient antecedents, which often represented living creatures; their most obvious model is the Great Serpent Mound in southwestern Ohio, which has been dated to the eleventh century but may be much older. Like many such constructions (unless they are cut into a hillside) their patterns are most discernible from overhead, and thus Lin's "Earth Drawings" are not as fully comprehensible at ground level as her wave fields, which exert a far stronger effect on the viewer.

Since 2008, Lin has been represented by the New York–based Pace Gallery, one of the four so-called megadealers (along with Gagosian, Hauser & Wirth, and David Zwirner) that have increasingly monopolized the very high end of the international art trade since the start of the millennium. One of the principal motivating factors behind Earth Art was to create works whose environmental, site-specific nature would negate the commercial commodification that disturbed many young artists during the late 1960s. However, in order to finance such costly undertakings as Michael Heizer's massive earthworks or Christo and Jeanne-Claude's grandiose wrappings, these visionaries also created salable, domestically scaled objects to underwrite their endeavors. Furthermore, since the greatest examples of Earth Art—including Robert Smithson's *Spiral Jetty* on Utah's Great Salt Lake, Walter De Maria's *Lightning Field* in western New Mexico, and James Turrell's *Roden Crater* in Arizona's Painted Desert—tend to be in remote locations, more physically accessible manifestations of such colossal conceptions are essential to gain critical and financial support for projects that otherwise might remain intriguing hypotheses on paper. Lin, for her part, is the most ethical of artists and there is nothing venal about her assertion that "I wanted to transfer what I was exploring in my outdoor installations to the confines of a museum."

Her *Around the World x 3* (2014) is a twelve-foot-wide floor piece comprising three concentric rings of white marble, an arrangement that immediately suggests Richard Long's circular aggregations of rough-hewn stones on a flat surface. The upper surfaces of this tripartite, target-like composition are naturalistically carved at various heights to suggest comparative elevations of points around the globe including the North Pole, Iceland, the Ural Mountains, the Bering Strait, New York City, Ecuador, Indonesia, Kenya, and the Democratic Republic of Congo. Given several other recent conceptual pieces by Lin that address the crisis of climate change, rising sea levels, and the disastrous effect that global warming is already having on the world's coastlines, one assumes that the aim of this beautiful object is to dramatize that present threat in readily comprehensible form. What is certain is that the elegant surface Lin achieves here—which attains a level of suave semi-primitive effect reminiscent of Isamu Noguchi's half-raw, half-polished stone sculptures—can also divert attention from the urgency of her important if inchoately articulated message. Her desire to bring the grandeur of untamed nature into a gallery setting can seem a bit too self-defeatingly well-mannered compared to grittier efforts of other Earth artists, especially Long and Heizer.

In 1996 Lin married the pioneering photography dealer Daniel Wolf, whose New York gallery, which opened in 1977, was among the first in the US to specialize in nineteenth-century images. They have two daughters and divide their time between a Manhattan apartment and a vacation house in southwest Colorado built for Wolf in 1988 by the architect Ettore Sottsass, the founder of Milan's breakaway Memphis Group. This brightly colored, busily massed caprice is antithetical to Lin's very few residential designs, including her Box House of 2008 in Telluride, Colorado, a wood-clad, flat-roofed rectangle of an almost Shaker-like restraint. In 2013 the couple bought the former Yonkers City Jail, just north of New York City, and converted that ten-thousand-square-foot facility, which abuts the Hudson River water-front, into art studios and galleries.

In 2015 Lin completed her largest architectural project until then, the Novartis Institutes for BioMedical Research in Cambridge, Massachusetts, commissioned by the multinational pharmaceutical giant. She designed the master plan for this expansion of the firm's enclave adjacent to the MIT campus, as well as two of the three buildings (the third is by the architect Toshiko Mori). As indicated by her series of twenty-eight study models, she finally settled on a format that assigned laboratories to a glass-walled medium-rise slab set at an angle against a low-rise street-front volume with ground-floor commercial spaces and offices above. The evident aim is to encourage a lively engagement with pedestrians that is often missing along this sometimes barren stretch of Cambridge's biotech corridor on Massachusetts Avenue.

The obliquely angled façade of the scheme's lower portion, which reflects the irregular intersection of the surrounding streets, is clad with pale stone blocks worked into porous patterns meant to evoke microscopic sections of coral or bone. The top story is wrapped in a continuous horizontal band of glass beneath a projecting flat roof, which brings to mind midcentury modernism of a superior sort that might have been executed in Miami or Rio de Janeiro, or by Jacques Herzog and Pierre de Meuron, whose Switch House addition to their Tate Modern gallery in London, which opened in 2016, has a not dissimilar exterior of perforated brick.

Lin came of professional age at the conjunction of two immense changes in architectural culture: the increasing acceptance of women in a field that had long restricted them to subsidiary roles, and a renewed sense that what during the modern period had come to be seen primarily as a technical discipline was an art form as well. Thanks to her culturally supportive upbringing, youthful acclaim, and preternatural self-confidence in following multidisciplinary pursuits without a careerist agenda, Lin has freed herself from the entrapments of the infernal fame machine. If all her experiments do not lead to a breakthrough as momentous as her defining hour in 1981, she nonetheless has established herself as a model of what architecture can become in the hands of a woman unafraid to pursue a different path.

Illustration Credits

Front endpapers: Louis I. Kahn Collection, University of Pennsylvania and Pennsylvania Historical and Museum Commission. Photo by George Alikakos.

Back endpapers: Mary Evans/Süddeutsche Zeitung Photo

Frontispiece: New York Daily News/Getty Images

1a: Copyright © Michael Yamashita

1b: gigi_nyc

2b: Catalunya La Pedrera Foundation

3a: Copyright 2018 Frank Lloyd Wright Foundation. All Rights Reserved. Licensed by Artist Rights Society. [2904.001]

The Frank Lloyd Wright Foundation Archives (The Museum of Modern Art/Avery Architectural Fine Arts Library, Columbia University, New York)

3b: Copyright 2018 Frank Lloyd Wright Foundation. All Rights Reserved. Licensed by Artist Rights Society.

Digital Image © The Museum of Modern Art/Licensed by Scala / Art Resource, NY.

The Frank Lloyd Wright Foundation Archives (The Museum of Modern Art/Avery Architectural Fine Arts Library, Columbia University, New York)

4a: Copyright © Claudio Susani

4b: akg-images/viennaslide/Harald A. Jahn

5a: Annabel Watts Collection

INDEX

Albert Speer presenting a model of his German Pavilion for the 1937 Paris International Exposition to Hitler, who in 1942 would name him Reich Minister of Armaments and War Production, a job that Speer, the Führer's favorite architect, fulfilled with murderous efficiency.